2 00

Morrissey

Ten years on this book are dedicated to
Joey Stefano,
Mark Nicholson and
Les Enfants de Novembre
N'oublie pas . . .
La vie sans amis
c'est comme un
jardin sans fleurs

Scandal & Passion

Morrissey

DAVID BRET

ROBSON BOOKS

First published in Great Britain in 2004 by Robson Books, The Chrysalis
Building, Bramley Road, London W10 6SP

An imprint of **Chrysalis** Books Group plc

British Library Cataloguing in Publication Data
A catalogue record for this title is available from the British Library.

ISBN 1 86105 787 3

Typeset by SX Composing DTP, Rayleigh, Essex
Printed by Creative Print & Design (Wales), Ebbw Vale

Contents

Acknowledgements

Writing this book would not have been possible had it not been for the help, inspiration, criticisms and love of that very select group of individuals whom I will always look upon as my true family and *autre coeur*. Barbara, Irene Bean, Marlene Dietrich, Roger Normand and Dorothy Squires, *que vous dormez en paix*. René and Lucette Chevalier, Jacqueline Danno, Héléne Delavault, Tony Griffin, Axel Dotti, Betty Paillard and Gérard, Annick Roux, Terry Sanderson, John and Anne Taylor, François and Madeleine Vals, Caroline Clerc and Charley Marouani.

Very, *very* special thanks to the munificent Mark Nicholson. What you don't know about Morrissey and Elvis isn't *worth* knowing! Thanks also to Jeremy Robson, Jennifer Lansbury, Robert Dimery, Melanie Letts and the staff at Robson Books for putting up with me. It never gets any easier!

For their help and contribution to this book I offer *un grand chapeau bas* to Jean-Daniel Beauvallet, Peter Burton, Richard Smith, Murray Chalmers, Adrian Deevoy, Christophe Devos, Ruth Edge, Nicole Garrison, Iestyn George, Dirk Van Gils, Andrew Harrison, Martin Hunt, Kanako Ishikawa, Gianfranco, Danny Kelly, Sandy Lee, Kris Kirk, Stuart Maconie, Gary Day, Nigel Thomas, Boz Boorer, Paul Morley, Tristan, Mark Nevin, Kirsty MacColl, Tony Parsons, Manuel Rios-Sastre, Linder Sterling, Emmanuel Tellier, Pierre Siankowski, Mark Hooper, Jennifer Ivory, Paul Williamson, Robert Mackie, Alain Whyte, Robert Sandall, Michael Bracewell, Johnny Bridgewood, Peter Adams, Spencer Cobrin and Andy David.

Final thanks go to my loyal agent, David Bolt, to my wife Jeanne, who is still the keeper of my soul . . . and to Steven Patrick Morrissey for being so much to so many.

Foreword

He is placed upon a pedestal and worshipped; alternately, he is derided and loathed by detractors. There is rarely room for compromise. The British press call him 'The Pope of Mope', the French 'le coqueluche des mansards-branleurs'. The Americans find it impossible to adequately define him; though currently residing among them, he will never belong on the wrong side of the Atlantic, because he is and always will remain a quintessentially English monument.

He is arguably the *only* English entertainer to have successfully created his own culture, a personal world filled with foibles, likes and dislikes, and above all unsuppressable opinion: the bizarre obsessions with old films, camp icons, obscure entertainers, rough trade, the gay heroes he promoted and emulated, and his hatred of authority, politicians and royalty.

He claims to have loved rarely, his sexuality has been the subject of acres of press coverage for over twenty years, but if his personal life has been intensely private (barring a few press slip-ups), his greatest love affair – with his audiences, who have religiously followed his every pitfall and triumph – has been unashamedly flaunted and reciprocated since the moment he first stepped on to a stage. These are the faithful, many of whom often go to quite extraordinary lengths to flock to his travelling shrine, braving hardship just to attend the extra concert. They hang on to his every word. When he despairs, they despair too; when he hurts, they share his pain.

He is unique, the greatest singer-songwriter of his generation. His is a story of scandal . . . and passion.

He is Morrissey, and this is his story so far.

Introduction

There'll Always Be an England

'I have had nearly everything bad said about me. I can't really be accused of anything else now, except murder, and I'm sure that's bound to come at some stage.'

– Morrissey

Sheffield City Hall, 11 December 1992. This was a whole new world to me. Not so long before we had stood on these same steps, guests of Peggy Lee, the greatest American singer of her generation. Tonight it was Morrissey, perhaps the greatest British singer of *his* generation. Then, it had been suits and cocktail dresses – the show had been filmed for television. Champagne bottles had been cracked open at the bar and the talk had been of how well Ms Lee had looked despite her recent illness. And now . . .

'I never expected it to be like this,' my wife Jeanne observed as we surveyed this devoted crowd of youngsters whose average age could not have been more than eighteen.

We had entered the strange, undeniably exciting, and for someone of my profession potentially dangerous world of Steven Patrick Morrissey. It was raining, yet apart from ours there was not an umbrella to be seen. There was a plump, unsmiling Chinese woman, barely five feet tall, clutching a bunch of daffodils that had seen better days. There was a lanky youth from Amsterdam in a soaked, translucent Arsenal T-shirt and a leather-clad, brash but beautiful gay porn star from Chicago,

1

Gianfranco, who pronounced without stopping for breath, 'Moz's buddy did a couple of porno movies, you know, but it was such a disappointment meeting him because he wasn't that nice, and straight after the show I'm off to the airport because tomorrow I've got a shoot in Rome, Italy!' Then there was a painfully thin man from Arizona, and a young Spanish teacher complaining about the ad for hamburgers that was printed on the back of his ticket: 'We're vegetarians, for God's sake. *He's* a vegetarian!' – to which the fan from Arizona opined, 'He's also a *god*!'

By the end of the evening I, the eternal sceptic, was inclined to agree with him, for the object of our being there, primarily as part of my research for this book, had joined the ranks of my other singer-songwriter *monstres sacrés* of the recital stage: Barbara, Brel, Brassens, Piaf and Aznavour.

Prior to this revelation I had been compelled to endure the prejudices of the press when, unable to cope with the excruciating support band (The Well-Oiled Sisters), my wife and I had spent thirty minutes at the theatre bar. Here, two very well-known music journalists from the opposing end of my entertainment spectrum had been engaged in a spirited banter over which of them would write the most vitriolic account of the event we were about to witness. 'I saw him last week,' one said. 'He was bloody good, the best concert I've *ever* seen in my life, but the editor still told me to say he was crap.' To which his companion added, 'I don't care *how* good he is. He won't be getting a good review!'

The atmosphere within the auditorium was surprisingly hushed, the air heavy with the scent of flowers – almost like one of the many Dorothy Squires concerts we had attended. There were more males than females, allegedly mostly heterosexual – to a great many people's way of thinking, no one could possibly worship a man like these people did and not fancy him even a little bit. And Morrissey's management had ensured that Jeanne and I would be in full public view too: ours were the so-called 'key seats', those in the balcony that traditionally face the precise centre of the stage. The city's florists, I later learned, had record sales that day, and seemingly thousands upon thousands of these blooms rained down like missiles the moment Morrissey stepped on to the stage – heralded by a dire Klaus Nomi overture, itself quickly drowned by the toneless but stirring chanting of Morrissey's name to the tune of the football chant 'Here We Go'.

He was bigger than I had anticipated, nowhere near as thin as in his early photographs. And he had *talent*, not a word I would use often to describe modern entertainers – the real, heart-stopping brilliance of a hardened trouper who has worked his way through the fleapit ranks to *earn* his success. No male singer since Fritz Wunderlich, or Elvis crooning 'Love Me Tender', had brought such a lump to my throat.

Looking decidedly shy and uncomfortable during his opening song, he overcame this obstacle by transforming the microphone cord into a bullwhip, thrashing the boards and monitors with frenetic abandon during this and several subsequent hard rock numbers. In so doing, he encouraged several crowd surfers to negotiate the steepish drop into the empty orchestra pit, hug their man for a few seconds, then fall prey to the burly, know-all bouncers. Then, having expended enough of his energy on the bullwhip, in a potently Continental soliloquy, Morrissey balanced his hunky frame on one of the monitors, took the spotlight full in the face, and during a tender ballad reached out to brush fingers with the first wave of sweaty, now gently gyrating followers. And, even more impressively, he was wholly unashamed of opening up and displaying his feminine side – of disproving the tenet that big, stiff-upper-lipped Englishmen, excepting the vanquished on the soccer pitch, are not permitted to express emotion by shedding a tear or two.

Most of the songs in Morrissey's set were taken from his innovative new album released that summer – *Your Arsenal*, a pun intended for the irreverent British music press if ever there was one. The album had shot to the upper echelons of the charts, adding lustre to the 'moon-June' lyrical dross more usually found there. Morrissey himself – never backwards at coming forwards when it comes to barbed put-downs – had told Dermott Hayes of *Rage* at the end of the previous year (and subsequently repeated the gist of this time and time again) that 'Most pop personalities are literally so plain and dull, that anyone who appears to have a vaguely working brain comes across as conniving.'

As probably the most intellectually gifted and imaginative lyricist of his generation, Morrissey could always be relied on for a memorable quote or a sharp, witty one-liner. That said, his relationship with the press had rarely been less than problematic. His appearance at Madness's reunion concert at Finsbury Park earlier that year had seen him accused of racism. Music paper *NME*, formerly a fervent champion both of The Smiths and Morrissey the solo artist, had taken to pillorying him for his presumed flirtation with the political Far Right and the lyrics of songs such as 'Bengali In Platforms' and 'Asian Rut'.

In January 1991 he had told Jean-Daniel Beauvallet:

> Newspapers make up stories, hoping to bait me into calling them with *my* version of events. That's how low these people have sunk in order to get an interview. I prefer to leave them to it, hoping the readers will work out for themselves the difference between truth and lies. Even so, I've been terribly, terribly hurt.

Beauvallet explained to me how, prior to meeting him for the first time, he had been forewarned by one British journalist that Morrissey was difficult, very bad-tempered, dangerous and rude. But Beauvallet told me:

> I can honestly say, hand over heart, that he was one of the politest, gentlest men I ever met. The so-called *mauvaise reputation* is solely the invention of the British music press. He's so calm and collected, even when angry. It would be easy to run out of superlatives describing him. England should be proud of him.

The British fans *were* proud of him, but this persistent bile spouting had taken its toll and sowed the seeds of doubt in Morrissey's mind: so far as the British music press were concerned, he could do nothing right. In November 1989 Nick Kent had asked him, 'Don't you feel that England is a doomed country now?', and his response had been that it was 'shambolically doomed'. However, he *had* added optimistically, 'I feel I have to stay. I feel that I have to go down with the ship if that's what must happen. Anything else would be too much like desertion.' Sadly, that 'desertion' was eventually to come to pass, though it would take a good deal more anguish, soul-searching and press butchery to get him to pack his bags and cross the Big Pond, following in the footsteps of P G Wodehouse (whose house he would later live in), Tom Jones, Engelbert Humperdinck and Quentin Crisp.

Shortly after this Herculean upheaval, Morrissey would tell his close pal Michael Bracewell:

> The England that I have loved, and I have sung about, and whose death I have sung about, I felt had finally slipped away. And so I was no longer saying, 'England is dying.' I was beginning to say, 'Well, yes, it has died and here's the carcass' – so why hang around?

It had taken him almost forty years to desert the sinking ship . . .

1

Heir Apparent: Heroes and Villains

'The permutations and contradictions which Morrissey throws in the face of all who seek to analyse him would tax the mightiest machine IBM could produce.'

— George Byrne, *Irish Sunday Independent*

Morrissey was born of Irish stock on 22 May 1959, at Manchester's Davyhulme Park Hospital, the second child (after daughter Jacqueline) of Elizabeth (Dwyer) and Peter Morrissey, who had emigrated from Dublin a few years earlier and married at the city's Moss Side Catholic Church. Ironically, he shares his birthday with cult Russian silent film actress Nazimova – champion of Henrik Ibsen and Oscar Wilde – a *narcissiste* par excellence who became the doyenne of Hollywood's infamous lesbian Sewing Circle after producing and starring in a version of Wilde's *Salome* made by a gay cast and crew.

He was baptised Steven Patrick, the first name after the brooding, famously hirsute and hedonistic American actor Steve Cochran, who had appeared with Mae West in her Broadway revival of *Diamond Lil*. Mrs Morrissey had particularly enthused over Cochran's portrayal of the mobster Nick Prenta, opposite Joan Crawford in *The Damned Don't Cry* (1950). In some shots the physical resemblance between Cochran and the adult Morrissey is uncanny.

Morrissey came into the world when northern England was in the throes of artistic change with the belated introduction of the Expressionist film genre (one such had been the aforementioned Crawford film), which had taken America by storm a decade earlier. Controversial productions such as *Saturday Night And Sunday Morning* and *A Taste Of Honey*, with their gritty plots and dialogue, were riding the crest of their own particular wave, narrowing the chasm in the North/South divide previously exacerbated by the Gracie Fields and George Formby comedy-dramas of the previous generation.

Television soaps were also about to enter a new lease of life. For years, the country had been monopolised by *The Grove Family* – Britain's first authentic soap, set in Hendon – but now Manchester was fighting back with *Coronation Street* (to which the teenage Morrissey would unsuccessfully submit at least one script idea). Soon too there would be a short-lived explosion of Mancunian home-grown musical talent, entertainers who would initially give Liverpool and The Beatles a good run for their money: Freddie and the Dreamers, Wayne Fontana and the Mindbenders and Herman's Hermits.

At the end of 1965, however, while the Morrisseys were ensconced at 17 Harper Street, in the city's Hulme suburb, something happened that imbued Manchester with an infamy it could well have done without: the Moors Murders, about which Morrissey would later conduct a personal crusade.

These particularly abhorrent crimes traumatised a nation. They were perpetrated by Ian Brady – a Glaswegian aficionado of Nazi memorabilia, fascism and the depraved works of the Marquis de Sade – and his lover, Myra Hindley. The couple had tortured, killed and then buried several children on Saddleworth Moor. Morrissey was seven when the evil pair were locked up for good, and though media reports at the time were not as graphic as they are today, these gruesome slayings (one of which was taped) were explored in great depth in Emlyn Williams' book *Beyond Belief: The Story of Ian Brady & Myra Hindley*, published in 1967. One can only assume the effect this had on the 300,000 morbidly curious people who bought it, or on the mind of the impressionable boy who would later use the subject matter of the tragedy to produce a startling and moving reflection on the Moors Murders, a unique achievement in the pop canon – and find himself pilloried for it.

Morrissey recalled the Manchester of the sixties as having been a violent place. On one particular occasion, at a fairground in Stretford, he was hit by a thug simply because he had been standing in the wrong place at the wrong time: 'You accepted it, there didn't have to be a reason.' According to Morrissey, life at St Wilfred's Primary was no bed of roses, but he tolerated whatever crises winged his way and years later used these experiences to sow the seeds for a career that might otherwise have been as bland as those of his less talented contemporaries.

In 1970, as part of an estate clearance operation, the Morrisseys relocated to another council house at 384 King's Road, in Stretford, and Morrissey was enrolled at St Mary's Secondary Modern. His miseries here are said to have been recounted in 'The Headmaster Ritual', a cataloguing of physical abuse that would not be tolerated today, but which in many such establishments (and I speak from personal experience) was par for the course back then: the thwack on the knees, the knee to the groin, the 'good hidings' in the shower block. There were protests from the Greater Manchester Education Authority who declared that none of *its* teachers had ever acted with such brutality and tried – but failed – to get the record banned. When The Smiths put out the song on a single, it was Morrissey's intention to hammer home his point by having a cover-shot of one of his idols, Terence Stamp, in the film *Term of Trial* (1962), hand outstretched, getting six of the best from Laurence Olivier and obviously enjoying the punishment. Both actors objected.

Morrissey tended to disagree with the education authority. 'I can remember being forcibly kicked by a teacher,' he argued. 'I'd taken the ball off him. His response was to ignore the game, ignore the ball, ignore the pupils and just kick me. I stood quite still.' Future Smith Mike Joyce, who attended St Gregory's Grammar School, described his school years as similarly 'barbaric', telling *Select*'s David Cavanagh early in 1993, '*I* had teachers who'd lift you up by the neck and he'd get his knuckles and he'd start knocking on the back of your head as hard as he could, until I was on the floor. Now I mean, was that education?'

The school was run by a rather military headmaster named Vincent Morgan, a stalwart Catholic, who came down hard on anyone, pupils or staff, caught using strong language or discussing sex. 'I was raised with the notion that excitement and exuberance and extremities were something other people did and were not for me,' the singer told *Details* in 1994, recalling a solitary sex education lesson delivered by a 'gung-ho rugby-type' master, who told him, 'You know penis? Well, it's your dick. What more do you want to know?'

According to Morrissey's later admissions, he does not appear to have been particularly happy at home with his warring parents. In August 1987, when Chris of *Les Inrockuptibles* asked him if 'Barbarism Begins At Home' was based on personal experience he replied:

Yes. I was beaten as a child – with umbrellas or whatever came to hand. Discipline was very strict when I was small, less as I grew older. As a child I had no freedom. For poor children like us, there wasn't enough room to flourish. I just built this wall around myself.

In April 2003 he would more or less repeat this story to Andrew Harrison of *Word*, adding that most of the time he had probably deserved that occasional clip around the head: 'I was a very noisy child. I always stood in front of the television. I wouldn't go to bed, and then I discovered music at the age of six and played it loud, constantly . . . which must have been unbearable. I was surprised they were so tolerant of me, to be honest.'

In the same *Inrockuptibles* interview, Morrissey appears to have attempted to throw a veil over his past by actually denying that he had had a conventional education, adding, 'I didn't go to school very often. I failed all my exams and I *never* attended a secondary school. It was easier educating myself, reading the books I wanted to read, developing my own interests. I couldn't tolerate authority, I was completely undisciplined. *Nobody* could tell me what to do.'

This reinvention of himself and his legend would occur repeatedly over the years: sometimes to throw the press off a particular scent; sometimes, it has been said, so as not to offend members of his family, his mother in particular, who might have frowned upon his youthful activities. As with many great stars who have become *monstres sacrés*, all we know of their youth, mis-spent or otherwise, is largely what they themselves have remembered since achieving fame, and Morrissey appears to be no exception. Few have come forward to speak of knowing him as a child or teenager; the anecdotes of those who have are clouded and influenced by his fame. There have been no interviews with his closest friends or with members of his family. His lovers also have remained dutifully silent. In his early interviews, when he could not possibly imagine what a huge star he would become, he makes no reference to crippling loneliness and celibacy never enters the equation; he is relatively open about matters sexual and does not appear to have an acerbic bone in his body. This does not necessarily mean, of course, that he has anything to hide or be ashamed of, and he may only be admired for keeping up a Garboesque stance and preventing his personal life from being splattered across the tabloids – even more so when one considers how he has treated those he feels have wronged him. What we are sure of regarding his youth was that he was blessed with the redeeming quality of an overactive imagination, and an ability to jot down these vibrant thoughts and ideas. 'Being able to write was *better* probably than having friends,' he told Chris of *Les Inrockuptibles*, adding that he had carried his notebook everywhere, even into the bathroom. Long before his tenth birthday he was drawing inspiration from retro heroes such as Gracie Fields, George Formby, Jimmy Clitheroe and Hylda Baker.

Some of his biggest heroes, however, were the tormented gay or bisexual ones: Billy Fury, James Dean, Oscar Wilde – the ones he could have 'safe' relationships with, as he explained in his *Inrockuptibles* interview:

> People who possess *that* much allure, no matter what they produce or do with their lives, are very rare. I *hate* ordinary people. I was a strange child who couldn't function in ordinary society. It's easier to fall in love with images and myths. They don't answer back, they don't deceive you. There's no danger. I've taken precautions choosing them, and I have *such* good taste!

Liverpool-born Billy Fury (né Ronald Wycherley) was an ethereal-looking young man who had always wanted to be a rock star and enjoy the hedonistic lifestyle that went with it. Perhaps terrified of his sexuality becoming public knowledge, he had more or less taken over Johnnie Ray's 'tears on my pillow' mantle, and found fame with heartfelt ballads such as 'Halfway To Paradise' and 'I'd Never Find Another You'. Morrissey included Fury's photograph on the sleeve of The Smiths' 'Last Night I Dreamt Somebody Loved Me' (but wisely refrained from etching 'Eaten By Vince Eager' on the vinyl, a reference to one of Fury's stable-mates, when warned of the possible repercussions). He also championed Fury in 'Paint A Vulgar Picture'. Both tracks were recorded in the spring of 1987 for *Strangeways Here We Come*.

'Paint A Vulgar Picture' takes as its theme the 'death = profit' aspect of the recording industry – though to be fair, when a much-loved artiste dies, especially of a heart-attack at just 41 as Fury did, the fans expect this kind of thing, and would be offended if it did not happen. From Morrissey's point of view, however, the 'sycophantic slags' at the board meeting who probably could not stand the singer while he was alive are intent on making a fast buck, and argue among themselves as to which one of them was responsible for putting him on the map. And the song ends with Morrissey expressing the feelings he has suppressed until now, because death has rendered his idol untouchable. 'They cannot hurt you my darling,' he laments. Stirring stuff! 'He's virtually the same as James Dean,' Morrissey told *Sounds* in June 1984, speaking of Fury. 'He too was entirely doomed, which I find quite affectionate.'

James Dean was, of course, *the* archetypal rebel and loner par excellence. When asked if his beyond-the-grave bonding with Jimmy was more than simple admiration, Morrissey told *Sounds*, 'Profoundly more. James Dean was more than the actor in *Rebel Without A Cause*. He was a great symbol. There was nothing that remarkable about his acting in my opinion, but he always seemed in control of every situation. People like that are only too rare. That man's life was so wonderfully perfect.'

If cynics suggested that by making such comments about Dean and Fury, Morrissey was leaving himself open to criticism by exposing his 'feminine' side, nothing could have been closer to the truth. Even the staunchest opponents of Freud and Kinsey cannot deny that all men have a feminine side, just as all women have a masculine side – it's nothing whatsoever to do with sexuality. That said, neither authority would have been capable of pigeon-holing the testosterone-charged, massively talented, equally temperamental, pre-Brat Pack prima donna from Fairmount, Indiana, whose death at 24 had brought about the biggest outpouring of national grief since the death of Rudolph Valentino in 1926.

Morrissey later retraced Jimmy's footsteps – as if, like Atticus Finch in *To Kill A Mockingbird*, he wanted to climb into the actor's skin for a little while. During The Smiths' first ill-fated trip to New York, he insisted upon the group staying at the Iroquois Hotel (next door to the Algonquin, of 'Round Table' fame) where Jimmy had resided for a while with his producer-lover, Rogers Brackett, during *his* first visit to the city – though by the time The Smiths arrived the establishment had gone downhill, and cockroaches were reported in the bedrooms. Two years later, a pre-fame snap of seventeen-year-old Jimmy, taken by a schoolfriend, graced the cover of 'Bigmouth Strikes Again'.

It would be insulting to Oscar Wilde to suggest (as have some of the singer's more fanatical admirers) that Morrissey is his reincarnation – and equally offensive to the Stretford bard to state that he is not a man of similar wit, verbal aptitude, a scribe and raconteur of considerable understanding and insight into the human condition, and above all a man who does not suffer fools gladly. Neither can one deny that he has, albeit in a lesser way than Wilde, been ostracised and pilloried, some-times on account of his own folly, largely on account of misinter-pretation – not always by moralists, but by the barbed quills of the British press. 'As I blundered through my teens,' Morrissey told *Sounds* on one occasion, 'I was quite isolated. In a way he became my companion, and as I get older the adoration increases. I'm never without him. It's almost biblical, like carrying your rosary around with you. He had a life that was really tragic, yet it's curious that he was so witty.'

Wilde nurtured a passion for flowers, notably the white lily, which he adopted as his emblem, for it symbolised purity, beauty and death; his rooms at Oxford were rarely without the flower. Morrissey wanted to follow suit, but settled for the more easily affordable gladiolus or daffodil, depending on the season. He studied Wilde's life intently and became fascinated by the so-called artistic depravity of it all. Wilde and his lover, Lord Alfred Douglas, were fanatical about 'chickens' and 'dollies' – the rent boys who plied their trade around the Earls Court and Piccadilly areas of London; one only has to watch the superb biopic featuring Stephen Fry and Jude Law to see *how* fanatical. So too was Morrissey, though not for the same reasons.

There is a misconception today that these young men were invariably underage, but one has to remember that there *was* no age of consent at the time – all homosexual acts were against the law and, in Wilde's day, an imprisonable offence. The average age of a 'Dilly Boy' was 23, and a great many of these were married and needed the money to support their families. As a mature artist, Morrissey was to champion 'age-gap sex' and 'sex for sale' in numerous songs, with absolutely no suggestion that anyone was underage. He did this sometimes quite brazenly with The Smiths, more subtly as a solo artist, but the one song ('Piccadilly Palare') that commends him by linking Wilde's favourite pastime to modern-day man-to-man sex is maybe more daring than its predecessors, and will be discussed in greater detail later.

There were also the musical heroes and heroines. At six, Morrissey had bought his first 45 rpm vinyl singles: Françoise Hardy's 'Another Place', and Marianne Faithfull's 'Come And Stay With Me'. At some stage, The Smiths are known to have taped two Faithfull songs, their own arrangements of 'The Sha La La Song' and 'Summer Nights'. Morrissey also liked Dusty Springfield, but he was *passionate* about two-hit wonder Twinkle, and barefoot contessa Sandie Shaw. 'I really, really did love these people,' he told *Select*'s Mark Kemp early in 1991, 'I gave them my life, my youth. Beyond the perimeter of pop music there was a drop at the edge of the world.'

Twinkle's 'Terry', like Edith Piaf's 'L'Homme A La Moto' and The Shangri-Las' 'Leader Of The Pack', had attracted fierce criticism in sensitive days because the central character of each had been a maniac motorcyclist who had paid the ultimate price for wreaking terror on the neighbourhood. The song that really impressed Morrissey, however, was 'Golden Lights', Twinkle's 'ode to despondency' which she had written upon the break-up of her romance with Declan Cluskey of The Bachelors. A few years later Morrissey began writing to her, and in 1986 she gave permission for The Smiths to cover the song, one of their most harmonious arrangements, which saw Morrissey duetting beautifully with Kirsty MacColl. 'I think he's wonderful,' Twinkle later told *NME*. 'I've never met him, and I know he has a strange reputation, but he must be very kind underneath because like me he loves animals. I'm very grateful to him for all that he's done.'

Sandie Shaw was one pen pal whom Morrissey would eventually meet. He had been eight when the Dagenham-born chanteuse had won the Eurovision Song Contest with 'Puppet On A String', her third chart-topper; the title of The Smiths' 'Heaven Knows I'm Miserable Now' would be based on her little-known song of 1969, 'Heaven Knows I'm Missing Him Now', and Shaw would respond with a tribute of her own, 'Steven, You Don't Eat Meat'. Early in 1984 she replaced Morrissey to perform a cover of the group's first failed single, 'Hand In Glove', with the three other Smiths. This provided her with her first Top 30 hit in fifteen years. She performed the song with the band on *Top Of The Pops*, the gimmick being that while she wore black and emulated Morrissey's movements by writhing about on the floor, the musicians appeared barefoot. Shaw also covered The Smiths' 'I Don't Owe You Anything', while Morrissey duetted with her on a never-released cover of her 1964 hit 'Girl Don't Come'. There was also a lavishly orchestrated singalong version of 'Please Help The Cause Against Loneliness', though arguably her best work with Morrissey was her duet with him on 'Jeane' – for whereas she unquestionably strains to reach the top notes in 'Hand In Glove' (the 1988 solo rendition is positively dreadful), her delivery in 'Jeane' is breathtakingly simple and emotional to the point that it sends shivers down the spine.

Like Gracie Fields' signature tune 'Sally', 'Jeane' is also a man's song sung to a woman, but without any hint of sexuality. In 1985, Sandie Shaw told *Gay Times'* Kris Kirk that she had once lived with a woman so that they could combine budgets between marriages and better support their children: 'It was a very real closeness. Sex wasn't involved at all but the relationship was really passionate, like that between Morrissey and Johnny Marr. There's no thought of sex in their relationship, just an absolute closeness between them in which they've found they best express themselves.'

Exactly why the alliance between Morrissey and Sandie Shaw ended so abruptly is not known, save that a few years down the line he would be saying, 'I don't hear from her any more. It wasn't exactly a friendship made in heaven . . . let's just put it that way without saying any more.'

As the seventies dawned, Morrissey's musical tastes were developing apace. Already a fan of Roxy Music and Mott The Hoople, he latched on to Nico, the tragic German singer who performed briefly with Lou Reed's Velvet Underground – all but wearing out the grooves of her *Desert Shore* and *Chelsea Girl* albums. 'Yes, the poor Velvets,' he told pen pal Robert Mackie, 'I spent my entire twelfth year locked in my bedroom with *All Tomorrow's Parties*. I was such an incendiary child. Nico's voice paralyses the imagination.' He also became an aficionado of glam rock, with its colourful wardrobe, platform shoes and grossly outspoken, frequently sexually ambiguous frontmen such as David Bowie, with whom he would one day work but not particularly like, and T. Rex's Marc Bolan. Whenever he could, he attended glam concerts at the King's Hall, Belle Vue.

No one, however, had as profound an effect on the teenage Morrissey as perhaps the weirdest outfit of them all: The New York Dolls, one of the most controversial punk acts ever. Morrissey saw them for the first time in 1973, on the BBC's *Old Grey Whistle Test*. 'At my school, you had to be passionate about Bowie or Bolan. It had to be one or the other, never both,' he told journalist Nick Kent in December 1984. 'For me, it was the Dolls because I found traditional rock and rollers stupid, brainless, hyper-machismo soup-sellers. The Dolls were absolutely *male*, not in the least effeminate. They were personalities you didn't treat lightly because *they* were the rock and roll Mafia!'

Three of the Dolls came to tragic early ends. Drummer Billy Murcia drowned in his bathtub after an alcoholic binge in 1972, aged just 21. Guitarist Johnny Thunders (born John Genzale) left the group in 1975 to front another Morrissey favourite, The Heartbreakers, and embark on a never-ending series of drink-drugs benders. Thunders' 'speciality' was to get his friends to play Russian roulette with syringes, not knowing which one contained water or heroin. It was he who famously got Sid Vicious hooked on the drug by taunting, 'What are you, man or mouse?' In April 1991, Thunders overdosed on methadone, aged 38, in a New Orleans hotel. The Dolls' new drummer, Jerry Nolan, died of a stroke nine months later while undergoing treatment for drugs-induced bacterial meningitis.

Almost in the same category was the extraordinary German counter-tenor-rock singer Klaus Nomi, whom Morrissey had also seen on *The Old Grey Whistle Test*. Born Klaus Sperber (his stage-name was an anagram of OMNI, the name of his favourite sci-fi magazine), he had relocated to New York in 1972 and become part of the new-wave performance scene: in his time he would work as a backing singer for David Bowie and Madonna, among others. Nomi had had some success in 1981 with his debut album, a mixture of contemporary rock, sixties pop and opera – his speciality in this field being Purcell and Saint-Saëns, both of which opened Morrissey concerts of the nineties. On stage he was impressive: almost seven feet tall in his platform boots, his hair styled into three points, wearing the most garish make-up and *Blake's Seven*-style costumes. Nomi made several albums, all moderately successful, and a number of promotional videos – the one for Lou Christie's 'Lightnin' Strikes' has to be seen to be believed. Then, just as he was on the threshold of major international stardom – not unusual at forty, when classical singers reach their peak – everything fell apart after he was diagnosed with Kaposi's sarcoma. In 1983, Nomi became one of the first show business personalities to die from AIDS, and until 'revived' by Morrissey had been almost forgotten.

In similar vein was Jobriath (né Jobriath Boone), the inspiration behind Marc Bolan's 'Cosmic Dancer', who had launched himself on New York's underground scene at the same time as Nomi. In 1972, claiming to have signed a $500,000 contract with Elektra, Jobriath commissioned a 41 x 43-foot airbrushed nude poster of himself to be pasted on a Times Square hoarding. This led to him being discovered by a French impresario, who compared him with the infamous Texan man-woman Van der Clyde. The latter visited Paris in 1925, met Cocteau and changed his name to Barbette. Appearing in a nude revue at the Folies-Bergère, he had executed a perilous tightrope routine in a blond wig and dress – removing the first to reveal a totally bald head, the second to reveal that he was a man!

Promoting his debut album, Jobriath had opened at the Opéra de Paris in 1973. The curtain rose on him dressed as King Kong, scaling a 50-foot phallic-shaped Empire State Building! Thereafter he had danced out of his monkey suit, and in various states of undress had sung a clutch of off-beat songs, revealing a hunky frame. He finished his act (to rapturous applause each evening) wearing only a spangled posing-pouch. Some believe Morrissey emulated Jobriath with his later displays of narcissism – the diaphanous or shredded shirts, the flaunting of flesh – though unlike his American hero he always kept his trousers on.

Jobriath's star had shone but briefly, and according to his publicist he 'vanished without trace' shortly after releasing his second album, *Creatures of the Street*, in 1975. In fact, he had not disappeared at all. Failing majestically to become the world's first openly gay superstar – no one would engage him and risk being prosecuted when he threatened to make his lyrics explicitly sexual – Jobriath resigned himself to a life of drugs and debauchery at New York's infamous Chelsea Hotel, famed first for its association with Andy Warhol and thereafter for its celebrity deaths – Nancy Spungen, Sid Vicious and drag queen Christina had all expired there. In 1985, desperately ill and following a bungled suicide attempt, Jobriath was evicted from his tawdry room at the hotel and taken to a local hospital, where shortly afterwards he died of an AIDS-related illness. His last words, from one of his songs, are reputed to have been, 'Please hold that sunrise below, if you don't mind.' In his memory, Morrissey would later adapt and perform 'Cosmic Dancer'.

Because he was a loner, and like many loners spiritually and artistically on a completely different wavelength to his classmates at St Mary's, Morrissey submitted himself wholeheartedly to the worship of these rather oddball heroes. And in an environment that he felt did not understand his world and its foibles, he used his pen as a beacon to make contact with the rest of humanity. To do so he often drew on songs that were an early inspiration to him. 'This Town Ain't Big Enough For Both Of Us', by the American group Sparks, was a big hit in early 1974. It contained the couplet, 'The rain is pouring on the foreign town/The bullets cannot cut you down', which Morrissey would later amend to, 'The rain falls on a humdrum town/This town has dragged you down' for The Smiths' 'William, It Was Really Nothing'. Sparks' keyboard player was Ron Mael, a rake-like individual with staring eyes, slicked back hair and a Hitler moustache. Vocals were provided by Mael's brother Russ, who attacked the song in a piercing falsetto. Fifteen-year-old Morrissey so liked the single, and the group's debut album *Kimono My House* (a pun on the old Rosemary Clooney song 'Come On A My House'), that he wrote a letter to *NME* about them. The editor, at a time when literary merit still counted for something among members of the British music press, was impressed. Not only did he publish the letter, he added a coda of his own:

> Conviction oozes from every sentence like the very ichor of life from the metal life-support systems of the Bronze Giant of Fengorak. The eyes of Mr Morrissey gleam with a missionary zeal that shames into submission the cringing doubts of those yet unconvinced.

Morrissey, the intellectual daydreamer-poet, left St Mary's School during the summer of 1975 with no formal qualifications. He enrolled at Stretford Technical College to read Sociology, English Literature and General Studies, though music was still his be-all and end-all. The following year he latched on to The Sex Pistols, catching their Manchester debut at the Lesser Free Trade Hall (their mentor, Malcolm McLaren, had managed the Dolls for a while). Despite being impressed, the youngster was contemptuous of their attire. In a letter to *NME* he wished them eternal fame, 'So they'll be able to afford some new clothes which don't look like they've been slept in.' His Sex Pistols phase, however, was brief.

It was probably during the summer of 1975 that Morrissey visited the United States for the first time, staying with an aunt in New Jersey. At around the same time, the so-called 'Karen Quinlan Affair' was attracting attention Stateside – a lengthy procedure summoned by the courts to decide the fate of a young woman who had been hooked up to a life-support system for over a year. After much campaigning by religious groups, and with the lawyers battling it out on behalf of the family, the life-support was switched off. Quinlan was moved to a nursing home, where nature was allowed to take its course. Morrissey was later to draw on this for The Smiths' song 'Girlfriend In A Coma'.

The young Morrissey's waspish tongue and his criticism of anyone who did not happen to be on his wavelength was much in evidence not long after his return home from the States, when he became infatuated with the American punk-poet, Patti Smith, whose album *Horses* would remain one of his perennial favourites. Though struggling to keep afloat on unemployment benefit, he managed to travel to Birmingham to see Smith in concert, had a letter published in *Sounds* declaring that the album 'showed more promise than just about any release in recent memory' – then promptly attacked the same publication's reviewer, John Ingham, for his stinging denunciation of The New York Dolls, telling him, 'Stick with The Sex Pistols, whose infantile approach and nondescript music will no doubt match your intelligence.'

Morrissey's bubble would burst during the spring of 1978 when, as a regular contributor to the fanzine, *Kid's Stuff*, he attended a press-conference Patti Smith gave in London. He later told *Sounds*:

She farted four times, and the room was crowded with young, impressionable people. There was one boy at the front who was no more than seventeen. She walked up to him . . . and loudly asked him an extremely vulgar question about how sexually endowed he was . . . The lesson here is that sometimes it's better to cherish your illusions about people you admire than it is to meet them.

When *NME* refused to acknowledge the brilliance of the Mancunian quartet The Buzzcocks, Morrissey penned a withering missive to the editor of the *NME* – almost as if he were gazing into a crystal ball and getting in the first punch:

Buzzcocks differ in only one way from their contemporaries: they possess a spark of originality . . . and their music gives you the impression that they spent longer than the customary ten minutes clutching the quill in preparation to write. Indubitably, Buzzcocks will hardly figure strongly – or even weakly – in the *NME* poll, and in these dark days when Patti Smith, Loudon Wainwright or even The New York Dolls fail to make any impact on Radio 1 DJs, common sense is therefore not so common. But for now they are only the best kick-ass rock band in the country. Go and see them first and then you may have the audacity to contradict me, you stupid sluts.

In this instance, the editor gave as good as he got, though Morrissey was no doubt tickled by his response. After assuring him that a feature on The Buzzcocks *was* on the stocks, he dismissed him with, 'Now go away, you nasty little brat!'

Life in the Morrissey household had not been easy for some time, and finally, on 23 December 1976, when he was seventeen years old, Morrissey's parents separated. Peter Morrissey moved out, and the children stayed at home with their mother. 'Which I actually think is quite natural,' Morrissey told *Details* eighteen years later, adding, 'I love them both very much, but I didn't raise them, and I can't alter the past. Millions upon millions of people come from damaged backgrounds, as they say. Mine wasn't so much damaged as merely *nothing at all*.'

Early the next year, with his parents' divorce very much on the cards, Morrissey began working as a clerk for the Inland Revenue – hardly the sort of employment one would expect a self-confessed anti-Establishment figure to enjoy. The extra money, however, enabled him to widen his musical sphere by attending concerts by Talking Heads, The Ramones and Blondie. Again, as a very vocal anti-royalist, he supported The Sex Pistols' contra-feting of the Queen's Silver Jubilee, which saw Malcolm McLaren and his protégés hosting a hugely irreverent boat party on the Thames opposite the Houses of Parliament, attended by numerous Pistols fans in T-shirts depicting Her Majesty with a safety-pin through her nose. When Morrissey's turn came to insult her some years later, he used the memorable image of 'Her very Lowness with her head in a sling.'

Morrissey is thought to have participated in a local anti-royal demo during the Jubilee year, waving a BAN THE JUBILEE banner and paving the way for some very barbed comments about the Windsors. In *Sounds* in March 1985, he launched an attack on Princess Diana for what he thought was her extreme extravagance:

> To me there's something dramatically ugly about a person who can wear a £6,000 dress when at the same time there are people who can't afford to eat . . . The statement she is making to the nation is, 'I am the fantastically gifted royalty, and you are the snivelling peasants.'

Few people would have agreed with him on this point. It's equally valid to argue that Diana's 'extravagance' was an essential tool of her trade as an ambassadress for the human suffering; that she had to look like a million dollars to raise the vast amounts of money she tirelessly raised for charity; that she remains one of the best-loved Englishwomen in history. That said, Morrissey's anti-royalist stance would be enduring and would later be used to create great art in the form of The Smiths' finest album, *The Queen Is Dead*.

Of course, a wildly imaginative lyricist with strongly held views and a cutting sense of humour is all very well and good, but without a band to provide the music . . .

2

The World Will Listen

'There is more to it than Johnny's guitar sound and Morrissey's lyrics. There was always that naked expression about life and death which was put so eloquently.'

– Geoff Travis, Rough Trade

The eighteen-year-old Morrissey seemed to have already resigned himself to a life of near-loneliness. He had few friends, it would seem, trusting mostly those such as pen pals whom he could keep at a suitable distance. With amazing foresight, a dozen years on from then he would observe, 'I will live my life as I will undoubtedly die – *alone*.' Yet in common with that other great exponent of solitude, Greta Garbo, he seems to have been aesthetically contented with his lot – indeed, to have gleaned great pleasure from it rather than have it fight against him.

An early correspondent was Billy Duffy, a Wythenshawe guitarist whom Morrissey met for the first time in November 1977. Duffy, a huge New York Dolls fan, had just joined the newly re-formed Nosebleeds, who were on the lookout for a vocalist. Morrissey's biting, witty lyrics – particularly those of 'I Think I'm Ready For The Electric Chair' – ensured that he was given the job. The rest of the line-up included Vini Reilly, the gifted guitarist who would later feature on Morrissey's debut solo album. The new Nosebleeds played Manchester Polytechnic on 15 April 1978, and appear to have been well received: among the Morrissey–Duffy collaborations were 'Peppermint Heaven' and 'I Get Nervous'. They played a few weeks later at the Ritz, where Morrissey hit on the novelty idea of tossing sweets into the audience. Also on their set-list was the old Shangri-Las hit, 'Give Him A Great Big

Kiss'. Interestingly, Morrissey did not change the gender in the song, suggesting that he may have been aware and proud of his sexuality, or merely taunting the crowd, or perhaps already singing in character as he would in years to come.

The event earned Morrissey his first mention as a non-scribe in the press: Paul Morley, then writing for *NME*, observed, 'Steven Morrissey has charisma'. Not that this prevented The Nosebleeds from disbanding soon afterwards. Morrissey, who had given up his job with the Inland Revenue, now signed on. His closest friend in those days – as now – was Linder (Linda Mulvey, aka Linder Sterling), born in Liverpool in 1954, and in the late seventies one of the celebrities of Whalley Range, the Manchester suburb known as 'the home of the bedsit' – which Morrissey would evoke in 'Miserable Lie'. Where and how they met is not known: for three decades their friendship has been free from media scrutiny and tabloid sensationalism.

Linder was the vocalist with Ludus, a punk-jazz ensemble who enjoyed moderate success in concert halls and particularly at the Hammersmith Odeon. One of their most popular numbers was the Morrisseyesque, 'I Can't Swim, I Have Nightmares', but his favourite appears to have been 'Breaking The Rules', which he chose as one of the tracks for his *Under The Influence* compilation album in 2003. 'Linder has an *enormously* sexual voice and is also *enormously* underrated,' he told *Word* upon the album's release, adding, 'I find these lyrics remarkable, suggesting that all forms of love are wonderful, whether it's three women together, four men together. Why can it not be so?'

The pair seem to have been on the same spiritual and intellectual planes – foils for each other's search for artistic and poetic inspiration amongst the grimy tangle of Manchester backstreets. A favourite haunt for reflection was the iron-gated South Cemetery, in West Didsbury, the subject of The Smiths' 'Cemetry Gates' – deliberately misspelled as it is spoken, and a work of some charm. For who has *not* ambled amongst the tombstones in some ancient city graveyard, if not in search of karma then in search of deceased celebrities one never would have had the hope of 'seeing' otherwise? Oscar Wilde, Colette, Chopin and Victor Hugo did so in Paris's Père Lachaise, and ultimately chose it as their final resting place. And on Wilde's cumbersome Jacob Epstein tomb, one invariably finds Morrissey quotes daubed in felt-tip pen.

After a brief spell behind the counter of a record shop, Morrissey followed in his father's footsteps and worked (equally briefly) as a hospital porter, only to throw in the towel when asked to collect and clean the surgeon's blood-spattered boots. Once again he returned to the solace of his room, writing letters to the music press (which would later defile him) in praise of Ludus and his other favourites, and penning witty neo-Wildean epistles to a young Scot named Robert Mackie, of whom nothing is known save that one had answered the other's 'Musical Tastes' advertisement in *Sounds*.

Had Morrissey never achieved international fame, these half-dozen letters, clumsily written and with many words deliberately misspelled, would not have seen the light of day. As he did achieve it, however, Mackie subsequently photocopied them into a crude booklet, *Words by Morrissey*, and this provides a fascinating insight into the man's mind back then. It is as if he was *so* self-assured that he would become an icon that he had become The Great Morrissey while still an unknown, for while other Manchester youths were out on the pull, doing pub-crawls and generally letting their hair down after their working week, this particular young man was content to stay in his room, inadvertently or not gleaning information from old Joan Crawford films, Ealing comedies – a host of details from 'the good old days' that would later crop up in his work.

The letters are as irreverent as they are funny, but never vulgar. They are alternatively addressed to Sir Laurence, Paganini, Tugboat Annie (the character in the famous Marie Dressler film of the same name) – and signed Natalie Wood, Oscar Wilde or Ronald Reagan. The first sees Morrissey gently rebuking Mackie for calling him Steve ('It reminds me of the Bionic Man.') – and the last one is signed off Steven, shortly before he dispensed with the moniker for good.

In a letter dated 13 October 1980, Morrissey berates Mackie for not having seen David Bowie, whereas he has seen 'Him' fourteen times between September 1972 and May 1976. He claims to have been born in Odessa and adds, Wilde-like, that he does not work except on his genius. Denouncing Mackie's favourite singer, Kate Bush, he declares that the nicest thing he can say about her is that she is unbearable. He closes with, 'I'm glad you liked me in *Rebel Without A Cause.*' In his missive of 22 October, he enthuses over Lou Reed, but pulls no punches over his hatred of Orchestral Manoevres In The Dark's frontman, Gary Numan, and concludes that to him, all electronic music is a sad accident.

In his next letter, Morrissey callously tells Mackie how sorry he is to hear that Mackie has lost his sister – this is careless, he says, and he wishes he could lose his. In another he laments the death of Mae West – at just 88, it was such a waste! He asks Mackie to send him some pornography, if he has a girlfriend, if he *likes* girls. He says that he has a girlfriend called Annalisa, that they are both bisexual, but that he hates sex! The girl in question was most likely Annalisa Jablonska, who later sang backing vocals on The Smiths' 'Suffer Little Children' and 'Pretty Girls Makes Graves'.

Taking a swipe at 'pretty-boy' music, Morrissey assures Mackie that there are worse groups than Duran Duran, though he is damned if he can think of any. Then he adds, 'Adam Ant bores the shit out of me.' In his letter dated 10 December he combines his sadness over John Lennon's murder with his loathing of Margaret Thatcher, technically his first attack on her before his opinionating got him into hot water. He tells Mackie that he *almost* cried, that he has none of his records and did not care about The Beatles – only to add that he was disturbed that someone who had devoted part of his life to peace could be shot five times for it. Concluding that the wrong people always die he adds, 'Nobody would assassinate our dear prime minister. Is all life sad?'

Robert Mackie was one of the first to be informed, in March 1981 upon Morrissey's return from his holiday in Philadelphia, of the imminent publication of his first biography, *The New York Dolls*. The 24-page booklet, published by Manchester-based Babylon Books, may have been scoffed at by Morrissey's later detractors, but during that summer and despite the limited appeal of its subject matter, it sold over 3,000 copies – a figure not often achieved by mainstream publishers of music books back then. It contained forty photographs of the group, one of Morrissey himself – and the audacious coda added to the Preface, 'Many thanks to Steven Morrissey – watch out for his James Dean book.'

In the meantime, big things were about to happen on the musical front. In one of his last letters to Robert Mackie, Morrissey announced that he was about to form a group, Angels Are Genderless, of which absolutely nothing is known. Why the friendship with Mackie ended is also a mystery. The pair had spoken for the first time on the telephone, and maybe this had put paid to the mystique: on the subject of Mackie's Scots accent Morrissey observes that he would have enjoyed their conversations more, had he been able to understand what Mackie had been talking about. Then, having invited Mackie to Manchester he tells him that there are lots of 'Thoroughly Modern Millies' in the vicinity who look like extras from Fellini's *Satyricon* – therefore if he does not find *him* funny, he can laugh at someone else.

The pair had exchanged photographs – and while Morrissey was undeniably vain and almost ethereally good-looking, his only compliment to Mackie was to observe that he looked as though he had a dead caterpillar on his upper lip. Mackie's own letters to Morrissey have never been seen, but Morrissey's responses to him are suggestive at times, almost like one elderly Noël Coward scene-queen writing to another – as if *daring* a relationship, should they meet, that might transcend the platonic. So far as is known they never did and from now on Morrissey would conduct himself, personally and within his work, with the same degree of guarded titillation – seemingly flaunting his sexuality on the one hand, but always acting defensively when directly questioned about it; feigning lack of experience or celibacy, which many believed was but a cover-up for the fact that he was just another normal young man with normal desires. It is an undisputed fact that just about everyone who meets him, young or old, male or female, enemy or fan, finds him physically irresistible despite his occasionally *un*attractive views.

Morrissey's closest male friend was James Maker, a slightly older Londoner of Mancunian parentage. The singer mentions 'Jimmy' in one of his letters to Robert Mackie, saying that he is going to spend the weekend at Maker's flat in London, adding, 'We often sit on the balcony looking for UFO's. We're such a wild pair (yawn) . . . one so modern as you would find us boring, but most people find us *très* amusing.' James Maker was flagrantly effeminate, possessed of matinee-idol looks, was self-confessedly sex-mad, has admitted to appearing in two gay porn films – *Bike Boys Go Ape* and *Well-Hung Studs* – and in a varied career has fronted several bands. Peter Adams, who ran The Gemini Club in Huddersfield (an ex-local where, amusingly, one had to press a buzzer and be 'vetted' through an upstairs window before being allowed in) was certain that there was something between the two men. He told me:

We used to run Saturday evening trips to the gay village in Manchester. First we would take in a pub – Dickens, where the trannies hung out, or Stuffed Olives where the drinks were cheaper than anywhere else. When we were feeling especially brave we'd try the Thompsons Arms or the Union, where all the rough stuff congregated – you'd never believe *how* rough! Then we would go on to a club, or maybe the Church in Bolton. In some of those places Jimmy Maker was unmissable: drop-dead gorgeous, showing off on the dance-floor. Morrissey wasn't known in those days. He was your typical shrinking violet, hanging around in the background or sitting at the bar. I never saw either of them cruising. Jimmy could have had the pick of the club. He didn't. He and Morrissey always arrived together, and they always left together, which certainly said something to me.

Much later, Morrissey himself spoke to *Melody Maker*'s Frank Owen about an incident that can only have been an attempted gay-bashing involving himself and James Maker, though by all accounts not the first. Owen had caught up with The Smiths in Cleveland, Ohio, on 8 August 1986, and interviewed the singer shortly before the group were about to go on stage. Morrissey complained bitterly when Owen published his comments in the paper's 27 September issue, yet in all honesty he had seen Owen's tape recorder sitting on the table between them, and should have exercised caution. He did not, and as such had no one to blame but himself, for this certainly *was* a classic case of Bigmouth Strikes Again.

Describing the incident as the worst night of his life, Morrissey explained how he and Maker had been heading for Devilles (a gay club, Owen made a point of stressing), but had begun their evening at the Thompsons Arms. Between the two watering holes, in a car park near the Chorlton Street bus station, they had encountered 'a gang of thirty beer monsters all in their late twenties, all creeping around us'. The pair had taken to their heels, but the mob had caught up with Maker and started kicking him around. He had not been too badly hurt, however, and had managed to get away, and running in different directions in the hope of losing their pursuers they had met up in Piccadilly bus station and jumped on to a bus marked Stretford – only to find it driverless. By now, the thugs had caught up with them again. 'We had all these coins and we just threw them in their faces and flew out of the bus,' Morrissey told Owen, next explaining how he and Maker had rushed across the road, boarded the nearest bus *with* a driver, and encountered more trouble: 'Suddenly the emergency doors swing open and these tattooed arms fly in – it was like *Clockwork Orange*. The bus is packed, nobody gives a damn. So we run upstairs and the bus begins to move and we end up in Lower Broughton. For some reason we get out and we're in the middle of nowhere – just hills.' Morrissey concludes by explaining how he and Maker were compelled to walk back to Manchester, after failing to find a telephone at the nearest house – the door of which had been opened by a 63-year-old Teddy Boy, 'We came back home to my place, finally, at something like 5 am, and listened to *Horses* by Patti Smith and wept on the bed.'

Owen, as if attempting to defend himself, observed how, in Manchester in those days, in order to seek sanctuary from gay-bashers who might pick on the wrong person, one had 'little alternative but to seek refuge in the gay clubs, like Dickens (a sleaze pit where your feet stuck to the floor when you walked in), or the gay pubs, like the Thompsons Arms, the Rembrandt or the Union (the hippest spot of degeneracy in town – full of trannies with plastic legs).' This cannot be right: most heterosexual men would not have been seen dead in this part of town, let alone its clubs and pubs. And Morrissey was very definitely and enthusiastically speaking 'boys-town' from experience when he took Owen on a trip down memory lane:

> The gay scene in Manchester was a little bit heavy for me. I was a delicate bloom. Do you remember the Union? Too heavy for me, as was [the] Dickens. The Rembrandt I could take. It was a bit kind of craggy. There was no place, at that time, in Manchester in the very early stages, that one could be surrounded by fascinating, healthy people – fascinating healthy bikers, for example. It was always like the cross-eyed, club-footed, one-armed, whatever! . . . Do you remember Bernard's Bar, now Stuffed Olives? If one wanted peace and to sit without being called a parade of names then that was the only hope. Bernard's Bar was fine for a while, but what I was really into was the music. That's where punk fitted in . . . I never liked the Ranch. I have a very early memory of it and it was very, very heavy. I never liked Dale Street. There was something about that area of Manchester that was too dangerous.

It probably goes without saying that there must have been *some* attraction between himself and James Maker, added to which was their common bond of wit, high intellect, gross outspokenness and the aforementioned love of danger and recklessness. Morrissey's *New York Dolls* is inscribed, 'This book of mine is dedicated entirely to James Maker, who lives it.' Listening to Maker speak, and reading transcripts of his interviews, he is *so* similar to Morrissey that one may only wonder who influenced whom in their acquiring of carefully nurtured campology mannerisms. Speaking of the young Morrissey, Maker told David Cavanagh of *Q* in January 1984:

> Life had fashioned a Spartan, crushingly monotonous biscuit-coloured pattern for him. His life was hugely unelaborated. He turned to his own contemplations and he sought expression in the ideology and ritual of his own life. He breathed for art . . . depended on nobody but himself. At the age of seventeen he was possessed of great intellect and humour. His presence was entirely unassuming

but he could lay people waste with laughter at a sentence, effortlessly.

Morrissey's final letter to Robert Mackie ended, 'Life is a terrible, terrible thing, Robert. Going Down Slow.' There would soon be another man in his life; however, this relationship would never be considered as anything other than very definitely platonic: Johnny Marr.

The Americans had had Rodgers & Hart, Lerner & Loewe, Simon & Garfunkel, Leiber & Stoller. Britain had had Lennon & McCartney. On the continent there had been Jacques Brel & Mort Shuman. In the wake of these, the very unlikely partnership of Morrissey & Marr would influence *their* generation – failing to attract an international coterie of stars covering their work (unlike these other great collaborators) only because *their* work was so insular and personal to its lyricist. Loosely equating with Barbara – France's biggest ever singer-songwriter, whose songs were similarly intimate – absolutely *no one* can put over a Morrissey lyric other than Morrissey himself. This is why so few artistes have tried, and why when they *have* tried, the results have generally been mediocre at best.

Born on 31 October 1963, Johnny Marr (né John Martin Maher) was, like his future partner, the son of Irish immigrants who had moved to Manchester; since 1973 he had lived in Wythenshawe. He had attended a better school than Morrissey (St Augustine's Grammar), but had not fared as well, and certainly had not acquired the same intellectual standing. Marr's chief interests at school had been football (at one time he'd played for the Manchester Boys and was offered a trial with Manchester City) and music. The first record he had bought had been T. Rex's 'Jeepster'. Not as outspoken as Morrissey, though no shrinking violet and something of a precursor to the Gallagher brothers where expletives were required to make a point, Marr told *NME*'s Danny Kelly in April 1991, when fame was largely behind him, 'I was one of those kids who always got the *plastic* guitar for Christmas. Everybody knew me as "that cunt who walks around with a guitar-case who thinks he's gonna be a big success." I developed a thick skin.'

Marr, a guitar virtuoso at twelve, was also a serious New York Dolls/Patti Smith fan. Cocky and sure of himself, he knocked around with Andy Rourke, a long-haired classmate from Ashton-upon-Mersey who, it later transpired, was already experimenting with soft drugs. The pair, notorious truants, spent much of their time jamming at Rourke's house to recordings of heroes Rory Gallagher, Nils Lofgren, Marc Bolan and Keith Richards – Marr on guitar/harmonica, Rourke on acoustic guitar. By 1977 they were playing semi-professionally with their group, The Paris Valentinos, augmented by two schoolfriends: drummer Bobby Durkin, who spent some time with the Manchester Youth Orchestra, and on vocals/bass, Kevin Williams, who later changed his surname to Kennedy and played Curly Watts in *Coronation Street*. Though their repertoire was excessively tilted towards rock (notably Thin Lizzy and Tom Petty) they performed mostly at church functions before splitting up. Marr later played briefly with Sister Ray, though by the end of 1979 he, Durkin and Rourke had joined White Dice, who *almost* landed a record deal with F-Beat, in London. The failure to do so knocked Marr back sufficiently to warrant him temporarily readjusting his sights and studying for his O Levels at Wythenshawe College – an enterprise he soon abandoned to form another short-lived ensemble, Freaky Party, before taking a job behind the counter at X Clothes, a clothing store in Manchester's Chapel Walks.

By this time, Marr had moved out of his parents' council house and was lodging with Granada Television producer Shelley Rohde, who allowed him use of her sound-proofed attic for rehearsals. Another new pal was Matt Johnson, who later achieved some success as The The, and who came close to persuading the youngster to join *his* group – which, of course, is what eventually did happen in 1989. Then there was Joe Moss, the rag-trade baron who owned the Crazy Face fashion chain and also supplied other outlets (including one where this author worked – we met during the late sixties) with cheap denim jeans. It was Moss who urged Marr to form a group, which he said he would back. Marr therefore set about finding a suitable vocalist and lyricist.

Johnny Marr had apparently already read some of Morrissey's biting lyrics, courtesy of Billy Duffy, but Duffy had fallen out with Morrissey and now refused to have anything to do with arranging an introduction. Some years later, after joining The Cult (then known as the Southern Death Cult), Duffy commented, 'Morrissey hated me because he thought we'd *stolen* some lyrics from him, which we probably had.' Marr therefore acquired Morrissey's address from another source, along with a warning: the Stretford bard could be tetchy and unapproachable. Marr decided to take his chances.

Leiber & Stoller, arguably the greatest American song-writing partnership of the fifties, had written a staggering roll-call of million-sellers for artistes as diverse as Elvis Presley, Peggy Lee, Edith Piaf and The Drifters. According to Mike Stoller (the composer), one morning he had opened his front door to find Jerry Leiber (the lyricist) standing on his doorstep with the announcement, 'Hi! Why don't we start doing songs together?' Poetically romantic, if therefore unoriginal, is the only way of describing the landmark meeting between Morrissey and Marr. The latter, with his foppish X Clothes garb, late sixties hairstyle and charm-the-birds-out-of-the-trees patter, must have been as much of a culture shock to Morrissey as the lanky, soft-spoken, bequiffed and bespectacled Morrissey must have been to Marr. One also gets the impression that the angelic-looking teenager may have been afraid of the older, bigger and tougher Morrissey – or at least apprehensive of having the door slammed in his face. Legend has it that Marr had piped up, 'This is how Leiber and Stoller met. I'm a fabulous guitar player and I'm interested in forming a group. Let me in!' Morrissey's response was a polite, 'What kind of music do you like?' – and the biggest 'musical marriage' since Lennon & McCartney had got off to a promising start, as Morrissey observed with typical Formbyesque fervour to *Sounds* a few years later:

> Johnny came up and pressed his nose against the window . . . it left a terrible stain. I think he'd been eating chocolate. He seemed terribly sure of what he wanted to do, which I liked. He said, 'Let's do it, and do it now!' So we did it! Then!

It is quite possible that neither account is accurate. Naturally, no witnesses were present at the time and, besides, both were speaking after their particular bubble had burst – romanticising the facts may have helped cushion the blow of their split. This is immaterial: all that matters is that they *did* meet.

The pair's working methods mirrored Leiber's & Stoller's, in that they rarely sat down together to produce a song. Morrissey, the trouper, maintains that his happiest moments have been spent in front of audiences, where reaction to his work is instantaneous. Johnny Marr, however, has always preferred the close confines of the studio, and from the outset of their professional relationship had the unenviable task of slaving away with the other members of the group for hours on end, day or night – to dutifully present the patron with arrangements for him to set his lyrics to, or so that he might pen new ones. This may explain why, in some of their songs, Morrissey sounds desperate to fit so many words into the shortest bar – Freddie Mercury-like – or grossly extend others, a system he uses to this day and which gives his work a unique extra dimension.

The day after their historic encounter – Morrissey's 23rd birthday – and allegedly surveyed by the James Dean poster in his bedroom depicting the actor's 'crucifixion' pose from *Giant*, the pair produced their first two songs. These were 'Suffer Little Children', and 'The Hand That Rocks The Cradle', the latter title possibly inspired by a 1917 US birth-control short of the same name. Its message ties in well with the theme of Hindley and Brady in 'Suffer Little Children'. The voice of a typical sixties parent promises the child protection from the horrors of a recurring nightmare, but probably makes matters worse by reminding him what these contain: the bogey man, the meat cleaver, the terrifying shapes of the darkened furniture. And Morrissey's *pièce de résistance* is the clever weaving of Al Jolson's 'Sonny Boy' into the closing stanza – an innocuous action that would later bring undue criticism from the tabloids.

The two songs were put on to demo tapes at Manchester's Decibel Studios, with the engineer, Dale Hibbert, playing bass and Freaky Party's Simon Wolstencroft on drums. From this point, things moved quickly. While Morrissey was jotting down lyrics on every conceivable subject, Johnny Marr set about arranging the group's first engagement – though effectively there *was* no group at this point. He secured a spot at the Manchester Ritz, supporting the ten-piece ensemble Blue Rondo A La Turk whose most recent album, *Chewing The Fat*, had been part-produced by Clive Langer; some years later, he would work with Morrissey, the solo artiste. Marr also accepted responsibility for finding the combo backing from a reputable record company, travelling down to London and sleeping on the floor of Matt Johnson's flat to save on hotel bills. For his part, Morrissey chose the name for his group, eschewing the latest fad for fancy names by picking a nomenclature that identified with his Northern roots and basic ordinariness: The Smiths. 'This is real music played by real people,' he would soon be telling journalists, 'There's no façade. We're simply here to be seen as real people.'

He also took the important step of dispensing with his Christian names – declaring that, as history had so often proved, poets worthy of their salt were only ever remembered by their surnames. This was taking a grandiose, indeed a blatantly arrogant stance that, had he fallen flat on his face with his adventure, would have made him a laughing stock. Fortunately, it was as if he had seen his guardian angel standing over his shoulder.

As a frontman, Morrissey would prove a determined, if not ruthless taskmaster. Because *he* had lived a straightforward, reasonably sanitised life, he was anxious that anyone who worked with him should follow his example. The New York Dolls and The Rolling Stones had lost members through drugs and debauchery. Jimi Hendrix, Janis Joplin and Jim Morrison had all self-destructed before thirty. Manchester's 'golden boys', Joy Division, had recently been devastated by the death of their singer, Ian Curtis: that good-looking, sad young man had made a spectacular exit by *carving* a smile on his face with a Stanley knife before hanging himself. Morrissey, unenthusiastic about the group, upset more than a few New Order fans by commenting, 'I saw them just before "the death" and I was astonishingly unmoved, as were the audience.' The Smiths would therefore be solidly anti-drugs, anti-violence and free from vice – albeit that Morrissey himself was *the* champion of thuggery in his lyrics and, cynics might say, not as sexually inexperienced as his self-proclaimed press liked to make out. Like him, the other members of the group would have to be pro-Northern, intelligent to a degree, and supportive of *his* views on issues such as politics and vegetarianism. Had he known of the drug habits of one of his future band mates, of course, The Smiths' line-up may have been entirely different: not only would he have rejected Andy Rourke, but also quite possibly the man who recommended him – Johnny Marr.

The drummer, Mike Joyce, was the first to be recruited. A few months older than Johnny Marr, this slightly frowning Fallowfield youth had played with punk band The Hoax before leaving school. More recently he had joined Victim. His audition for The Smiths took place at Spirit Studios, where Morrissey and Marr were so amazed by his 'balls-out' playing to their new song, 'What Difference Does It Make?' that they hired him on the spot, thereby signalling Victim's demise. What they did not know was that Joyce's frenetic performance was allegedly on account of his having just eaten magic mushrooms.

The Smiths – comprising Morrissey, Marr and Joyce, with Dale Hibbert on bass – made their public debut at the Ritz on 4 October 1982. Morrissey engaged James Maker as MC/go-go dancer: wearing a sixties-style suit and women's high-heels, he introduced the group in French! They performed three of their own songs ('The Hand That Rocks The Cradle', 'Suffer Little Children' and 'Handsome Devil') – and The Cookies' 'I Want A Boyfriend For My Birthday' without raising any eyebrows. Mike Joyce got carried away and burst a drumskin, and there was a problem with the microphone, which would not detach from a stand set far too low for the six-foot Morrissey, who spent the whole time on stage with his shoulders uncomfortably hunched. Even so, the group were well-received by the 300-strong, mostly gay audience, while James Maker pranced back and forth, alternating between the tambourine, the maracas, and flinging handfuls of confetti into the crowd.

'Handsome Devil' would bring condemnation from so-called moralists, but widespread approval from the gay community, who would quickly adopt Morrissey as an icon for almost a decade demanding, 'Is he or isn't he?' – until an ill-timed remark to a journalist from *The Face* appeared to give them their answer. His fascination with the subjects of rent boys, age-gap sex, car backseat dalliances, and even the fact that The Smiths' record label was actually *called* Rough Trade cannot be ignored, though this of course did not necessarily imply that Morrissey practised what he preached or extended his interests beyond the lyrical – tough-guy actors leave their characters behind on the film lot before heading home to their families, after all. It is an indisputable fact, however, that over the coming years The Smiths would immerse themselves in more gay and camp imagery than any other show business act. On the other hand, in these formative years, it should also be remembered that Morrissey was first and foremost an 'interpreter of situations', as near as damn it to France's Georges Brassens, who always performed his neo-pornographic vignettes in character.

The lyrics to 'Handsome Devil' pull no punches, but they are literary rather than vulgar, and would set Morrissey apart from out-to-shock contemporaries such as Frankie Goes To Hollywood. A teenager stops an older person (maybe a policeman – 'I say, I say, I say!') in the street to ask the time, but the elder character knows what the teenager *really* wants and declares, 'Let me get my hands on your mammary glands.' Then, having obviously 'scored', the older person offers to lend a hand to help see the teenager through examinations, adding, 'And when we're in your scholarly room, who will swallow whom?' Delectably poetic, but hardly subtle!

'Handsome Devil' was one of two songs recorded on to demo tapes at Chorlton's Drone Studios a few weeks later: the other was the only slightly less suggestive 'Miserable Lie', which contained the choice locker-room line, 'I look at yours, you laugh at mine.' By this time, Andy Rourke had replaced Dale Hibbert on bass. The Smiths, however, still lacked a recording contract. There were rumours that a deal *might* have been forthcoming from Factory Records. The company had been founded in 1979 by Tony Wilson, the former Cambridge graduate turned television presenter (*Granada Reports*) who also owned the Factory Club in Hulme, and the Beach Club. Wilson had booked all the big Manchester groups, including Joy Division and Ludus. He saw The Smiths at Manhattan Sound in January 1983, but possibly on account of the high-camp nature of their act, he merely offered them a thirty-minute spot at his newest acquisition – the Hacienda, on Whitworth Street West, which had opened the previous May. This catered largely for gay audiences, and was famed for its notorious 'Gay Traitor Cocktail Bar' cruising area. The group performed eight songs at the Hacienda including the newly composed 'Jeane', 'These Things Take Time' and 'Hand In Glove'. The latter boasted the phrase, 'The sun shines out of our behinds', informing would-be competitors, the audience (many of them high on poppers) and Tony Wilson especially, that they were *not* witnessing the latest five-minute sensation who would end up as last year's news.

The Hacienda's auditorium was gloomy, to say the least, which is why the group turned up with armloads of flowers to add a little colour. 'Flowers are virtually as important as the sound system,' Morrissey once said in a radio interview that was preceded by Dorothy Squires' 'Say It With Flowers'. Tony Wilson appears to have been suitably impressed by The Smiths' music that night, but a few years after the event he fell victim to the sharp end of Morrissey's tongue. Claiming that he had once seen a one-act play written by Morrissey, he compared him with lesbian scribe Jeanette Winterson, adding, 'He's a woman in a man's body – she's a woman in a man's body.' This was hardly a compliment and Morrissey hit back below the belt, with, 'He's a *pig* trapped inside a man's body. The day somebody shoves Wilson into the boot of a car and drives his body out to Saddleworth Moor, that's the day Manchester music will be revived.' When the critics took him to task over this, he compromised an apology, declaring that the first part of his statement had been misquoted – that he had actually said, 'Wilson's a *man* trapped inside a *pig's* body!' He also strenuously denied the claim made by Wilson's business partner, Richard Boon, that he had heard a pre-Smiths tape of Morrissey, unaccompanied, performing 'The Hand That Rocks The Cradle' with a different melody to the more familiar one, and (if such a tape does exist, with uncanny synchronicity bearing in mind that this was two years *before* he met Johnny Marr) Bessie Smith's blues classic, 'Wake Up, Johnny'.

With or without Wilson's help, The Smiths had crashed on to the Manchester scene and now began acquiring a cult following – or rather

Morrissey did, with his songwriting partner running a close second. For just as the likes of Queen were nothing without the flamboyance of Freddie Mercury, so The Smiths would have been 'just another group' without their flower-waving leader. The Smiths would prove themselves the most innovative British group since The Beatles and The Rolling Stones; in Morrissey they had a peerless lyricist. Despite their later gimmicks and overt campness they were never gender benders like Adam and the Ants and Culture Club. On the continent, *réaliste* singers were nothing new: death and unrequited love were as much a part of life as the daily diet. For the first time since the fifties, British audiences were to be treated to articulate, meaningful and inspirational lyrics set to stylish musical arrangements. The quartet *were* attractive to look at, of course, but attractiveness was not the key component of their being – as happens with today's grossly inferior boy bands. The Smiths always offered considerably more than glamour.

Such traits, so far as the more insular British were concerned, did have certain drawbacks, largely because as far as blinkered critics were concerned, intellect and commercialism did not always mix. Most of The Smiths' early eighties peers, particularly Duran Duran and Adam and the Ants, made up for a lack of lyrical know-how by making the most of the promotional video. Adam and the Ants' video of 'Prince Charming', with its superb characterisations and the bonus of an appearance by Morrissey favourite Diana Dors, becomes just another bland, repetitive ditty when heard on the humble turntable. For this reason The Smiths vowed that they would never make videos – and with few exceptions, never did.

An unwelcome guest at their early shows appears to have been Morrissey's father. Writing in March 1988, the editor of *Rock Sound Français* repeated a story that Morrissey had told him:

> There was this man of a certain age who, behind his whiskers and alcohol-ravaged pallor, looked incredibly like Morrissey. He would jump on to the stage and try to dance with the group. This was Morrissey's father. He used to hang around a lot backstage, trying to pick up girls. He became such a terrible embarrassment for the

singer, who ended up barring him from all The Smiths' future concerts.

Morrissey, meanwhile, was faced with a quandary when Babylon Books published his second biography, *James Dean Is Not Dead*, commissioning an initial print-run of 5,000 copies and effecting an option contract for a follow-up, to be provisionally entitled *Exit Smiling*. This was to have been a compendium of lesser-known (in Morrissey's opinion, though not that of the Hollywood box office) kitsch icons such as Sandra Dee, Agnes Moorehead, Thelma Ritter, William Reynolds and Sal Mineo – and rounding off the fifty-plus-page tome, 'Slush Be My Destiny', an essay on the deliciously outrageous Tallulah Bankhead. This was placed on the backburner, then abandoned completely in favour of The Smiths' debut single, 'Hand In Glove'/'Handsome Devil' – recorded during the Hacienda show and, financed by Joe Moss, mixed at the Strawberry 2 Studio.

On 23 March 1983, The Smiths made their London debut at the Rock Garden, in Covent Garden. Here, they were actually billed 'A Mancunian Five-Piece'. Both Joe Moss and Johnny Marr had urged Morrissey to dispense with James Maker: his 'exotic' dancing was acceptable in the Manchester gay clubs, but Moss in particular felt that his on-stage antics were distracting and he was afraid of inciting trouble from the anti-gay element that flocked to the Rock Garden on Wednesday nights. The songs, of course, were still the same, and not for the last time Morrissey, in his Evans Outsize Shops blouse, attracted wolf-whistles from some of the establishment's precursors to lager-louts. Even so, the evening was a success, and, clearly en route towards national recognition, The Smiths supported the notorious Sisters of Mercy on 6 May at the University of London. A little later, they supported Altered Images at the Hammersmith Palais. They *should* have appeared at the Leeds Futurama Festival, but Morrissey allegedly threw a tantrum and cancelled upon learning that the proposed headliner, former Buzzcock Howard Devoto (at one time Linder's boyfriend), had been replaced by The Bay City Rollers, whom, critics say, he could not stand.

The Smiths' very first interview for *NME* appeared on 14 May, headed CRISP SONGS AND SALTED LYRICS (an allusion to the famous Smiths potato snacks) and conducted by Cath Carroll, who had seen them at the Hacienda. She aptly observed, 'Smithville could be anywhere, a timeless zone where high-school and low-life collide. They're the young generation and they've got something to say.' Though the Wildean quips and Marr expletives were not in evidence that day, Morrissey and his partner were very sure of themselves, with the other two members of the group barely getting a word in. 'Songwriting just isn't there any more and that's why we're important,' Morrissey expostulated. And when questioned about the 'meaningfulness' of 'Handsome Devil', without wishing for the conversation to get around to sexuality, Morrissey chimed in, not for the first time hoping to avoid being asked *that* question, 'The lyrics I write are specifically genderless. I don't want to leave anybody out. Handsome is a word that people think is applied to males . . . but I know lots of handsome women. After all, there *is* such a thing as a pretty male.'

'Hand In Glove'/'Handsome Devil' was released that same month as part of an anticipated temporary contract with Rough Trade, whose headliners in those days were the now largely forgotten Aztec Camera, until something better came along. In March 1994, the company's director, Geoff Travis, recalled his very different meetings with Morrissey and Marr to Brian Boyd of the *Irish Times*: 'There was something about Johnny Marr. He didn't look or act like all the other hapless musicians with demo tapes in their hands.' And of Morrissey he said, 'He had a very striking presence and he seemed to bear down on me. He said, "I want to know everything that is going through your head. The first Smiths single is being recorded. This is a very important day in my life."'

Later, when it was all over, Travis changed his opinion of the 'nice Manchester boy', telling the same interviewer, 'I've seen Morrissey in a lot of different states over the years, both good and bad. As an artist I have nothing but the highest respect for him – as a human being I think he has some way to go in certain areas.'

The single did well in the independent charts, got nowhere in the national, but has since more than made up for this. Most importantly, it got The Smiths noticed. The sleeve, setting an important camp-classic precedent, caused even more of a stir than the lyrics: it depicted a nude, rear-view shot of gay porn star Leo Ford, one-time lover of the outrageous diva Divine, who appeared at the Hacienda around the same time as The Smiths. In the shot, Ford is leaning against the locker-room wall on the set of one of his films. The Huddersfield Gemini Club's Peter Adams, who witnessed the group's Hacienda show, recalled, 'Leo Ford wasn't restricted to films. He did jerk-off shows all over the world, including one in Manchester which The Smiths were invited to. I very much doubt their manager even gave them the message. Still, it was a nice sentiment seeing as they'd used his arse to their advantage, so to speak.'

Morrissey stirred the pot of dissension in July 1983 by telling *HIM* magazine's Catherine Miles:

> I adore the picture. It evokes both sorrow and passion. It could be taken as a blunt statement against sexism, yet in using that picture I am being sexist. It's *time* the male body was exploited. Men need a better sense of their own bodies. Naked males should be splashed around the Co-op. I'm sure this would go a long way towards alleviating many problems, even that of rape.

'Hand In Glove' and 'Handsome Devil' are songs about unconventional love, possibly gay love. Certainly, as The Smiths made the transition from clubs to mainstream venues, Morrissey's flirtation with gay culture escalated. Yet the more famous Morrissey became and the more he flaunted such frequently beautiful, plaintive stanzas, the more reticent he would be when expected to discuss the rumours he had nurtured.

In later years, as a solo artiste with an indisputably 'laddish' air to him, Morrissey would not have discussed the merits of gay nudity with anyone, let alone *HIM* magazine – which, in the early eighties, was the biggest-selling such publication in the country. During this first balmy summer of Smithdom, however, when fame and fortune were just beckoning, he spoke freely with the gay press. When Catherine Miles remarked that even openly gay rock stars would never take the risks he was taking with his lyrics, Morrissey responded, 'Obviously people don't want to insert cyanide in chocolate because it won't sell. Pop *is* tame.' When asked if, in view of The Smiths having been engaged for Manchester's *September In The Pink* celebrations, he would like to play more specifically gay venues, he replied, 'To me, it's just people with ears. We're a group that doesn't recognise any boundaries. I don't want to get up on a soapbox. I detest sexual segregation. One of the things that separates The Smiths from other bands is the concern with words.'

It was the group's 'concern with words', in the days before Morrissey's interviews were peppered with such words as 'loneliness' and 'celibacy' – or at least it was the three other Smiths' willingness to follow, seemingly without question, the path their frontman had marked out for them – that had endeared them to the gay community in the first place. Before The Smiths, known gay or bisexual stars such as Johnnie Ray, Michael Holiday and Billy Fury had *always* addressed their love songs to women, though more often than not they were singing them with men in mind. But what did Morrissey actually think of the gay scene at the time – and did he still go clubbing? His response would endear him to thousands more gay men:

I had a brief spasm some time ago. Hmph. I was never terribly popular. The gay scene seems so full of hate in all directions. Then there's the heterosexist behaviour of a lot of gay men. Before clonism, the scene was extreme in being so totally *female*. Now some of the men are undistinguishable from Tetley Bittermen. Obviously gays shouldn't be frightened of *rock*, but again it comes down to wanting as many people as possible to hear our music. I want to be pinned on everybody's wall – or pinned *against* everybody's wall. Could you possibly make me a sex symbol?

Morrissey certainly liked exploiting his own body, regularly whipping open his shirt to expose his finely tuned torso as often as not inscribed with some potent message, or occasionally he would shrug the garment back over his shoulders to titillate, while always staying well within the bounds of Catholic decency. In his definitive biography of James Dean,

The Mutant King (Plexus, 1974), David Dalton writes of his subject's androgyny and the fact that he obviously fancied himself – and might just as well have been describing Morrissey. All one has to do is swap their names around and substitute 'singer' for 'actor':

> Androgyny is the traditional sexuality of the classic performer. Jimmy's interest in his own body has the autoerotic quality of all great actors. The relationship of an actor with his audience takes place in a zone of sexually-charged reciprocal currents, and the androgynous character of Jimmy's roles is a fusion of both male and female elements. It was the material out of which he created, composed his polymorphous body. All vices have claws and can be traced through the unerasable hieroglyphics of the features and gestures . . .

It was during The Smiths' show at the University of London that they were 'spotted' by John Walters, the producer of Radio One's *John Peel Show*, who invited them to record four songs for the programme's 31 May edition – which remains one of the series' most memorable and most-repeated by public demand, though much of the fuss centred around the airing of one of Morrissey's most controversial lyrics, the stunning 'Reel Around The Fountain'.

Again, when discussing the song, one has to consider that Morrissey may be singing in character. Fifty years earlier, Gracie Fields sang, 'Marry me, Sally, you're more than the whole world to me', while Al Jolson once crooned, 'I'm just wild about Harry . . . the heavenly blisses of his kisses fill me with ecstasy.' No questions had been asked, no stones cast. Though it's doubtful, when one considers his knowledge of Polari slang, Morrissey may not have known that the title of his song was also a gay porndom term for oral sex (running the point of the tongue around the tip of the penis until ejaculation occurs), though 'Shove me on the patio, I'll take it slowly' coming straight after: 'It's time the tale were told of how you took a child and made him old,' should be self-explanatory. What also must be taken into consideration, bearing the widespread but erroneous theory that the song is about paedophilia, is that it is the younger of the two who is taking the initiative to importune/seduce the older one, and not the other way around. Also the line, 'You can pin and mount me like a butterfly' is purloined from the film *The Collector* (1965), the line delivered by lepidopterist Terence Stamp to Samantha Eggar, at a time when the word 'mount' had a different connotation than today. Years later, when asked for his idea of perfect happiness, Morrissey would respond, 'Being Terence Stamp!'

Following their runaway success on the *John Peel Show*, The Smiths were given a spot on the similarly high-rating *David Jensen Show*, also on Radio One – but with one proviso: they were not permitted to perform 'Reel Around The Fountain'. Someone connected with the programme who knew *exactly* what the term meant contacted the *Sun*, resulting in a badly researched feature appearing on 25 August headed, CHILD-SEX SONG PUTS BEEB IN A SPIN. Its author, who obviously cannot have listened to the song, observed, 'it contains clear references to picking up kids for sexual tricks' – and worse still added, 'As part of their live act, they also do a version of "Climb Upon My Knee, Sonny Boy", about picking up a seven-year-old in a park.' Not only was all of this wrong, the latter statement was blatantly slanderous. The other tabloids followed suit, accusing The Smiths of condoning paedophilia, again seemingly without listening to the song. Plans to issue the track as a single were aborted, and Morrissey hit back with a press statement of his own, saying that the author 'has misinterpreted the facts. Quite obviously we don't condone child molesting or anything that vaguely resembles it. What more can be said?'

Morrissey's only support came from Alex McKenna, *HIM*'s news editor, who had watched the singer fend off hundreds of admirers with a massive bunch of gladioli at London's Venue on 15 September. In the magazine's November 1983 issue (appearing too late, on account of the monthlies' lengthy printing set-up, by which time much of the fuss had died down), McKenna observed, 'Out-gay Morrissey wrote the lyrics of "Handsome Devil", which cloth-eared journalists on the *Sun* and *Sounds* magazine, enlisting the help of Tory MP Geoffrey Dickens, have tried to allege is about child-molesting. Buy [the record] and see why The Smiths' office told *HIM*, "It's such a ridiculous thing to say that none of us even bothered to read the articles."'

For once, silence might have been the better policy, for though the lyrics of the song definitely do not suggest child molestation, the sexually active narrator leaves us with no doubt that he *does* want to have sex with the older person (not necessarily a man) he has long been fascinated with – adding to the equation that, in cases like this, it is frequently the younger party, regarded as the 'victim' by the unknowing, who does the chasing.

Because Morrissey did not argue with the BBC themselves over the banned song, The Smiths were invited back on the *John Peel Show*. Of their new songs, aired during their brief recent summer tour, 'This Charming Man' was considered the best of a good clutch, and was chosen as their next single. Produced by John Porter and coupled with 'Jeane' (produced by former Teardrop Explodes guitarist Troy Tate), it was released in November 1983 in a cover that, though less controversial than its predecessor, was no less striking.

Morrissey had requested a still from Jean Cocteau's avant-garde film, *Orphée* (1949), featuring Cocteau's lover, Jean Marais, face and hands pressed against a mirror as if embracing his own image. Regarded by cinema-goers at the time as The Most Beautiful Man In France, Marais granted permission to use the still, originally used to promote the film on playbills, but strongly disapproved of what Morrissey did with it – turning it on its side and 'adding' sand, so that the actor looked like he was lying down at the edge of a pool. 'Cocteau would have turned in his grave,' Marais told me in 1990. 'By changing the photograph he completely misinterpreted and *ruined* the message of the scene. I wish I had never given permission for it to be used.'

The song, preceded by a stirring introduction by Johnny Marr, is yet another tale of age-gap sex – the story of the 'jumped up pantry boy' (a later Victorian term for a rent boy) who, after his bicycle gets a flat tyre, finds himself being picked up by the nice man whose car has smooth leather seats, but who ultimately cannot understand why someone so handsome should *care* about him.

The Smiths made their *Top Of The Pops* debut with the song on 24 November 1983, shortly before their return visit to Manchester's Hacienda. It brought them instant national recognition, and reached number 25 in the charts. Sting, The Police's frontman, thought he was doing the group a favour by asking them to support The Police on their forthcoming tour. Johnny Marr's response to this was a sharp, 'We're a hundred times more important than The Police will ever be.' The group's success also saw them parting company with Joe Moss, who wanted to spend more time with his family. As for Morrissey, when asked to explain The Smiths' cult following, he rattled a few more cages by responding, 'People are dedicated to us because we deserve it. It's all quite natural because I really think we merit a great deal of attention.'

Unable to find a major record company, despite their success, Morrissey and Marr had re-negotiated a clever fifty-fifty deal with Rough Trade – not dissimilar to the ones some of the major American movie stars had signed upon the collapse of the studio system – which also offered them a share of the profits. The money they subsequently earned for the company is more than the company ever thought possible. The hurricane speed with which The Smiths moved, and the idolatry bestowed upon their singer, was alarming. Their 7 December performance at Derby's Assembly Rooms – exciting to watch, but with Morrissey persistently half a tone off-key throughout – was filmed, and two days later broadcast on BBC2's *The Old Grey Whistle Test*. For the first time, it would appear, the proceedings had been brought to an early conclusion when dozens of mostly male fans invaded the stage to *hug* Morrissey – their actions were initially (and in later concerts, often purposely) misinterpreted by security staff, whose rough handling of the situation resulted in several injuries. Whether any of these pasty-faced apostles actually understood the message of 'Reel Around The Fountain', which astonishingly did not end up on the cutting-room floor, is not known. The programme led to a doubling of the group's fanbase.

In December 1983, reluctantly it would appear, The Smiths made their first trip to America: a dance mix of 'This Charming Man', along with several remixes, had been released against their wishes by New York producer Francois Kervorkian – and on the strength of this they had been booked at the city's Danceteria on New Year's Eve. Professionally and personally, the occasion was a disaster. Mike Joyce caught chickenpox; Morrissey tripped during the performance and fell off the stage. The group were offered a brief tour of the East Coast, but turned this down and flew back to England – Johnny Marr to his flat in Earls Court and Morrissey to his new Kensington home. The only good thing to have emerged from their American misadventure, they later said, was 'Heaven Knows I'm Miserable Now', written in their dingy room at the Iroquois Hotel. Released in May 1984, the single would reach number 10 in the charts.

Also in December 1983, The Smiths were given the official seal of approval by the gay press when the legendary Kris Kirk of *Gay Times* included them in his annual *New Year Gay Alphabet* round-up, describing Morrissey as gay:

> What a gay chart we have at the close of the year with Marilyn, Georgie, Frankie Goes to Hollywood, Tom Robinson, Elton John, and the sensational Smiths plus a large number of closet cases crowding out the single scene. *S* stands for Sexy and The Smiths which, in my book, are synonymous. Gay lead singer Morrissey has one of those voices which makes you feel horny and want to burst into tears at the same time . . . Mark my word, they'll be HUGE in '84.

Meanwhile, The Smiths' next single, 'What Difference Does It Make?'/'Back To The Old House' (according to one *Les Inrockuptibles* interview, the former was the one Smiths song Morrissey truly *loathed*), was released in January 1984, and reached number 12 in the charts. Continuing his fascination with the 1965 film *The Collector*, Morrissey commissioned a still from the film of Terence Stamp, holding a lepidopterist's chloroform pad. Stamp objected, and a hasty cover-switch was effected with Morrissey himself emulating a near-exact pose – quiffless, and holding a glass of milk!

Voted Best New Act in the *NME* poll, at the end of the month The Smiths began their first international tour: by the summer they would have played over fifty dates in England, France, Belgium, Holland, Germany and Scandinavia. Part of their show at the Amsterdam Meerward was released on a bootleg album, and an edited version of their longest show so far (25 songs) at Hamburg's Markthalle was filmed and broadcast on the hugely popular *Rockpalast* magazine. On 9 May, Morrissey donned a gold-lamé jacket and eschewed his quiff for a Brylcreemed Teddy Boy hairstyle when The Smiths took to the stage at L'Eldorado, on Paris' Boulevard de Strasbourg. Beforehand, there had been considerable outrage when the director of this, one of the city's most hallowed music halls, had been accused of 'cashing in on mediocrity' by hiring a little-known foreign pop group to follow in the footsteps of immortals such as Piaf, Mistinguett and Chevalier. The performance itself, part of which was screened on the French showcase *Les Enfants Du Rock*, was dire on the whole, though there was a fleeting special moment when Morrissey, en-profile in the legendary silver spotlight, inadvertently raised his eyes towards the rafters. It was a magical instant. As an audience member myself that night, it reminded me of the dated but still potent images that survive on old newsreel footage of the period fondly remembered by the French as *Les Années Folles* – and made up for the mediocrity of everything else that had transpired that evening. I remember telling a journalist friend at the time, 'The group probably won't survive the decade, but their singer certainly will!' Several years later, as a solo artiste with a string of hits tucked under his belt, Morrissey would prove me right by triumphing at another bastion of Parisian working-class culture, L'Elysée Montmartre, receiving a ten-minute standing ovation for what many French fans saw as his signature song, 'Will Never Marry'.

In those early days, it is extremely doubtful that Continental fans with an astute knowledge of the English language grasped the *full* meaning of most of Morrissey's lyrics until these began appearing on record inserts. Once this happened, one song that had a particular impact, especially in France, was 'Pretty Girls Make Graves', with its theme of an older, voracious woman attempting to 'straighten out' the timid man, using the 'quick and easy way', despite his plea, 'I'm not the man you think I am!' Later on in the song, when she has almost succeeded in dragging him to the end of the pier, he confesses his impotence – 'He will not rise for *anyone*!' – and she latches on to another stud who may satisfy her needs.

The Smiths only performed twice on French soil. They always refused to play the out-of-town arenas favoured by their Gallic contemporaries because, they declared, these were impersonal. Yet the Olympia, the Palais de Congrés, and the Théatre de Chatelet would have nothing to do with them because of the brouhaha caused by their engagement at L'Eldorado. My friend Fernando Lumbroso, who ran the Mogador, said, 'I *almost* booked them, but I valued my beautiful red velvet seats. And their manager was one of the *rudest* men I ever spoke to!'

Foreign audiences, accustomed to the more conventional *chansonniers*, were bemused to witness Morrissey gyrating about the stage with a bunch of flowers sticking out of the back pocket of his usually baggy denims. The fans loved the gimmick, while serious rock fans used to the more stylised performances of Johnny Hallyday and Eddie Mitchell scoffed because these movements usually detracted from Morrissey's lyrical voice and frequently made him sing flat. In Britain, the flowers were once eschewed for a miniature bush, and in one *Top Of The Pops* appearance the 'gormless Lancashire lad' effect was completed with a pair of NHS spectacles. Morrissey claimed that this was his way of displaying that the entire British music scene was way over the top, and added with deliberate George Formby double-entendre, 'I don't mind if people remember me for my bush, so long as it's for artistic reasons.'

As had happened in New York, The Smiths felt uneasy performing away from home, much of this being down to the strictly vegetarian Morrissey and Marr trying to cope with over-rich foreign food. Even so, they might have thought about that before undertaking the tour, and they earned themselves few favours when, after flying back to London for a *Top Of The Pops* appearance with Sandie Shaw, they cancelled their remaining dates in Germany, Switzerland and Austria.

3

Oscillating Wildly: A Band of Brothers

'He's childlike, very extreme in his emotional reactions to people. I feel
he's been indoctrinated against trusting people at some stage in his life.'
— Jo Slee

The Smiths had arrived back in England to tremendous acclaim: their
debut album, simply bearing their name, had been released on 20
February. The group had originally put down ten tracks in a Wapping
basement studio, run by Troy Tate, during the summer of 1982 *before*
their first stage appearance. These had subsequently been scrapped, and
the whole concept re-recorded with additional material in new sessions
produced by John Porter at Manchester's Pluto Studios. Three of the
songs taped by Tate – 'These Things Take Time', 'Handsome Devil' and
'Accept Yourself' – were replaced by 'Suffer Little Children', 'Pretty Girls
Make Graves' and 'Still Ill'. In the latter, Morrissey champions the dole
queue, cockily declaring, on behalf of those who know the system and
are getting enough cash from the state to make working for a living
unnecessary, 'England is mine and it owes me a living.'

The album, which reached number 2 in the charts, arguably contained more gay themes and references than straight ones, and its cover
was graced with a doctored photograph of Andy Warhol's in-house 'wet
dream-hustler-stud' Joe Dallesandro, taken from the 1968 underground
movie *Flesh*. Nicknamed 'Little Joe' on account of his phenomenal
endowment (inasmuch as Little John had been so named because he

had been very tall), Dallesandro had started out posing for beefcake pictures for the Athletic Model Guild before being discovered by Warhol producer Paul Morrissey, and put into a series of semi-pornographic films, best described by the title of the one he made in 1970 – *Trash*. In *Flesh*, Dallesandro plays a rent boy whose customers, unappealing as they are, are still far better-looking than him. The still acquired for The Smiths' album depicts him bare-chested, six-pack rippling and head down, perched on the edge of the bed next to a young client (Louis Waldon), who is licking his lips in anticipation of what is on offer.

Much of the imagery and Morrissey's lyrics appear to have been rather alien to the other members of the group. Mike Joyce and Andy Rourke were so thrilled to be part of a high-profile pop unit that they took potential sleeve photographs and demo-tapes home to impress their families, who apparently *did* understand some of what was going on. Joyce recalled to David Cavanagh of *Select* early in 1993, 'Johnny said to me, Uh, I've got the cover of the new album. And it's a picture of a bloke going down on another bloke. So I'm like, GREAT! FAN-TAS-TIC! Hey, Mam, look what *I've* been doing for the last eight months!'

There was no way, of course, that The Smiths would have got away with using the whole shot: Dallesandro's image was therefore blurred slightly and Waldron removed completely. Even so, it caused a stir – largely because the tabloids informed a generally unknowing public *where* it had come from.

The 'gay issue' was alluded to on 7 June when *Rolling Stone* published a feature on The Smiths. That evening the group were giving a concert at the Hammersmith Palais, and a somewhat weary-through-rehearsing Morrissey spoke of his literary interests and dashed off a perfunctory attack against Margaret Thatcher: 'She's only one person and she can be destroyed. I just pray there is a Sirhan Sirhan somewhere. It's the only remedy for this country at the moment.' Morrissey's sexuality, however, was foremost on journalist James Henke's agenda. He began his piece, 'He goes by a single name . . . He calls himself "a prophet for the fourth gender", admits he's gay, but adds he's also celibate.' Given his propensity for privacy, one cannot imagine Morrissey making so direct a statement, and he laughed off the situation later by saying that the 'gay' tag had been wishful thinking on the journalist's part.

More press attacks came in May 1984 when, promoting 'Heaven Knows I'm Miserable Now', Morrissey appeared on *Top Of The Pops* wearing his usual baggy shirt, denims, NHS spectacles and beads – and dangling an unconnected hearing-aid. The tabloids accused him of mocking the afflicted; more knowledgeable viewers may have imagined he was emulating another idol, fifties 'Nabob of Sob' Johnnie Ray. Morrissey said that the gesture was his tribute to a deaf fan who had written to him, professing the miseries brought about by such a handicap. He added, 'I did it to show the fan that deafness shouldn't be some sort of stigma that you try to hide.' Even so, many die-hard fans copied him.

On the flipside of 'Heaven Knows I'm Miserable Now', The Smiths placed 'Suffer Little Children', a work of astonishing sadness and conviction by Morrissey, simply but effectively orchestrated by Johnny Marr – quite possibly the first truly great British *réaliste* song. The piece denounces Hindley as the more evil of the two murderers – because she supplied Brady with his victims, luring them to him – and the dialogue alternates between the spirits of the children who plead, 'Over the moors, take me to the moors – dig a shallow grave and I'll lay me down' and the censurer (Morrissey himself), who reminds Hindley that her crimes will haunt her until the day she dies, then darkly concludes, 'Manchester, so much to answer for . . . but fresh lilaced moorland fields cannot hide the stolid stench of death.'

The title for the song came from a feature about Hindley that had appeared in the *Sunday Times*. Under the heading THE WOMAN WHO CANNOT FACE THE TRUTH, the editorial claimed that the murderess was unable to leave her prison cell without the other inmates chanting from the Bible, 'Suffer the little children to come unto me!' 'Suffer Little Children' was also the title of Chapter 20 in Emlyn Williams' book *Beyond Belief: The Story of Ian Brady & Myra Hindley*; Chapter 13 was headed, 'Hindley Wakes', also quoted in the song, as is the line, 'Wherever he has gone, I have gone . . . whatever he has done, I have done,' spoken by Hindley at her trial when asked about her involvement with Brady.

The song got Morrissey into hot water with the media. It refers to the children by name – paying especial attention to the 'pretty white beads' worn by Lesley-Anne Downey at the time of her death. When relatives of another victim, John Kilbride, heard the record on a pub jukebox, they contacted the *Manchester Evening News*, which led to a very much overblown attack on Morrissey being syndicated to the national press. The *Sun*'s Jim Oldfield quoted the dead boy's surviving brother as saying 'Whoever wrote the song must be as sick as the killers. It's just blood money', while Lesley-Anne Downey's mother, Anne West, accused The Smiths of bringing back the horrors of the worst incident in the city's history. Neither they, nor the *Sun* journalist, can have listened to the song.

Morrissey was personally denounced as 'grossly insensitive' for including a photograph of Myra Hindley on the record sleeve. In fact, had any of these people taken the time to read the caption on the reverse they would have realised that the photograph, taken around the same time as the Moors Murders, of the hard-featured young woman with the badly peroxided hair, standing in front of a row of grimy terraced houses, was actually 'Spend! Spend! Spend!' pools winner Viv Nicholson, returning to her home town of Castleford after her husband's death in a car crash. Nicholson's picture had been substituted at the last minute when Morrissey's original choice, Albert Finney, had refused to be depicted with the slogan, 'Heaven Knows I'm Miserable Now', at a time when he was at the peak of his career. However, and again without listening to the lyrics to see what all the fuss was about, several major outlets removed the record from their shelves.

Not for the first time, Morrissey found himself the victim of a smear campaign, very much in the vein of the spate of celebrity rape or child abuse allegations that would clutter the tabloids twenty years down the line: often groundless accusations, bandied about indiscriminately, resulting in the limitless prejudice against the 'accused', who suddenly becomes the victim while the accuser is permitted to remain anonymous, even if the allegations are dismissed. Morrissey's press office released a statement that explained what should have been obvious in the first place:

The song was written out of a profound emotion by Morrissey, a Mancunian who feels that the particularly horrendous crime it describes must be borne by the conscience of Manchester . . . It is a memorial to the children and all like them who have suffered such a fate.

Morrissey made it blatantly clear that the song was a tribute to the children, that the photograph on the record sleeve was *not* the loathsome Hindley. He also contacted Anne West and John Kilbride's family – the former for two decades the unofficial spokeswoman and campaigner for the families of other murdered children. Morrissey and Mrs West met and became friends after she realised how truly sincere he was. She also realised that he was just as keen as she was that Hindley should rot in jail, despite the relentless efforts of campaigners such as Lord Longford who believed that if she was released, rehabilitation and counselling would put her back on the straight and narrow. Mrs West died before Hindley, still desperately worried that this monstrous woman might be granted her freedom.

As for Viv Nicholson, Morrissey was very much taken with the rags-to-riches-to-rags story of the coarsely spoken West Yorkshire housewife who had scooped over £150,000 on the football pools – an enormous amount in those days – blown the lot on a series of spending sprees and then, after her husband's death, become a Jehovah's Witness. Her ghost-written autobiography *Spend! Spend! Spend!* had been turned into a television drama, and would later be transferred to the legitimate stage. Nicholson's photograph appeared also on the cover of The Smiths' 'Barbarism Begins At Home' that was originally issued as a 12-inch promo in the UK – she looks very unladylike in a home-crocheted 'fanny-belt' mini-skirt, and is depicted standing in front of a Castleford pit. Morrissey actually met her: the pair were photographed strolling along Blackpool's promenade; he borrowed the line, 'Under the bridge we kissed [and] I ended up with sore lips,' from her book and included it in another song, 'Still Ill'.

Viv Nicholson also sang Morrissey's praises in *The South Bank Show*'s Smiths documentary, filmed at around the time their friendship ended quite abruptly. Having already expressed her delight at appearing on two of the group's sleeves, Rough Trade assumed that she would be pleased to make the hat-trick when Morrissey commissioned the cover for a Dutch CD of 'The Headmaster Ritual' in 1987. In the picture she is seen painting at an easel. According to Rough Trade (see Jo Slee's *Peepholism*, 1994), however, Nicholson objected when the CD was released in Britain – as a Jehovah's Witness she 'was embarrassed by the expression "spineless bastard" on the track 'Headmaster Ritual''. Many who knew Nicholson were surprised by this: on the two occasions that I encountered her, her own language was colourful to say the least.

The inimitable Morrissey wit was harnessed for a rare non-singing television appearance at around this time when he guested on the arts programme *Eight Days A Week*, alongside Wham!'s George Michael and DJ Tony Blackburn. *They* may have been enthusiastic about *Breakdance: The Movie*, but Morrissey put on his best Sitwellian voice to denounce it with a deliciously snappy, 'I find it almost *impossible* to care!'

The Smiths' next single, released in August 1984 – at a time when singles were not taken from albums commercially milked for all they were worth – was a new song, 'William, It Was Really Nothing'. It reached number 17 in the charts and caused another controversy with its cover: a homoerotic 'morning-after-the-night-before' shot of a nearly naked young man sitting forlornly on the edge of his bed. The photograph was tasteful, inoffensive. Even so, Rough Trade was instructed to change it, and subsequent pressings of the record were housed in a sleeve featuring a no less exploitative still of Billie Whitelaw from the 1967 film *Charlie Bubbles*. As for the subject of the song, the more gullible believe that it was Billy Fisher, the central character played by Tom Courtenay in *Billy Liar* (1963) – the story of a young man who evades a dull life by daydreaming that he is treading the gold-paved streets of London, in the days when such a myth existed. A more likely theory is that the subject is Billy Mackenzie, the bisexual singer from The Associates. Morrissey had met him earlier in the year, describing him as 'a whirlwind', whereas Mackenzie apparently told friends how much he *fancied* The Smiths' frontman. If so, Morrissey was arguably flying the gay flag when, as the narrator, he urges the eponymous hero to ditch his 'fat girl' and marry him instead. Simon Goddard observed in the June 2003 issue of *Record Collector*, 'Legend has it that [Mackenzie] paid a visit to the singer's flat only to abscond with a *James Dean* book and one of his shirts. "It wasn't my favourite," Morrissey lamented, "but these things are sacrosanct."' The devilishly attractive Mackenzie would respond with a song of his own: 'Steven, It Was Really Something'. Suffering from depression following the death of his much-loved mother, paranoid about his rapid hair loss and addicted to cottaging (picking up men for sex in public toilets), Mackenzie was found dead of a Paracetamol overdose in January 1997.

Meanwhile, in the wake of an Irish tour blighted by seasickness, dietary problems and flu (Johnny Marr became so ill that he was hospitalised), and with their second album, *Meat Is Murder*, nicely underway, Rough Trade put out *Hatful Of Hollow*. This was a comfortably assembled mid-price compilation album, a mixture of rarities and songs from the Peel/Jensen sessions, the whole packaged within an attractive gatefold sleeve depicting a pre-war Cocteau model reproduced in a French magazine from 1966. Inside the package was a photograph of The Smiths, snapped in their dressing room at Glastonbury: Morrissey bespectacled and wearing his controversial hearing aid, and Mike Joyce, himself looking Ortonesque in his under-shorts. 'For all their sexual ambivalence and lyrical unorthodoxy,' *NME* observed in those Morrissey-friendly days, 'Morrissey's songs are universal in the vulnerabilities and desires they seek to express.'

Morrissey's outspokenness and much-discussed *causes célebres*, which had alienated him from some sections of society but endeared him to many more, were challenged at around this time by the emergence of three very different gay-orientated ensembles: Bronski Beat, Culture Club and Frankie Goes To Hollywood. Boy George, as effeminate as they came, made headlines by professing that instead of sex, 'I'd rather have a cup of tea!' Bronski Beat's Jimmy Somerville discussed in the greatest anatomical detail the physical aspects of gay sex. Frankie Goes To Hollywood said everything in their lyrics – the BBC's ban of 'Relax', which championed fellatio, only sent it zooming to the top of the charts.

Of course, record companies, including Rough Trade, were interested in this 'pink explosion' not because it applauded specific issues, positive or otherwise, but because these groups were bringing in *money*. Peter Burton observed in the August 1984 issue of *Gay Times*, at a time when the charts were dominated by Hi-NRG records and hits by bands with a gay orientation:

> Is the high-visibility of gay men in the pop charts going to bring about a change in attitudes? Will queerbashers drop their weapons because they happen to like [Bronski Beat's] 'Smalltown Boy', 'Relax', or any of the string of The Smiths hits? Somehow it doesn't seem very likely. Will struggling gay bands suddenly find themselves snapped up by greedy record companies? Maybe – but it will simply be bandwagon jumping rather than enterprise. And – after all – the music *has* to be good to make an impression and sell.

The Smiths saw no point in trying to compete with these outfits, whose chief selling points were (certainly in Frankie Goes To Hollywood's case) vulgar lyrics and raunchy, no-holds-barred videos. When questioned by Martin Aston of Dutch magazine *Oor* in November 1986 about the elements of camp and camp humour in his songs, in comparison with the songs of these rivals, Morrissey would reflect, 'I worship camp humour and the several levels of it, but there's the very frivolous "You old queen" level that I never indulge in. Alastair Sim and Margaret Rutherford – *that's* the campness I idolise.' The Smiths declared themselves a smut-free zone, and believed that they possessed sufficient originality to outlast any rival, which of course is ultimately what happened, long after their demise, with the record-buying public.

Morrissey, for whom commercialism had never been the be-all and end-all, was also astute enough to think carefully before speaking to journalists, now that his group was the biggest in the country. In January 1985, leading reporters from several music publications joined forces with *Gay News*' Neil Bartlett for a feature on the latest gay attack on the charts, and *NME*'s Neil Spencer singled out Morrissey – who after eighteen months of being labelled gay had neither categorically admitted nor denied the fact, but given some less-than-subtle hints to the affirmative – as his role model. 'The only way we cover gay issues more is with people being willing to talk about their sexuality,' Spencer observed. 'Morrissey put it well in our Christmas issue. He said, "I'm not heterosexual, homosexual, bisexual, asexual – just sexual."' His change of 'tactic', however, displeased the same magazine's Janice Jaye, who scathingly awarded The Arthur Rimbaud Misunderstood Genius Award, 'To Morrissey of The Smiths, who would like us all to think he is, without having to prove it.' Jaye concluded by predicting that by the end of the following year the group would have 'faded gently into obscurity . . . The only thing left that will make him a legend now is suicide.'

That same month, Rough Trade put out another ode to loneliness which, though it only reached number 24 in the charts, remains just as memorable as anything these other groups released – *and* which has since caught up with their chart-toppers, sales-wise.

'How Soon Is Now?', of which *Melody Maker* remarked, 'Rarely has catharsis been tinged with so much regret – and shared with such purity,' was housed in a sleeve featuring an obscure actor named Sean Barrett, and which is controversial only in that he is cupping his crotch in both hands (actually, *praying* in Leslie Norman's compelling war film of 1958, *Dunkirk*). For this reason – ignorance *not* being bliss once more – the sleeve was banned in America and replaced by the *Hatful Of Hollow* insert from Glastonbury, minus of course the 'athletic' shot of Mike Joyce. The lyrics to the song were not as hard-hitting or suggestive as Morrissey's previous forays into same-sex attraction, and were a refreshing anodyne to some of the smut in the charts. The narrator knows of a club where one can find love, if this is what one wants, though so far *he* has been unsuccessful and feels that he always will be. And for the detractors there was the message, 'You shut your mouth . . . I am human and I need to be loved!' Lovely!

The Smiths' next two singles, 'Shakespeare's Sister' and 'That Joke Isn't Funny Anymore', offered the group something of a commercial lull, charting at 26 and 49 respectively. The former, an invitation to clifftop suicide, had as its inspiration an essay by Virginia Woolf: in Morrissey's case, the narrator is urged by the rocks to throw his skinny body down so that he and the singer he once loved may be reunited in death. The singer is believed to have been Tim Buckley, the manic-depressive singer-songwriter who had died of a heroin overdose in 1975, aged 28. Buckley's equally famous singer son, Jeff, thought so: he reportedly carried a torch for Morrissey for years, and was so inspired by the tribute that he recorded the most exquisite cover version of a Smiths song, 'I Know It's Over'. This was played in June 1997 over newsreel footage of the police recovering Buckley's body from the Mississippi, near Memphis, after he had tragically drowned.

'That Joke Isn't Funny Anymore', marginally less grim but equally fascinating, dealt with death inspired by solitude. The song appeared on The Smiths' next album, *Meat Is Murder*, which more than made up for the commercial lameness of the previous few months by rocketing to the top of the charts, 'dethroning' Bruce Springsteen. For seemingly no reason at all, Morrissey now hit out at the 'Born In The USA' rocker, declaring, 'Springsteen calls out to the philistines of America, and naturally there is a huge response.' The album's February 1985 release coincided with certain problems within the group, largely because Morrissey was now becoming belatedly aware of Andy Rourke's heroin addiction. 'Things are bloody horrendous at the moment,' Johnny Marr told *The Face*'s Nick Kent, 'Morrissey's just found out about Andy and he's going frantic demanding he leave the group. And I'm in the middle, trying to hold everything together.' Perhaps not surprisingly, given Morrissey's wizardry for keeping personal matters personal, the matter was kept out of the press. His main concern right now was getting over the new album's message. From his point of view, there were no ethical differences between child abuse, death in military action, and the killing of animals for human consumption. 'I don't *hate* meat-eaters,' he told *Sounds*, 'But I've found that if I say to certain journalists that I'm a vegetarian, they immediately assume that I detest to the point of death anybody that eats meat.'

The album cover, almost as important to The Smiths as the goods it contained, depicted a doctored still of a US soldier from Emile de

Antonio's anti-Vietnam film of 1969, *In The Year Of The Pig*. The caption on his helmet that had read MAKE LOVE NOT WAR (amended in some prints to MAKE WAR NOT PEACE) now read MEAT IS MURDER. Morrissey drove the point home by launching an attack on animal rights organisations for being too peaceable, his point being that they would only truly get their point across by giving the meat industry magnates a taste of their own medicine. Though he later threatened Norfolk turkey baron Bernard Matthews with legal action for using a Smiths poster in a television campaign, for the time being he only 'attacked' Matthews' contemporaries by declaring that if he ever met Kentucky Fried Chicken's Colonel Sanders in heaven, he would effect a swift knee to the groin – hardly 'tough tactics' by Morrissey standards!

Morrissey remained fervently anti-Establishment, and his disdain for the Royal Family remained as intense as ever – witness this no-nonsense stanza from *Meat Is Murder*'s 'Nowhere Fast': 'I'd like to drop my trousers to the Queen/ Every sensible child will know what this means/ The poor and the needy/ Are selfish and greedy on her terms'. That same year, he caused outrage among royalists after watching a television news bulletin of the vast crowd outside Clarence House eagerly awaiting the walkabout celebrating the Queen Mother's 85th birthday on 4 August. 'If the woman had died, there would have been less,' he quipped to *NME* in September. 'And I would've been hammering the nails in her coffin to make sure she stayed there!' Shortly after repeating this particular comment in my book *Morrissey: Landscapes Of The Mind* I received a letter from the world's best-loved grandmother – the threat of a lawsuit, I told myself, as I slit it open with trembling fingers. But no, it was a request from the Queen Mother, asking me to keep her informed of the biography I was writing of her favourite (and, ironically, one of Morrissey's) entertainer, Gracie Fields. Even so, I would have been perfectly willing to publicly condemn him for what he had said, much as I admired him.

Of the album's other songs there was the wailing vignette of 'I Want The One I Can't Have', in which the narrator – Morrissey himself – bemoans the traditional working-class behaviour expected of men like him because this is how things have always been. He is actually in love with the thug who, when he was just thirteen, murdered a policeman – and further suggests that if the young man needs 'self-validation', then he should meet him in the alley by the railway station. 'My most personal songs,' he told *Les Inrockuptibles'* Mishka Assaya during the summer of 1986, 'These are "Stretch Out And Wait" and "I Want The One I Can't Have". They just about sum me up.' There is more sexually linked thuggery with 'What She Said', the story of the literate woman who is sexually dead, smoking herself into an early grave, until her eyes are opened by a tattooed boy from Birkenhead.

The key statement on *Meat Is Murder*, of course, is the title-track itself, strategically placed at the end of the album so that by the time one reaches it, bearing in mind Morrissey's intention for the listener to experience the ten songs chronologically, one has received an education in just about every emotion in the book. Even so, it is a far from morbid excursion. The album's crowning glory, 'Meat Is Murder' is said to have genuinely terrified many Smiths fans out of eating meat – those who, so obsessed with their singer and willing to follow his every word to the letter, were not abstaining already. And while Andy Rourke later confessed to not eating meat only when Morrissey and Marr were around, Mike Joyce also turned vegetarian 'by fear'. It is a tremendously disturbing *chanson-grise*, whether one supports its sentiments or not: the buzzing of electric saws, the sharpening of knives, the authentic sounds of baying beasts as they are being led to the slaughter while Morrissey opines, 'Heifer whines could be human cries . . .'

Neither was Morrissey's powerful protest transitory. Seven years later, when asked by American reporter David Keeps, of *Details*, to define evil, he would pull no punches:

I do see McDonald's as the core of modern evil because it is the death industry. I just feel rage that they will promote themselves from every possible angle, but they will not show the process by which the hamburger is made. They will not show the cows' throats being slit, the bull trying to commit suicide by banging its head against the stone floor.

Not all Smiths fans, however, were enthusiastic. Hugh Miller of *Gay Times* loved the album, but found the title-track 'patronising', adding, 'While people should be able to express their preferences, lyrics as loaded as this come across as empty as a policeman's speech. With clichés such as "the unholy stench of MURDER" the song makes a sharp contrast to "Nowhere Fast" and makes the listener wonder if these two songs were written by the same person.'

The Smiths' *Meat Is Murder* tour opened in Cheltenham three weeks after the album's release. The group frequently appeared in I DON'T EAT MY FRIENDS T-shirts, while Morrissey attempted to prick the consciences of the uninitiated by being photographed holding a kitten on a plate – the fake hearing-aid deflecting the seriousness of it all. There were 23 dates, all sell-outs, and each night – setting a precedent for extravagantly effective Continental-style entrances – the group were played on to the stage by Prokofiev's 'March Of The Capulets' from *Romeo And Juliet*. Memorable moments – aside from the nightly stage invasions always directed at Morrissey and never the other three (and one occasion when someone flung a string of sausages at him!) – included Morrissey's impromptu duetting of 'Barbarism Begins At Home' with Pete Burns, the Liverpool-born singer from Dead Or Alive. Morrissey courted controversy by telling *Sounds* of the event, which took place on 6 April, at the Royal Albert Hall, 'I felt a great affinity with that situation. He's one of the holier saints that ever walked the earth.' He also joked over their recent exchange of birthday 'gifts', though many believed that with these two anything might have been possible. 'He sent me twenty-six roses. I sent him forty-eight naked sailors.'

The diminutive Burns had caused something of a commotion in March 1984 when he had told *HIM*'s Kris Kirk, 'The pop chart is full of faggots, myself included to a degree,' adding, 'I'd prefer to see my face staring out of *HIM* than *Record Mirror* and know that I'm appealing to people who've got more in common with me than ten-year-old girls with wet panties.' On top of this, in just about every interview he gave, Burns was unabashed at confessing that he shared his bed most nights with his wife and a live-in lover named Steve.

Morrissey's close friendship with Pete Burns did not go unnoticed by the gutter press, and more than a few less knowledgeable journalists jumped to the wrong conclusion that Burns' love, Steve, and Morrissey could only have been one and the same – particularly Antonella Black, who interviewed Morrissey for *Sounds'* 20 April 1985 issue, though she was sensible enough not to refer to Burns by name.

One only has to read the introduction to Black's feature to see what Morrissey was up against, though he of course would not have known this at the time:

> Nobody told me that, in the flesh, Steven Patrick Morrissey looks like Judy Garland's understudy. Nobody informed me that Steven Patrick can't quite wrap his pretty tongue around the letter 'S'. Nobody unbridled the fact that my arse was to be booted out of Steven Patrick's boudoir once the interview reached a sticky consistency. Steven is celibate, yet Steven has a double bed. Steven isn't paranoid, yet now all his interviews are doubly recorded. Steven shrills long and loud about castrated cows and lambasted lambs, yet he confesses to finding leather seats highly erotic. Steven is a funny little kettle of fish.

Black wanted to know if Morrissey was a 'professional paranoid' and 'mega misery guts', and when he denounced the word 'mega' as 'very provincial', levelled at him, 'One more crack like that and I'll put you across my knee and wallop you!' He played straight into her hands by responding, 'At last! Prayers answered, prayers answered!' From here the tension increased, as mutual silliness allowed the interview to spin out of control. Black asked Morrissey what was preventing him from being happy – hardly giving him the chance to answer before doing so for him, immediately raising his hackles and bringing the outburst: 'Give me the chance to answer the question! Good heavens, that's the first time I've shouted since 1976! Now I've forgotten the question!' Morrissey calmed down at once, but as the banter took a turn for the juvenile, the situation grew increasingly more volatile.

MORRISSEY: I've been in every conceivable situation in human existence.

BLACK: You've had group sex on a rubber mat with a bowl of custard?

MORRISSEY: Daily. It's a terrible yawn.

BLACK: You have swung from chandeliers with black grapes in your teeth?

MORRISSEY: I do it every February.

BLACK: Don't you think that your frailty has become redundant?

MORRISSEY: Well, it always seems that way as soon as something becomes big business. How can it become redundant?

BLACK: In the same way as somebody like Prince has become nauseating in his fixation with fucking and rubber jockstraps.

MORRISSEY: It's not the same thing. I've never sung about a jockstrap.

BLACK: Do you think that *Meat Is Murder* is self-conscious self-flagellation for practising or latent homosexuality? Did you have a bad experience as a child?

MORRISSEY: (allegedly blushing) What – with meat?

BLACK: What do you find highly erotic at the grand old age of twenty-five?

MORRISSEY: As a child in the Sixties, when the seats of cars were made of leather, to me there was something highly erotic about actually being in a car. I have always found cars highly erotic. Not the driver's seat. There was just something about the old leather seats. The things I find erotic are certain situations. They don't ever have to be particularly sexual. I don't have to tell you! The erotic feelings I have are very conventional, I'm afraid . . .

BLACK: But if you have erotic feelings, why don't you sleep with anyone? Why don't you make it happen?

MORRISSEY: (getting anxious) I don't want to any more, I don't want to. I don't! No, I'm not going to instigate things any more . . .

BLACK: So you're telling me that if some dark man came up behind you in the hall, pulled your Marks & Spencers down, and . . .

Black got no further. The interview was over, and she was promptly propelled towards the door.

Morrissey's championing of strong women was akin to Alan Bennett's affection for the same demonstrated in *Talking Heads* and the American gay community's fondness for stars such as Crawford, Bette Davis and Judy Garland in the fifties – but in Morrissey's case the stars frequently had a rough edge to them. In May 1985 *Blitz* magazine unusually (for a pop publication) secured an interview with 61-year-old Pat Phoenix, for years the brassy tart-with-a-heart barmaid Elsie Tanner in Granada Television's *Coronation Street* – but with one condition: she should be allowed to choose her own interviewer. She chose Morrissey, whom she had never met, though she had been impressed by some of the nice things he had said about her, not only of her work in *Coronation Street*, but also in *The L-Shaped Room*, one of his favourite films. Later she would say, 'He's an astute, gentle young man, good-looking, intelligent, sincere. Mark my word, he'll go a long way in life.' Phoenix was so bowled over by the singer's 'deep-set charm' that she insisted on his photograph going on the cover of the magazine instead of one of them together.

Morrissey could have been referring to someone close from his own life when he wrote of her character, 'Elsie was the screen's first angry young woman, a wised-up, tongue-lashing cylindrical tempest sewn into cheap and overstuffed dresses, harnessed by severe poverty, staunchly defending her fatherless children, devouring a blizzard of temporary husbands in dour Salford council dwellings.' Later he observed, 'She was an absolute blizzard of professionalism – you simply wanted to rush towards her bosom and remain there for ever.'

At the end of that same month, when asked to select his own interviewer for a Smiths profile on Channel 4's controversial late-night magazine *The Word*, he plumped for Liverpool actress-siren and self-styled sexologist Margi Clarke, whom he had raved about as the sluttish heroine of the film *Letter To Brezhnev*, then on general release.

The interview/sketch, according to Morrissey, took place 'somewhere in the Scottish Highlands, near some ruins', and turned out to be a hoot with both stars 'taking the piss'. Morrissey announced Clarke as 'a luminary, a Venus who rises from the waves', and persistently called her 'Margox' (the name under which she had presented a 'what's on' Granada TV show in the late seventies). He confided that it had always been his ambition to act (a 'career' that had begun and ended with four lines in Phil Redmond's *Brookside* spin-off, *South*), and this of course was arranged with a re-enactment of a scene from *Letter To Brezhnev*. Clarke and a girlfriend are sharing a toilet cubicle in a nightclub, when Morrissey strolls in by mistake. 'He's frigging gorgeous, like that bloke from *Doctor Zhivago*!' she exclaims, after watching him re-arrange his quiff in front of the mirror. She then loans him her lip-salve – it is 'Choosy Cherry' – after which the action jumps to The Smiths' concert at the Glasgow Barrowlands.

In the middle of May 1985, The Smiths flew to Rome for a concert at the Tendetrisce. They should have made several television appearances, but owing to the nature of *Meat Is Murder*'s subject matter, these were cancelled at the last minute. The promoters, Virgin Italia, were less concerned with Morrissey's 'meat is murder' proclamations than they were with the age-gap/thug-sex content of some of The Smiths' other songs. In San Sebastian, Spain, the group themselves cancelled a show within an hour of curtain-up when the public-address system broke down with no guarantee that it would be repaired on time. For the first time, a riot erupted between agitated fans, theatre security and the police. All went well in Madrid: the 5 May concert, which formed part of the Paseo de Camoens Festival, was recorded and released on an excellent bootleg album that contains quite possibly the definitive version of 'Meat Is Murder'.

The Camoens Festival was by all accounts one of the few happy moments of The Smiths' European trip. Also in Madrid there was a row between the group and their then manager, Rough Trade's Scott Piering, which led to a parting of the ways. Not for the first time, Morrissey would be condemned for his searing perfectionism and demands that everything should be exactly right. Piering later told *Select*, 'On a professional level, he's a total nightmare. I don't think if he came to me on bended knees I would ever want to work with him again.' For his part, Morrissey would defend this regular to-and-fro of personnel, accusing managers of taking too much for granted by trying to inject creative ideas into the group, instead of staying behind the scenes and doing the job they were being paid to do. 'They can't resist meddling,' he told *Les Inrockuptibles* in 1991, 'thinking that they too are making the album, designing the cover. The Smiths was an absolutely closed society!'

Piering was replaced by Matthew Sztumpf, Madness' former manager, and it was he who finalised The Smiths' tour of America, which opened at Chicago's Aragon Ballroom on 7 June 1985. It was Morrissey's idea to hire a drag queen to open the proceedings by miming – badly – to a playback tape. A few minutes into his patter, the audience began pelting him with beer cans, and when this happened again in Detroit and Washington, he was unceremoniously dropped.

In San Francisco, on 20 June, Johnny Marr married his long-time sweetheart, Angela Brown. There was virtually no time for a honeymoon: The Smiths headed for Philadelphia, the city that was already preparing for what was predicted would be 'the biggest concert in its history' – Bob Geldof's Live Aid would be simultaneously relayed with the extravaganza he had organised to take place in London on 13 July. Bearing in mind what Morrissey had said about its predecessor, Band Aid, The Smiths were never even considered for the event, though this time it was Johnny Marr who had his 'five-penn'orth' about some of the artistes on the bill. Marr attacked Rolling Stone Keith Richards, declaring that he could no longer play the guitar, and accused Bryan Ferry of attempting to resurrect his flagging career by using the event to promote his new single. Then, leaving the US press to make what they wanted of this, the group played dates in Canada before flying home to more controversy. They had been booked for a guest-slot on the 19 July edition of *Wogan*, Terry Wogan's thrice-weekly television chat-show – an institution in the days when, by and large, stars were stars and questions were rarely vetted. Marr, Rourke and Joyce were at the studio and about to go into make-up when a call was put through from Morrissey: he had decided to give the show a miss. And yet only days later he complained in *Record Mirror* about the lack of airplay The Smiths were getting, adding, 'I'm tired of being broke!'

Also at this time, the Church was up in arms over the cover of the latest *NME* – Morrissey, complete with halo, and holding up one hand to reveal blood dripping from a stigmata wound. The banner headline read, FEAST OF STEVEN: MORRISSEY, FALLEN ANGEL OR DEMI-GOD. Within was another 'martyrdom' shot captioned, 'Tour of Deity: Moz Crucified By The Press, In Glorious Colour, Every Wednesday'. Interviewed by Danny Kelly at Manchester's Britannia Hotel, where for refreshment the singer ordered a samovar of hot chocolate, the talk had got around to Morrissey's inspirations: Oscar Wilde, James Dean, the heroes from his favourite old British films. 'I'm very interested in what emerges from the ashes of poverty or the bruises of torture, to see what people are capable of in extremes,' he told Kelly, in light of recent press attacks; ironically, seven years hence Kelly would be helping to launch the most vituperative attack of them all. 'People who achieve things artistically after persistent public floggings, after being roasted alive by the critics, interest me when they come out on top, smiling, in control, impregnable.'

In September 1985, The Smiths released another exploration of loneliness and unrequited love, quite possibly Morrissey's best example of this so far, and also the first to be promoted with a video. 'The Boy With A Thorn In His Side' had a cover depicting Smithsonian Institute alumnus-author Truman Capote, perhaps best known for writing *Breakfast At Tiffany's*. Capote had famously once said of his sexuality on a live American chat show, 'I was a beautiful little boy and everyone had me – men, women, dogs and fire hydrants!' – which ultimately led to Morrissey himself being photographed by Jurgen Teller, clutching the hydrant that still stands at the junction of Tench Street and Reardon Street in Wapping! The Capote picture, dating from 1949, was by the equally renowned Cecil Beaton – but only The Smiths' French fans would have picked up on the pun, intended or not, that *capote* is the old-fashioned French word for condom.

The record reached number 23 in the charts. Almost as exquisite was the flipside, 'Asleep', in which Morrissey was again accused of romanticising suicide. One is reminded of the death of Marilyn Monroe – who graced the cover of a Smiths bootleg album at around this time, *A Nice Bit Of Meat* – particularly the line 'Deep in the cell of my heart I will feel so glad to go', variations of which Monroe pronounced many times during her final months – though Morrissey was probably thinking of no one in particular when he wrote this. He told *Sounds* in August, 'There are many people who expect that I will be found dangling from some banisters, or swinging from the rafters of some darkened church.' Speaking of these 'sometimes quite agonising mood-swings', Kirsty MacColl told me in 1994, 'It's always been at the back of our minds that he might do something like that – that if he ever did, it would have to be something suitably Wildean or gothic. God forbid that he ever will!'

Morrissey's depressions and anxieties were rumoured to be at an all-time high during this autumn of 1985 when The Smiths embarked on a seven-date Scottish tour. Their next album, *The Queen Is Dead*, had been scheduled for a December release, but in-house problems resulted in this date being moved forward by six months. The group attempted to find another record company, but this only made matters much worse when Rough Trade served them with an interlocutory injunction – hardly the sort of thing to make them wish to stay with the company, though for the time being they were stuck with Rough Trade whether they liked it or not. By the end of the year, personal problems were exacerbated by a recurrence of Andy Rourke's heroin addiction. The bassist was now taking methadone substitute, and this had begun to affect his playing. In Dublin, after a poor performance, Morrissey told George Byrne of the *Sunday Correspondent*, 'I find heroin absolutely detestable, though a great many people who take it do so willingly. The more the authoritarian finger is wagged at these people, the more they are inclined to please themselves.' Those close to The Smiths – not least of all the fans – knew exactly who he was referring to. Then he went off at a tangent by actually attacking the Conservative government's anti-heroin campaign, adding, 'I found it very absurd that the British government could care about people on heroin, when they could scarcely care about people who are killing themselves because of unemployment.' And this coming from the man who, not so long before, had in one of his songs encouraged unemployed people not to bother looking for work!

Even so, desperate measures needed to be taken. Morrissey and Marr, who to all intents and purposes *were* The Smiths, ordered

Rourke to leave the group until he could convince them that he had kicked his habit. 'We told him to sling his hook,' Marr told *The Face*'s Nick Kent. He was replaced by Craig Gannon, a former guitarist with Aztec Camera and The Bluebells who was recommended by Marr's pal, Simon Wolstencroft.

Mere days after his dismissal, Andy Rourke was arrested for possession of drugs. Despite his comments to George Byrne, Morrissey was the first to rush to his aid, and soon afterwards a clean Rourke was taken back into the fold. For the time being, Craig Gannon was retained, and when The Smiths appeared on television in May 1986 to promote their new single, 'Bigmouth Strikes Again', as in the days of James Maker there were five of them.

There were also problems at around this time from 'stalker' fans, one in particular from northern England who spent a lot of time loitering around Morrissey's home – collecting such ridiculous 'memorabilia' as plants and leaves from his garden, pestering his mother, persistently ringing the doorbell and trying to take photographs through the windows. He is even thought to have secured the singer's telephone number. Morrissey was informed of his and several other fanatics' details, and dreaded bumping into them after concerts. However, because they did no actual damage to the property, he was unable to take action other than to inform the police. 'They're emotionally unbalanced,' he told *Les Inrockuptibles*' Mishka Assaya, 'I find it very hard dealing with them, wondering what to say or what not to say. These people think they know me. They say very personal things, and I can't respond to somebody I don't know. I just wish they would leave me alone.'

Even The Smiths' harshest critics would have to agree that *The Queen Is Dead* remains their finest album. Released in June 1986, it proved once and for all – if proof were needed – that Morrissey was the most articulate songwriter of his generation. And of course, because of the very nature of its title, it brought more media attacks than anything they had done since 'Suffer Little Children'. Johnny Marr told *NME*'s Dave Haslam in the spring of 1989, 'When we listened back to it, it made the hairs on the back of our necks stand up. It's what I'm most proud of with The Smiths and being involved with Morrissey, that juxtaposition of rock from a housing estate.'

The cover picture – French heartthrob Alain Delon, unrecognisable in a shot from the 1964 film *L'Insoumis* – caused no problems, but the gatefold's inside photograph of The Smiths posing outside the Salford Lads Club made up for this. The club's committee threatened Rough Trade with legal action unless the company made it patently clear that the group were in no way connected with the club itself, which the committee described as 'a Boy Scout Association type'. The fact that The Smiths had dealt with the subjects of unconventional sexual practices in their songs were the chief causes for concern, as were the contents of the album that the photograph was seen to be promoting: notably the title track, and 'Vicar In A Tutu' (with its guitar riffs reminiscent of Nancy Whiskey's 1957 hit, 'Freight Train') which tells the tale of a youth who, while filching the lead from a church roof, espies the priest prancing around in drag.

One might almost commend the Salford Lads Club committee for actually sitting down and listening to the record before voicing their disdain, which is not what happened elsewhere. Morrissey's ill-timed confession to the press that the group had been terrorised by ten-year-old girls while posing for the picture, and his comment, 'Everybody in the street had a club foot and a vicious dog', was brought to the attention of old enemy MP Geoffrey Dickens, who tried but failed to get the record taken off the shelves. It missed topping the charts by a hair's breadth. Support for The Smiths came from the unlikeliest source – Princess Diana, who had married into the very family Morrissey was lampooning, went public by declaring that they were one of her favourite groups. (Some years later, when the world had been made aware of her problems with 'the Establishment', a sketch on television's *Spitting Image* featured her puppet-caricature, introduced by Jimmy Savile, singing 'Heaven Knows I'm Miserable Now'.) Doubtless the princess was unaware of Morrissey's put-down, the previous year in *Sounds*: 'The writers and designers of *Spitting Image* should be unmercifully sued for making the Royal Family more attractive and intelligent than they actually are.'

Morrissey's supreme attack on the Royal Family, one that in retrospect overshadows The Sex Pistols' 'God Save The Queen', was 'The Queen Is Dead'. 'We don't believe in leprechauns,' Morrissey said at the time, 'so why should we believe in the Queen?'

In this instance, one did not have to be on his side to see his point. The song was witty, acerbic and above all intelligently structured. In the days of Oscar Wilde, Britain had been a mighty empire, thought of as invincible, but an empire built all the same on bloodshed, greed and racial prejudice – and times had changed. To many of its subjects, the present-day Royal Family were little more than figure-heads, albeit still much respected, and – in 1985 – pillars of the community that most people still looked up to. One shudders to even think of what 'The Queen Is Dead' would be like if Morrissey wrote it today, in the wake of the divorces and sex scandals.

Indeed, the Windsors were fortunate in that the song was just an attack on the Queen and Prince Charles. Morrissey launches his salvo with unfettered brilliance – reminding us of how life used to be in 'the days of yore' by using a snatch of 'Take Me Back To Dear Old Blighty' to prologue the piece before Johnny Marr's noisy chunk of feedback. The song was a World War I music-hall ditty, revived by Cicely Courtneidge (who sings it here); the version is taken from the soundtrack of *The L-Shaped Room*, one of Morrissey's favourite films, which had also starred Pat Phoenix. 'The Queen Is Dead' is a *chanson-grise* wherein the narrator, this time unquestionably Morrissey himself, bids 'Farewell to this land's cheerless marshes hemmed in like a boar between arches'. The latter is thought to be a reference, long before the 1992 *NME*-fuelled nationalism debacle, to the House of York's King Richard III (whose emblem was the White Boar) – one royal much revered by Northerners, who was based in the North and was wholly unafraid of doing things his way. Like Richard, who usurped the throne of his brother Edward IV and was succeeded by Henry Tudor, thereby changing the line of succession for ever, Morrissey stakes equal claim as the pale descendant 'of some old queen or other' – though the term queen is more suggestive here of its homosexual connotation than of anything monarchic. Morrissey then goes on to criticise Prince Charles for being so boring, asking whether he never feels the urge to do something spontaneous or outrageous, such as appearing on the *Daily Mail*'s front page dressed in his mother's bridal veil! He envisages himself emulating Michael Fagin, the man who had a few years previously broken into Buckingham Palace and chatted amicably to the Queen, sitting on the edge of her bed while awaiting arrest – save that in true *Carry On* tradition, in the song the narrator gains access to the royal bedchamber by means of a sponge and a rusty spanner. And finally, having touched on castration, poverty and the Church, he heads off to inform his gang, 'The Queen is dead, boys!' before rounding off the proceedings with the Garboesque quip, 'Life is very long, when you're lonely!' Superb!

Taken as a whole, the album represented a quite unprecedented diversity of emotions and mood swings. 'Frankly Mr Shankly' evokes the rich Northern humour of George Formby and Jake Thackray. It is allegedly based on the poetry-writing undertaker Mr Shadrack in *Billy Liar*, though one of the teachers at Morrissey's school – 'a flatulent pain in the arse' – had also apparently been called Shankly. Again, it deals with the 'I-want-what-I-can't-have' young man who returns home to his mother, sad and disillusioned after the break-up of a love affair that ended almost as soon as it began. Yet from his mother there is little sympathy – she reminds him that despite, or maybe because of, his wit, intelligence, fame and physical beauty he is still alone, sleeping in an empty bed while the lover who spurned him now languishes in someone else's arms. The conclusion, however, is that while it is easy to laugh and hate, it takes guts to be gentle and kind.

'Never Had No One Ever', a bad-English quip that often cropped up in the 1960s *Bootsie And Snudge* television series, explains in one elongated six-line stanza that he has not loved at all – and makes cryptic reference to a time (twenty years, seven months and 27 days) at which a particularly bad dream ended, though we are given no clues to its significance. 'Bigmouth Strikes Again', on the other hand, was an exercise in satire: Morrissey's way of getting one over on his critics by reminding them that he was not incapable of slapping himself down every now and again. More fun comes with 'Some Girls

Are Bigger Than Others', in which Morrissey borrows from *Antony and Cleopatra* – not the Shakespearean version but from *Carry On Cleo*, with Antony (Sidney James) quoting the song's title to Amanda Barrie as he opens a crate of ale. And the piece ends with the singer cheekily crooning a snatch of Johnny Tillotson's 1962 hit, 'Send Me The Pillow You Dream On'.

The song on *The Queen Is Dead*, so far as most of the fans and this author are concerned, is the penultimate track, the sublime 'There Is A Light That Never Goes Out'. The sentiment of actually dying for love was nothing new, of course. In 1949, after the death in an air crash of French boxing champion Marcel Cerdan, Edith Piaf composed and sang 'Hymne A L'Amour', proclaiming, 'If you die, I don't mind so long as I may die too.' The recording of this has sold over twenty million copies world-wide, and there is even a link of sorts with The Smiths: Jeff Buckley, who also sang it in French, declared that it was the only song better than 'I Know It's Over'. In Morrissey's case here, borrowing Judy Garland's utterance from the end of her 1961 Carnegie Hall comeback perfor-mance – 'I never, never want to go home!' – he is so in love for once that he wants to preserve the emotion by perishing with his grand amour after a last night on the town. How this happens is immaterial, and he very nearly asks his love to make it happen: 'To die by your side, such a heavenly way to die!' What makes the song even more poignant is that Morrissey claimed in one interview (for Dutch magazine *Oor*) that it was autobiographical. He told Martin Aston:

> There are three lines in that song I can't bear to listen to because I find them too personal: 'In the darkened underpass/ I thought, Oh God, my chance has come at last/ But a strange fear gripped me and I just couldn't ask.' I can't listen to those lines . . . I have to sit down. It's like someone hitting me with a hammer.

Aston went on to ask Morrissey about this realist's fascination with the darker aspects of life and suicide, and his response was in retrospect somewhat alarming, bearing in mind that in the not too distant future some Smiths fans would pick up on it and follow his credo to the letter.

Declaring that the ending of one's own life was not taking the coward's way out, he went on:

> It's the strongest decision an individual can possibly make, as it's so obviously very frightening. I dislike the term 'commit suicide' – it sounds like robbery, or something rude or bad. I admire people who take their own lives. I don't find fighting wars quite so very brave, or being in the army. To me, that's incredibly stupid.

One only has to see film footage of The Smiths' later concerts (and those of the solo Morrissey, some twenty years on) to witness how much 'There Is A Light That Never Goes Out' means to the fans: hundreds of young men, mostly, tears streaming down their cheeks as they join in with the refrain. One of these, the famous porn star who introduced himself to me in Sheffield, told me quite seriously, 'It's just like ancient Rome, when the emperor walks through the streets, points to someone and says, "Citizen, fall on thy sword!" Most of those apostles out there were so crazy with admiration for Morrissey, he could ask them to do anything.'

With the new album riding high in the charts, in July 1986 The Smiths embarked on their second major tour of the United States and Canada: 24 dates in concert halls, ballrooms and open-air theatres. The tour was a sell-out despite a severe lack of publicity: virtually nothing about the group appeared in the press; radio stations pronounced their records 'too depressing' for airplay save late at night, when there were fewer listeners. Some of the local independent radio stations showed interest, but only after hearing what had happened at a previous concert, and even then they only wanted to interview 'the tall guy with the flowers', as one put it.

On 29 July, Morrissey was interviewed by CHRW Radio, in Ontario – but only after the presenter had been 'briefed' as to who he was. For ten minutes, he struggled, responding only to the bland questions on the presenter's screen. After playing a track from *The Queen Is Dead* – the first time this presenter had heard Morrissey sing – he quipped, 'Your voice seems like a bit of a throwback to the era of crooners', bringing

the weary, unappreciated response, 'Yes, I listen to lots of people who
fall into that bucket. I even like Doris Day, so what hope is there for me?'

The tour ended prematurely when the last four shows were cancelled:
the problem was Johnny Marr, who had suddenly begun hitting the
bottle – at the time, he cited the pressure of work as the reason for his
lapse. Little did The Smiths know that after their 10 September concert
in Tampa, Florida, they would never visit America again as an ensemble.

The Chernobyl disaster of 26 April 1986, when the near-meltdown of a
nuclear reactor fogged the atmosphere with radioactive material,
brought widespread storms of protest from around the world. In the
United States, Barbra Streisand attacked the Reagan administration,
which she said was at least partly responsible for 'the proliferation of
nuclear plants and warheads' across the planet – and gave a concert that
raised $2 million to elect as many Democrats as possible to oust the
Republican government. In England, on a much lesser scale of attack,
and partly in response to Radio One disc jockey Steve Wright's ill-timed
playing of Wham!'s 'I'm Your Man' straight after the newsflash
announcing the Chernobyl disaster (many listeners inferred that Wright
may have been dismissing the event as 'just another overseas mishap')
Morrissey wrote 'Panic'.

The song was given more publicity clout by the fact that the
promotional video (itself a rare outing for The Smiths) was directed by
the hugely controversial Derek Jarman, of *Sebastiane* fame. Jarman did
The Smiths proud, incorporating not just 'Panic' but 'The Queen is
Dead' (the video's title) and 'There Is A Light That Never Goes Out' into
a fifteen-minute short, positively glowing with the violent imagery and
blatant homoeroticism for which the director was famed – two pretty
youths kissing, another blowing smoke into a skull, and the image that
would cause much less trouble for the director then than it would for
Morrissey six years on: a semi-naked woman flying the Union Jack.

Inasmuch as Streisand pulled no punches in denouncing Reagan, so
Morrissey went for Steve Wright's jugular, ending the song with the line
'Hang the DJ,' chanted by children in Jarman's film. The gist of the song
was twofold: the singer predicting how he imagined much of the

populace would react, should there be the equivalent of a Chernobyl disaster in Britain – and an attack on the uninspiring music they were churning out day after day on Radio One. The attack would reach its climax with Morrissey striding on to the stage at Carlisle's Sands Centre on 13 October, wearing a Steve Wright T-shirt and swinging a noose!

Meanwhile, in August 1986, *Melody Maker's* Frank Owen caught up with The Smiths in Cleveland, Ohio, while they were in the middle of their American tour. Owen's interview with Morrissey was published at the end of September, by which time it had been spiced up with some very personal comments.

Referring to the chasm that he said now existed between indie pop and 'black' pop – proof of which supposedly came from the number of complaints the music press received from the former each time a black face appeared on a front page – Owen accused Morrissey (not The Smiths) of widening this gap by releasing 'Panic', even though Morrissey said that the song was not about racism. Morrissey's original, full response to Frank Owen's question, 'Is The Smiths' music racist?' should therefore be studied in its entirety, and not bit by bit and way out of context, as picked up on by the tabloids:

Reggae, for example, is to me the most racist music in the entire world. It's an absolute total glorification of black supremacy. There is a line when defence of one's own race becomes an attack on another race and, because of black history and oppression, we realise quite clearly that there has to be a very strong defence. But, ultimately, I don't have very cast iron opinions on black music other than black modern music, which I detest. I detest Stevie Wonder. I think Diana Ross is awful. I hate all those records in the Top 40 – Janet Jackson, Whitney Houston. I think they're vile in the extreme. In essence this music doesn't say anything whatsoever. I don't think there's any time any more to be subtle about anything. You have to get straight to the point. Obviously, to get on *Top Of The Pops* these days one has to be, by law, black. I think something political has occurred among Michael Hurll [the show's producer] and his friends, and there has been a hefty pushing of all this discofied nonsense into the Top 40. I think, as a result, that very aware younger groups that speak for now are being gagged . . . If you compare the exposure that records by the likes of Janet Jackson and streams of other anonymous Jacksons get to the daily level of airplay that The Smiths receive – The Smiths have had at least ten consecutive chart hits and we still can't get on Radio One's A-list. Is that not a conspiracy? The last LP ended up at number 2, and we are still told by radio that nobody wanted to listen to The Smiths in the daytime. Is that not a conspiracy? I do get the scent of a conspiracy.

Morrissey *was* criticising black music, but only that of the eighties, which he felt in no way compared with the Motown boom of the sixties, quite simply because it was not as good. What Frank Owen and Morrissey's other detractors failed to mention was that Morrissey had also criticised Madonna ('Closer to organised prostitution than anything I've seen!'), George Michael ('I'm not impressed!'), Bucks Fizz ('One would hear more vocal passion from an ape under anaesthetic!'), Frankie Goes To Hollywood ('An entire career orchestrated by unseen faces!') – and many, many others had much less eloquently criticised him – but to blinkered detractors, the fact that he disliked certain artistes and types of music only pointed to the fact that it was on account of the colour of their skin.

In June 2003, when asked to select fifteen of his all-time favourite songs for the compilation album, *Morrissey: Under The Influence*, one of his choices was 'Swan Lake', by the bluebeat band The Cats. He told *Word*'s Andrew Harrison, 'I once said "Reggae is vile," did I? Well, several tongue-in-cheek things were said in those days which, when placed in cold print, lost their humorous quality. This track, along with "Double Barrel" and "Young, Gifted And Black" were staple teenage necessities to me.'

Morrissey, who like everyone else in The Smiths' camp was glowing with the tidings that *Spin* magazine had voted *The Queen Is Dead* Best Album of All Time, had returned home from the US tour to encounter more tabloid trouble with the publication of the *Melody Maker* interview, which Frank Owen had embellished with a few very personal comments of his own. Morrissey was alternately referred to as 'the

Queen' and 'the missing link between Norman Wisdom and Joe Dallesandro'. 'Morrissey doesn't need to have sex in private because he does it all on stage,' Owen wrote, adding that his British fans were 'grubby' and 'self-righteous'. He then opined, 'Morrissey's genital continence might be a strategy to rise above the debased form of rock 'n' roll sexuality we know today with its obsessive phallic focus . . . It wouldn't surprise me to find, in a couple of years time, Morrissey eulogising the joys of fist-fucking and water sports.'

Of Morrissey's reference in his interview to the 'dangerous' Manchester gay scene and his confessed love of punk, Owen levelled, 'You big jessy, you big girl's blouse, Morrissey. But he's right. It was dangerous and, with the increased media visibility of punk, the violence got worse. You see, punks were not only faggots, they were uppity faggots as well.'

What caused Morrissey the most humiliation was Owen's reference to cottaging – a subject which, to be fair to the journalist, Morrissey had brought up in the first place. 'I was born in Central Library – in the crime section,' he had observed. Then, after recalling all the happy hours spent here, the lunchtimes when he had hung around with 'the older bohemian set in the basement café', he had added, 'The toilets were guarded by uniformed gorillas. It was like guerrilla warfare going on in there – an awful, frightening place.' 'And what about Whitworth Street toilets?' Owen had asked, referring to the infamous cottage, to which Morrissey had responded, 'Aah, yes, Whitworth Street toilets. I never knew Bert Tilsley. But let's steer away from public toilets.'

Morrissey had been referring to the *Coronation Street* actor, Peter Dudley, who had been arrested at the aforementioned toilets and charged with importuning – and soon afterwards died of a stroke. These points, however, along with Morrissey's opinionated but valid comments about the glut of black music in the charts at the time, were picked up by the tabloids, who as per usual quoted chunks of the interview grossly out of context, thereby giving Morrissey's words an entirely different slant. Johnny Marr, slight and not known for being pugnacious, allegedly vowed that if ever he met up with Frank Owen, he would give him a 'good thumping'!

Gay Times, on the other hand, were interested only in satirising Morrissey in their November 1986 issue. The feature 'Who Do You Do?', in the wake of the popular television series, listed the personalities most likely to go down a storm at that year's seasonal fancy dress parties: Morrissey, Quentin Crisp, Tina Turner, Mother Theresa, Rock Hudson, Cilla Black and Japanese hara-kiri hero novelist Yukio Mishima! That Morrissey was included in such a line-up was a tribute in itself, and one gets the impression that he would have found the whole thing amusing. Emulators were advised to reel into the party emitting loud groaning noises, while clutching their forehead with one hand, then slump over the ice-box and sing 'Heaven Knows I'm Miserable Now'. Other points to remember were CLOTHES AND APPEARANCE: a baggy, unironed shirt covered in busy little paisley patterns, on no account tucked into one's appliquéd jeans. Also, one should cut random chunks out of one's hair with an electric knife. Then there were the ACCESSORIES: a biography of Oscar Wilde or James Dean, a 'frightfully conspicuous' NHS hearing-aid and a chastity belt. For a party piece, one was advised, 'Sit on the stairs crying. Refuse to join the end of the conga line or do the hokey-cokey. If there's any threat whatsoever that you might end up enjoying yourself, leave immediately – preferably unobserved.' In closing, participants were advised not to do this impersonation at a wedding reception!

It appears to have been Morrissey's decision, around this time, to sever The Smiths' association with Rough Trade. The group signed a lucrative contract with EMI, which brought with it much criticism – they were accused of using a small company to turn themselves into the biggest group of the decade, only to dump them. In fact, Rough Trade was only supposed to have been a stop-gap in the first place, and in any case, no one had *made* The Smiths: they had been created and nurtured by Morrissey and Marr. For now, however, contractual obligations prevented them from actually recording with EMI, and in October 1986 Rough Trade released 'Ask', coupled with 'Cemetry Gates' and housed in a cover featuring *George And Mildred* star Yootha Joyce, snapped in 1965 soon after she had appeared in *Fanatic* with Morrissey favourite

Tallulah Bankhead. Some thought that by using Joyce, who virtually no one knew had been alcoholic until after her death from cirrhosis of the liver, Morrissey was offering a veiled warning to Johnny Marr to curb his own drinking. The song, which reached number 14 in the charts, brings to mind Morrissey's pen-pal days: the narrator, too shy to venture out, spends 'warm summer days indoors, writing frightening verse to a buck-toothed girl in Luxembourg', but though he may be shy, if she wants to 'do' anything, he tells her, all she has to do is ask. There is, however, the typical Morrissey coda – for if love fails to bring the two of them together, the bomb will!

Morrissey formed another 'postal' friendship with Kirsty MacColl, the talented singer-songwriter daughter of Ewan MacColl, who had provided the backing vocals on 'Ask' and 'Golden Lights' (the Twinkle song appeared on the 'Ask' 12-inch). She told me of their first meeting:

> I was working in New York at the time. My manager called and said he's found the latest letter from Morrissey on the mat. All it said in that funny writing of his was, 'SING WITH ME!' I didn't know what to make of it. When I came home I found out which studio he was working at, and went down there and met Johnny Marr and his wife. Johnny said, 'Moz is in there. Go and sing with him!' I was terrified, but I did it. Morrissey greeted me as if he'd known me for years. I suggested that maybe he ought to hand the tapes over to my then husband [Steve Lillywhite] for mixing, which he did, though I'm not so sure the others liked that! He's one of the nicest, kindest men I've ever met.

The Smiths' autumn 1986 tour was infiltrated by a few royalists who had taken exception to The Queen Is Dead, and numerous incidents added to the general sense of ill-feeling within the group. Hecklers made their way to the front of the stage to hurl abuse and spit: one of these, pretending to be a fan, reached up to shake Morrissey's hand at Newport on 19 October, but instead pulled him off the stage; the singer hit his head on the floor and was taken to hospital with suspected concussion. A week later, at the Preston Guildhall, he was hit in the face by a coin. Taking no chances, he abandoned the concert and a fracas erupted in the auditorium, resulting in the police making fourteen arrests. There was also a massive row with Craig Gannon, who left The Smiths under a dark cloud at the end of the tour.

On 14 November, The Smiths should have topped the bill in the Artists Against Apartheid gala at London's Royal Albert Hall. They were forced to pull out when Johnny Marr wrote off his car in an accident in the rain near his Bowden home. Marr suffered whiplash injuries, and hurt his hands whilst stumbling away from the scene of the crash in a dazed state, so playing the guitar was wholly out of the question. Forced to wear a neckbrace, he was back on form for The Smiths' concert on 12 December at the Brixton Academy – where Morrissey delivered a severe, spine-tingling 'There Is A Light That Never Goes Out' and glared at his partner throughout. What the fans did not know was that they were watching their idols' very last UK performance. The combination of the pressure that had come to bear on Marr's too-slender shoulders and the burden of Morrissey's perfectionism – not to mention his mercurial temperament – had pushed their partnership beyond the point of no return.

More relaxed with foreign journalists who published his comments verbatim and, unlike many of their British counterparts, never twisted them to suit their own prejudiced agenda, Morrissey had already given the indication of changes afoot in an exclusive interview to *Les Inrockuptibles*' Mishka Assaya in July 1986:

> I'm afraid the day is coming when I'll have to bid farewell to the past, when I'm going to want to be somebody else. It hasn't come yet, but it will. It must. It seems inevitable that we'll split up one day because there's only so much in each of us to give. When it becomes hard for me to concentrate on writing songs, when I no longer feel I'm doing the right thing, then I'll stop.

Astonishingly, the contents of the French interview were not picked up on by the British music press. Neither did his comments reach The

Smiths' entourage, or their inner circle, where it was business as usual. In January 1987, Rough Trade released a new single, the quaintly titled 'Shoplifters Of The World Unite', which reached number 12 in the charts. The cover featured a very young Elvis, snapped on the set of *The Ed Sullivan Show* exactly thirty years earlier. Needless to say, the song was denounced by the tabloids: not content with championing criminals, animal rights and underage sex, they complained, Morrissey was now encouraging his fans to steal!

Lyrically, the flipside was much more interesting. 'Half A Person' tells of a fan's six-year attempt to meet his idol, to be afforded only a few seconds of his valuable time. It calls to mind a group of Morrissey fans I encountered in 1994: having spent most of their money on the air fare from America, there had been little left for food, so they had spent a whole day trekking the streets of London in the pouring rain in search of ad-hoc work so that they would be able to follow the rest of the tour! In this particular song, which may be Morrissey recalling his earlier excursion to see Patti Smith, a young man books himself into the YWCA (note that 'W'!) and timidly asks, 'Do you have a vacancy for a back-scrubber?' – an essentially Northern term used in backstreet seduction.

These two songs were included in a mid-price compilation album, *The World Won't Listen*, released in March 1987 – something of a misnomer, for where The Smiths were concerned, one had no option *but* to listen. The cover photographs, obtained at considerable expense, were from the Jürgen Vollmer Collection – the Hamburg-based artist who, having given The Beatles their famous haircuts, had gone on to photograph just about every European superstar, then turned towards street youth, as here with this group of fans at a 1962 Johnny Hallyday concert. A bonus for Smiths admirers was the previously unreleased 'You Just Haven't Earned It Yet, Baby', reminiscent of Marianne Faithfull's 1967 hit, 'Is This What I Get For Loving You?' The album reached number 2 in the charts, and coincided with the group's American record company, Sire, issuing their own compilation, *Louder Than Bombs*, with a cover-shot of the playwright Shelagh Delaney, of *A Taste Of Honey* fame. This contained 24 songs, but when fans complained that the imported album was too expensive, Rough Trade released a cheaper edition. This was a mistake:

coming out so soon after *The World Won't Listen*, it barely scraped into the Top 40.

On 7 February 1987, with Morrissey observing that this was what would have been the eve of James Dean's birthday, The Smiths participated in the San Remo Festival, sharing top billing with The Pet Shop Boys and Spandau Ballet; Martin and Gary Kemp of the latter would delight Morrissey with their portrayals of the Krays on the big screen. There was a new, short-lived manager: Ken Friedman, a 29-year-old American with big ideas who all too soon fell foul of Morrissey by daring to question his penchant for audience intimacy and suggesting that the group play in the stadiums where there was more money to be made. Johnny Marr told *Sounds*, 'Stadiums are fine for the likes of Dire Straits – boring people worshipped by even more boring people.' With Friedman hoping to turn The Smiths into another Queen, it was evident that his days would be numbered.

Rumours were now circulating of discord within Smithdom, and Rough Trade were intent on squeezing as much mileage out of them as they could – and out of the fans' already overstretched budgets. In April 1987 they released the single, 'Sheila Take A Bow', which reached number 10 in the charts. Exactly who the Sheila of the title is, is a matter for conjecture. Many think it was written in honour of Shelagh Delaney, though there is no direct reference to her. There was also a French singer called Sheila (pronounced 'Shay-lah'), a contemporary of Françoise Hardy, whose big hit had been 'L'Ecole Est Finie' (School's Out), which would tie in with the line, 'Throw your homework into the fire.' It is a very kitsch song. One might imagine any one of the *Carry On* stars saying, 'Sheila, take a bow – boot the grime of this world in the crotch, dear!' The song also provides the only example of gender-bending in a Morrissey song – 'You're a girl and I'm a boy . . . I'm a girl and you're a boy' – and featured Candy Darling (né James Slattery) on the cover. The transsexual Darling was one of Andy Warhol's in-house stars, though it is doubtful many Smiths fans had heard of her until now. She had appeared in *Flesh*, but the picture is from the 1971 film *Women In Revolt*. Unlike most of the Warhol discoveries, Darling died of natural causes (cancer), and she held a very special place in The Morrissey Camp

Hall of Fame. 'To be able to inflict Candy Darling on the record-buying public was a perfect example of my very dangerous sense of humour,' he told *NME*. It is also interesting to note that, with the release of the record, there was a sudden rush by Smiths fans to acquire the video of *Women In Revolt*, just as they had acquired *Flesh* and all the other films Morrissey liked, whether they liked or understood them or not. This was what made the complete apostle.

The song was coupled with 'Is It Really So Strange?', the story of a boy who relocates from the North to the South, experiences threats, prejudice and confusion, but only gets more of the same when he heads back to his roots. Better perhaps is 'Sweet And Tender Hooligan', Morrissey's hard-hitting but honest appraisal of a violent youth who swears that he will never get into trouble again – at least, not until the next time. He tries to convince us that the bludgeoning of an old man with an electric fire was an accident; that the woman he strangled was old and would have died anyhow. The narrator begs the jury to look into the boy's 'mother-me' eyes before reaching its verdict – after all, he only turned to crime because he was in debt!

The Smiths' final studio album, *Strangeways Here We Come*, was recorded at the Wool Hall, Bath, during the spring of 1987 – reputedly in a friendly atmosphere, though dissension appears to have set in as soon as the ten tracks had been canned. *The Face*'s Nick Kent dropped in on the group, allegedly to 'snoop' and see for himself if the in-studio picture was as rosy as it was being painted. The Smiths were sensibly playing their cards close to their chests, though Kent still headed his lengthy feature THE BAND WITH THE THORN IN ITS SIDE, summarised the personal problems of the last two years, referred to 'Mad Mozzer' as being 'Manchester's very own Whacko Jacko' (the mis-spelt 'whacko' amusing Morrissey, for this had been the title of Jimmy Edwards' hugely successful sixties television series) and concluded,

Smithdom in many respects is his version of Ambrosia, the fantasy land Billy Liar inhabited. It has given him a place to live out his adolescence; given him the fame he so craved yet which hasn't made him contented.

Faced by the pressure of success, he has often buckled and vacillated endlessly in matters of life as it is lived.

It was at this point that Johnny Marr, protesting that Morrissey was still his closest friend, informed him all the same that he wanted to end their partnership. What Andy Rourke and Mike Joyce had to say about this was immaterial, and it was Morrissey who made a last-bid attempt to keep the four of them together. They had fulfilled their contractual obligations with Rough Trade, and were now free to record for EMI in a reputed £1 million deal – and they were about to begin filming a retrospective of their career for *The South Bank Show*.

The split was postponed for the time being. In August, Rough Trade put out 'Girlfriend In A Coma', which peaked at number 13 in the charts. As mentioned earlier, the song had been inspired by the case of Karen Quinlan, a young American who had survived on a life-support machine in a comatose state for a year, during which the moral dilemma of whether or not to remove her from the machine provoked national debate in the USA. It is an immensely catchy but moving piece, which some journalists denounced as 'sick' for romanticising a deathbed scene. Morrissey caught the nuances of the scene beautifully: the familiar chit-chat of how the girl had been a handful at times ('There were times when I could have "murdered" her',) but that her parents would put all of that behind them just to see her come to – which, of course, is not going to happen. The song was very much in keeping with the songs by Juliette Gréco and Barbara (such as 'Vieillir' and 'Si D'Amour A Mort') dealing with harrowing subjects such as lung cancer and AIDS, that were storming the European charts at the time in countries where it was perfectly normal to sing about all aspects of life, even the worst kind, without being thought of as abnormal.

On the B-side was an old Cilla Black song, 'Work Is A Four-Letter Word', from the 1967 film of the same name that Black had made with David Warner; it was recorded at Streatham, along with Morrissey's 'I Keep Mine Hidden', which appeared on the 12-inch single. There was also a cover version of Elvis Presley's 'A Fool Such As I' – assigned to the Rough Trade vault because an engineer accidentally erased the introduction, though it has been restored, sounds good, and may resurface one day.

A few days after this session, Johnny Marr flew to Los Angeles, ostensibly for a break, where he bumped into Rolling Stones guitarist Keith Richards. The latter had obviously forgiven Marr's earlier press attack on him and was ready to offer some sound advice once the younger man had opened his heart about his woes with Morrissey: 'The music business isn't worth knocking yourself out for. It's not worth killing yourself or stepping on other people.' This was a rather strange statement coming from a man who would have been nothing without the music business, but Marr apparently heeded him, and over the coming weeks the British music press was awash with conflicting reports of The Smiths' demise. The then all-powerful *NME* ran the headline, SMITHS TO SPLIT, on 30 July 1987, though much of the editorial appeared to be supposition:

> Morrissey, when approached through his press office for a comment, said, 'Whoever says The Smiths have split shall be severely spanked by me with a wet plimsoll.' While *NME* news-hounds await the arrival of young Steven armed with soggy footwear, sources in both London and Manchester continue to feed us with snippets . . . Marr has reportedly told friends in Manchester that he and Morrissey are no longer pals, and he is sick of the singer acting the self-centred star . . . Morrissey is not pleased with the company Marr is keeping, acting the guitar hero and playing on albums by Keith Richards, Bobby Womack and Bryan Ferry. The final straw was allegedly Marr interrupting Smiths recording sessions to fly to the States to record with Talking Heads, and using Rough Trade money to pay for the trip. Insiders say Morrissey blew his top and declared it was the end of The Smiths, and he never wanted to work with Marr again.

Blitz more or less reported the same story, published a photograph of Morrissey and Marr that featured a dotted line and a pair of scissors down the middle so that Marr could be removed – suggesting, as had the statement, that he was now seen more as a dispensable guitarist than as co-founder of The Smiths. Whether Marr had ever used Rough Trade money is not known.

Morrissey and Marr each took it in turns to virulently deny they had leaked the story to the press, and it would take years for everyone to stop blaming everyone else. In 1992, one of *NME*'s contributors, Iestin George, told me, 'We did have one or two leads which came from neither Morrissey nor Marr, but by and large we were just spot on with our guesswork.' One of George's colleagues, who asked not to be named, claimed that it went much deeper than this:

> There have been four Jimmys in Morrissey's life – five if you count James Dean. Work the others out for yourself. There was a freelancer called Jimmy. In The Smiths' early days he was hanging around all of the time. He had this enormous crush on Morrissey . . . Then, as happens with everyone who gets close to Morrissey, Jimmy found himself dumped. Morrissey sent him a postcard with some silly quote in that daft handwriting of his. One of Jimmy's pals decided to get even on his behalf by leaking the news to us about The Smiths' split.

In April 1989, Johnny Marr told *NME*'s Dave Haslam:

> It was a hideous private explosion, but it was also a hideous public explosion . . . like a fantasy, turned into a soap-opera by the news-papers. Nothing that was said was true. People around us, both on my side and on Morrissey's, handled the whole thing so badly that it became their whole trip . . . the whole story. It had nothing to do with how I feel about Morrissey and how he feels about me, and that's true up till today. And that's really silly. I despise the way we became public property.

Marr should of course have realised that The Smiths *were* public property: made by the public, nurtured and made wealthy and famous by the public. 'Somebody should have grabbed hold of Morrissey and Marr and banged their silly heads together,' a *NME* spokesman told me.

'Then they should have banged Johnny Marr's head against the nearest brick wall for being so ungrateful!' Neither did Marr appear to have any sympathy for The Smiths' fans when he told Haslam:

> People seemed to think that the most important thing in the world was for their favourite group to stay together. They didn't know anything about the way things were. They'd have preferred me to have died, rather than split the group up. That was their sense of what mattered. But that wasn't what mattered to me.

The irreverence would intensify over time, with Marr achieving relatively moderate success in most of his subsequent musical projects, and with Morrissey going on to become an even more massive British institution on his own. 'He now refers to his former soul mate as "Dorissey",' Danny Kelly reported in the *NME* of 20 April 1991, 'and he has re-christened the limpid lad's [then] 45 ("Our Frank") as "Alf Wank".'

In the same issue of *NME*, Marr stressed almost defensively that The Smiths' more controversial songs had nothing to do with his or the other group members' beliefs: 'We were making music that said very different things about sex, politics and social stuff. The lyrics were unique to Morrissey, to his life, but the audience really picked up on them. It was brilliant. We were creating rock music with art in it.'

Effectively, Marr was shooting himself in the foot: what he was really saying was that Morrissey alone had been the artistic inspiration behind The Smiths. When Kelly confronted him with his drink problem ('seeing off a bottle-and-a-half of Remy Martin a day') and Andy Rourke's drugs dilemma – and asked what effect this had had on the group's collapse – Marr was similarly defensive:

> It was more complicated than that . . . I just stopped liking the other members of the group, and I stopped liking myself . . . We all wanted to be a success, make some money and have a good life. But that became all we lived for and that's the path to becoming completely self-obsessed, shallow and lonely. I thought we were all up our own

arse! We had completely inflated senses of our own importance. Ultimately, I was giving every single moment of my life to somebody else. I started to feel very unnatural and abnormal.

When asked if he was specifically referring to Morrissey, Marr's response was, 'Of course.' However, Kelly seems to have touched a sore point later in the interview when he prompted, 'You're very offhand about this: the last time I interviewed you, you said that you "loved" Morrissey.' Marr's response was a snappy, 'Did I? I must have been talking about my bottle of Remy Martin.'

In 1994, when the former partners were reputedly back on speaking terms, Stuart Maconie asked Morrissey on behalf of *Q*, 'Do you love Johnny Marr?' The response was, 'Yes . . . that's not a hard one. I loved and love Johnny Marr,' though he added, referring skittishly to the other members of The Smiths, 'but I feel tremendous indifference to Bruce and Rick.'

Danny Kelly meanwhile drew his own conclusions, particularly when taking into account Morrissey's attack on Marr's work with Electronic – and Marr's partner, Barney Sumner, of whom Morrissey had quipped, 'No talent whatsoever!' 'There is the unmistakable smack of thwarted love about these pronouncements,' Kelly opined, 'a sort of "If-I-Can't-Have-Him-Then-Nobody-Can" pathos, like the "best friend" mind games kids weave in playgrounds.' Marr's reply, pointing to the fact that he was clearly envious of Morrissey having made more of his Smiths afterlife than himself, was a sharp, 'I know it's an old phrase, now, but in Morrissey's case he should really get a life.'

Ten years later, on the eve of Morrissey's return to glory, Johnny Marr was interrogated in Manchester's Night And Day café by Andrew Harrison of *Word*. Discussing the numerous accounts that had circulated about The Smiths' split, he concluded:

There is, however, another version of the story which I've heard enough times over the years to make me think it is more than rumour. That the breakdown was personal . . . That essentially, Morrissey was in love with Johnny Marr. That he told Marr, in those typical hand-written notes left at his house, that Marr must choose between

Morrissey and his wife Angie . . . When I put this to Johnny Marr, he doesn't sigh or give any sign of surprise.

Denying that Morrissey was in love with him and that he had ever offered such an ultimatum, Marr's response was calm, but candid:

All the way through that time with Morrissey, I felt like the luckiest guy in the world . . . playing great guitar in a great band with people I love, a partner I love and the girl I love – and it's all working. Morrissey and I had a super-intense, close relationship, as close as it can get without being physical. He sent me correspondence all the time . . . but for him to have crossed a line would have been a serious misjudgement. For it to be suspected that I would have left my own band for a reason like that would be a complete insult to me and the work I put in.

*

In Britain, several distraught Smiths male fans, now bereft of their group, attempted suicide – though these had little effect on Morrissey, who believed that these people could only have been unbalanced before The Smiths came along. A group of enthusiasts in Arizona hired a coffin, filled it full of Smiths records and memorabilia, and held a wake. In Denver, Colorado, a fanatic entered a local radio station and held a disc jockey at gunpoint while forcing him to play the group's records for several hours. Handcuffed and led away by police officers, he sobbed to reporters, 'It was worth it for every minute I'm gonna spend in jail!' Unfortunately, the young man was sectioned and sent to an institution.

Meanwhile, on 28 September 1987, Rough Trade released the 'posthumous' *Strangeways Here We Come*. For some reason, Morrissey had wanted a sleeve photograph of Harvey Keitel from the 1968 film, *Who's That Knocking At My Door?* Although the studio owned the rights to the still, Keitel's permission was sought, and his alleged response – 'Who the fuck are The Smiths?' – at a time when he was location shooting in Scotland and their picture was in all the newspapers, did not go down too well with Morrissey, who immediately approached Richard Davalos, the blond actor who had played James

Dean's brother in *East Of Eden*. Davalos was happy to oblige, and supplied a picture of himself and Jimmy, taken on location while making the film, though by the time Morrissey and Jo Slee had finished with it – curiously 'de-homoeroticising' it by removing Jimmy, and using just part of Davalos' face – it looked little better than a blurred mugshot. When asked why he had chosen the title for the album, Morrissey replied tongue-in-cheek, obviously knowing something the press did not yet know, 'Because the way things are going, I wouldn't be surprised if I wasn't in prison twelve months from now. I don't have any particular crimes in mind, but it's so easy to be a criminal these days, I wouldn't have to look far!'

The album was superb, the perfect curtain-call for the greatest British pop group of their generation. The opening song, 'A Rush And A Push And The Land Is Ours' – the surrealist story of 'Troubled Joe', whose young life had ended on the gallows – refers to Morrissey's Irish ancestry and is based on the writings of Lady Jane Francesca Wilde, Oscar's hostess-poet-Nationalist mother who from 1845 wrote under the pseudonym 'Speranza'.

In 'I Started Something I Couldn't Finish', Morrissey becomes Wilde himself. In 1895, when his lover Lord Alfred 'Bosie' Douglas's father had accused Wilde of being a 'sodomite', Wilde had unwisely sued for libel, and had himself been prosecuted and imprisoned for homosexuality. 'I grabbed you by the gilded beams,' Morrissey pronounces, though Bosie is known to have been a very willing participant. And one cannot possibly imagine Wilde saying of his jail sentence, 'Eighteen months hard labour seems . . . fair enough.' The song became The Smiths' pen-ultimate single in October 1987, with a cover-shot of actress Avril Angers from *The Family Way* (1966), and might almost be regarded as the first Morrissey solo single: only he appeared in the rare promotional video, bespectacled and cycling around a chilly Manchester with a group of lookalikes. This song, and the plaintive 'Last Night I Dreamt That Somebody Loved Me', had introductions consisting of crowd noise from the 1984 miners' strike. Both records reached the Top 30, but the latter is by far the more poignant of the two. Morrissey's voice has never sounded more haunting and tortured, particularly when the piece reaches its crescendo. It is also perhaps fitting that the last Smiths release during their lifetime should feature a cover shot of Billy Fury, the object of Morrissey's apparent desire in 'Paint A Vulgar Picture', also on the album. What is surprising is that this truly astonishing pastiche never became a standard, as had happened with George Harrison's 'Something'. Both Shirley Bassey and Tony Bennett are thought to have been interested in doing cover versions, but their managements never got past that of The Smiths.

Murray Head, who had also appeared in *The Family Way*, was on the cover of 'Stop Me If You've Heard This One Before' (for which the aforementioned cycling video is used in the compilation *The Smiths: The Complete Picture*). Rough Trade planned to bring it out as a single and it was released as such in Germany and Holland, but cancelled after the BBC complained over the lines (after the drunken narrator has had an accident with his bicycle), 'And the pain was enough to make a shy, bald Buddhist reflect and plan a mass murder.' A witty observation when one seriously thinks about it. Not so long before, however, a man named Michael Ryan had gone berserk and shot seventeen people dead in Hungerford before turning the gun on himself; the sensitive Beeb felt, therefore, that the song might be considered in poor taste. Of course, that tragic incident had nothing to do with Morrissey or the song, which he had written some time before the event, and deservedly gave rise to a waspish comment by *NME*'s Len Brown in February 1988, 'They said people would instantly link it to Hungerford and it would have caused thousands of shoppers to go out and buy machine-guns and murder their grandparents.' Of the other songs on the album, 'Girlfriend In A Coma' has already been mentioned; of almost equal emotion are the veiled bitterness of 'Unhappy Birthday' and the abject indifference of 'Death Of A Disco Dancer' – the very real fact that when such tragedies become so commonplace, one more makes little difference.

The reviews for the album, mingling with the eulogies for the now-defunct group, were exceptional. *Smash Hits* observed, 'If you fail to be moved by songs like "Last Night I Dreamt That Somebody Loved Me", then you're missing out on a beautiful experience.' Giving the album 10 out of 10, *Record Mirror*'s Sylvia Patterson also singled out this song as its best, lamenting, 'And so for the last time, Morrissey brays his mournful billowings a-top the most skilled 'n' jingling guitar froths on this hapless globe.'

The South Bank Show aired on 17 October 1987. The group's split, on the cards when Tony Knox made the film but not made known to him, had necessitated a last-minute script rewrite. Many fans claimed that the documentary merely skimmed the surface in trying to get the Morrissey–Marr message across. It opens with George Formby performing 'Why Don't Women Like Me?' – not a subtle choice from the producer's point of view, for this ran straight into Morrissey gyrating in camp regalia to 'This Charming Man'. He, never one for personal interviews, seems lost. Journalist Nick Kent (whose feature in *The Face* was yet to be published), looking very emaciated, describes The Smiths as 'the first original English pop group', and predicts that by the end of the decade they will be held in the same esteem as The Beatles. Sandie Shaw, seen performing 'Hand In Glove' – and in a stylised shot with Morrissey at her feet, clutching a rosary – declares, 'He hides behind other people's experiences.' And Morrissey closes the proceedings by stressing that there will be no going back:

> I think this is more or less the end of the story. Ultimately, popular music will end. The ashes are already about us, if we could but notice them . . .

The Smiths' passing was lamented not just by their legion of fans, but by stalwarts of their own profession, though of the many 'obituaries', only that of Marc Almond made any sense and accurately forecast the future: 'Splitting The Smiths at their peak will ensure that their aura stays intact. Without doubt, Morrissey will go on to greater heights.' And in *NME*, an anonymous scribe borrowed a leaf from the Morrissey Book of Camp:

> Turned out finally that Morrissey and Marr weren't the soul brothers, the creative peas in a pod we'd imagined, but more like Dennis

The Menace and Walter, with Dennis fed up with wearing the tutu and bunking out, freelance, with various hoary old rock institutions.

Compared with what he achieved with The Smiths, Johnny Marr's subsequent career has been no great shakes. He worked with Quando Quango, Electronic, Everything But The Girl, Impossible Dreamers, Billy Bragg, Bryan Ferry and others – but he never did and never will find another Morrissey.

The absolute truth concerning the group's demise will probably never be known. There were so many contrasting stories. Morrissey blamed the split on immaturity – the fact that he had been five years older than the other Smiths. He also blamed bad management and their treatment by the press – citing one publication in particular. In February 1991, still annoyed, he told Jean-Daniel Beauvallet of *Les Inrockuptibles*,

> Nothing would have happened if the *NME* hadn't listened to certain rumours concerning Johnny's intentions. That paper is largely responsible for The Smiths' split. I was furious with them. They brought out the coffin long before the corpse was cold. Their attitude traumatised me. They printed so many lies about us – so much so that rumour became reality. If everyone had kept their mouths shut, our problems would have been resolved in private.

In November 1989, Nick Kent of *The Face* asked Morrissey what he would do if Johnny Marr called and asked him to work with him again. Without hesitation he responded, 'It's no secret that I would be on the next bus to his house. I don't feel, by saying that, that I have no confidence in my present standing as a solo artist. But he wrote great music and the union was absolutely perfect.'

In March 1991, when much of the heat had died down, Morrissey again brought up the age gap between himself and his fellow Smiths. 'When I first met them, they were teenagers and I was twenty-two going on twenty-three,' he told Mark Kemp of *Select*. 'It's a vast difference. I think The Smiths just snapped due to that kind of pressure, that boring old rock 'n' roll pressure.'

There would be a swansong, *Rank*, a live album of thirteen songs (whittled down from seventeen) and a Johnny Marr instrumental ('The Draize Train') recorded at the Kilburn National Ballroom on 23 October 1986. Housed in a stunning sleeve featuring *The Champions* star Alexandra Bastedo, its original title should have been *The Smiths In Heat*, which Rough Trade had considered too risqué. It was only on the publication of Jo Slee's *Peepholism* that the company found out that Morrissey had taken them for a ride with the new title. Slee includes a photostat of a handwritten note forwarded to her by the singer: 'Call me morbid, Call me pale, but I'm just not happy with the live LP TITLE and, trusting it causes little commotion, I newly nominate: 'RANK' as in j. Arthur.' In other words – 'wank'. Released in September 1988 and worth buying for one track alone – the definitive version of 'Rusholme Ruffians', which starts off as Elvis Presley's '(Marie's The Name) His Latest Flame' – the album peaked at number 2 in the charts.

The Smiths' rupture had been acrimonious and over the years the fighting would not merely continue, but would be augmented by a book that brought out the very worst in Morrissey's vituperative tongue. *Morrissey & Marr: The Severed Alliance*, subtitled *The Definitive Story Of The Smiths*, was published in the summer of 1992, and became an instant best-seller. Its author, Johnny Rogan, had previously published biographies of The Byrds, Roxy Music and The Kinks among others. The Smiths had provided him with his biggest challenge, however.

In his foreword, Rogan declared that it had taken him three years to research his book, that he had conducted over a hundred interviews, including several with Morrissey's relatives – and one with Johnny Marr which, according to Morrissey, his former partner had 'regretted enormously'. Many people were suspicious of Rogan and his more eccentric traits, particularly the pair's lawyers: the fact that he allegedly changed his address every ten weeks, that he had once written in total isolation for a whole year 'without speaking to another human being', or that he possessed neither refrigerator nor television, for example.

Morrissey might have ignored the book were it not for Rogan's claim to the press that he had once spoken to him, and that his book was therefore a 'true and unsanitised story of The Smiths'. Morrissey hit back with spectacular virulence, issuing the first in a trilogy of 'fatwahs' that simply resulted in Rogan receiving more publicity than ordinarily might have happened: 'Personally, I hope Johnny Rogan ends his days very soon in an M3 pile-up!' When Rogan responded that this was unlikely because he did not drive, Morrissey amended his death-wish: 'Okay, I hope he dies in a hotel fire!'

There had been a previous biography: *The Smiths*, by Mancunian journalist Mick Middles, in 1985. Middles had observed in his text, 'When I first approached The Smiths in regard to this book, although treated with sympathy by their manager, I was waved aside without so much as an acknowledgement.' It had originally featured a cover shot of Morrissey by Joelle Dépont: with his fingers threaded through his hair and his eyes starting out of their sockets, he had resembled a tormented Zachary Scott in an American Expressionist movie. Morrissey had said nothing about the book then, other than that he had disliked it, and had left Johnny Marr to launch the attack. In April 1989, Marr dismissed the book in *NME* as 'Hacienda cocktail bar hearsay'.

Morrissey liked everyone to believe that he had not read *The Severed Alliance*, but he confessed to Adrian Deevoy of *Q* that he had 'squinted at a friend's copy from across the room just to see who'd blabbed'. He did read the book eventually, however, and told Deevoy in July 1992,

Of course, the only definitive story is my story. Johnny Rogan has interviewed anybody who bears a grudge against me. Any of the people who've been close to me over the past decade he has not got near. Basically it's 75 per cent blatant lies. I made a statement when the book was published which said, 'Anybody who buys this book wants their head tested.' According to sales figures, a lot of people need their heads tested. A lot of people have bought it, and a lot of people will believe it.

The press gave the book mixed reviews. It covered the lives and careers of two men whose average age was only thirty, at three hundred pages extant of a well-researched discography, and was somewhat long-winded. 'After having waded through the book's first half,' observed Richard Smith of *Gay Times*, 'You feel ready to sit O-Levels in modern Irish History and the Stretford secondary system.' Tony Parsons, writing in the *Sunday Telegraph*, called it, 'A beautiful monster . . . a page-turner of the first degree.' Many criticised the poor editing and Rogan's frequently insensitive juxtaposing of events in Morrissey's life with the pop headlines of the day. Did we really need to know that he had come into the world on the very day that Elvis Presley had topped the charts with 'A Fool Such As I'?

Rogan claimed that Morrissey's 'fatwahs' had left him unperturbed, and that hundreds of people had written in thanking him for writing the book – including Mike Joyce, Andy Rourke and Morrissey's own father. None of these letters, however, were shown to the press.

In May 1993, in the wake of Johnny Rogan 'having the audacity' to interview Johnny Marr for Morrissey's own favourite publication, *Les Inrockuptibles*, Morrissey told the magazine's Christian Fevret:

If God exists, then Johnny The Rat will be gobbled up by his German Shepherds. I was furious. I haven't lost my sense of humour. I thought very seriously of what I was saying about him [when I made those announcements] . . . that his underhand enquiries prove him to be a dangerous person, one who writes only lies. I could discuss this with him, but why should I? I'm not afraid of confronting anyone, but not just any imbecile. I insist upon at least a minimum of intelligence!

Christian's colleague, Jean-Daniel Beauvallet, told me that *Les Inrockuptibles* had probably been wrong to publish the Rogan/Marr interview, but that the editor-in-chief had been hoping that Rogan might have made 'some sort of apology for what he had done to our favourite singer'. In effect, because this was a much-respected, Morrissey-friendly publication, the text had been cleaned up somewhat – Marr's expletives were removed – and the whole feature, aside from the singer being referred to as 'L'Ayatolla Morrissey', was generally laudatory. 'Let's get one thing clear,' Marr told Rogan, 'Morrissey and I were The Smiths. Mike and Andy could leave the studio when they'd finished. We couldn't.'

He went on to speak of their career highs and lows:

Only Morrissey could do justice to my music. I'll never forget his voice on 'I Know It's Over'. One of the most outstanding moments of my life, so moving. Also, he and I shared the same sense of humour, very dry, ironic. That last year was different. Everything was dead serious. Then our final session together for the B-sides of 'Girlfriend In A Coma'. I'd written 'I Keep Mine Hidden', and we'd done 'Work Is A Four-Letter Word', which I loathed. That's the drop of water which overflowed the vase. I hadn't founded a group to do Cilla Black songs! That and 'Golden Lights' were definitely our worst moments.

'Out of respect for Morrissey,' Jean-Daniel Beauvallet told me, 'we included just one photograph of The Smiths, the one which had appeared on their [bootleg] *Eldorado* album. There was no photograph of Johnny Rogan because he was terrified of anyone seeing what he looked like.'

Rogan hit out at Morrissey's latest 'fatwah' in a radio interview in July 1993, when *The Severed Alliance* was published in paperback: 'Morrissey's made a Freudian slip. I don't have German Shepherds – but Johnny Marr does!' Rogan's book (and my own too) were criticised by some sections of the press for not delving into Morrissey's sexuality, and though Rogan did not specifically 'out' him now, the hints were there in the revised edition – bringing the observation from *Gay Times*' Richard Smith that, 'La Mozz has already wished that Rogan dies in a hotel fire. When he reads this he'll probably run out and buy the matches. Excellent!'

The following year, Rogan brought out *The Smiths: The Visual Documentary*, promoted in *Select* with a photograph of Morrissey, in pre-quiff days, with shaggy long hair. Fans might have welcomed such

images and the day-to-day account of his life before fame beckoned –
the family trees, concert set-lists, the useful and extensive bootleg-
ography – but one imagines Morrissey must have been livid at this public
airing of so much dirty linen. 'No wonder La Mozz hates Johnny Rogan,'
Richard Smith wrote of this one, 'If someone knew this much about me,
I'd want to kill them too.'

Morrissey has always run the risk of certain aspects of his personal
life being made public knowledge by the other Smiths and their
respective families and associates, particularly in view of some of the
incredibly mean things he has said about them since the split. That his
was at least a partly self-fabricated persona goes without saying. In the
spring of 1987 he had told Mishka Assaya of *Les Inrockuptibles*, 'If I
don't work at being Morrissey for so many hours each day – if I stop at
say, five in the afternoon, to do something else – then I don't think
everything would be as significant, as strong as it is. I have to work at
being who I am.'

The singer was morally supported by long-time companion James
Maker. Adopting the stance of unofficial character witness, Maker very
grandly told *Q*'s David Cavanagh at the end of the year: 'Despite the
popular portrayal of Morrissey as an inhibited, retiring character, I know
him as a young man who was capable of great resolve and purpose . . .
He could be benignly considerate and gracious to those whom he
deemed disagreeable. He is the most self-actualised person I know.'

At the time, Maker was fronting the band RPLA, who had recently
released a single, 'The Absolute Queen Of Pop', dedicated to Morrissey.
The outfit had taken out a full-page advertisement in the November
1993 issue of *Gay Times*, depicting a posturing, black-clad, high-heeled
James Maker lounging across the top of a television set. Earlier,
Morrissey had turned up for the group's performance on *The Big E* and
heard Maker tell the audience, 'He's a very good friend of mine. I love
him. So, I dedicated a song to him, yeah!'

Morrissey's and Maker's friendship has reputedly weathered its fair
share of ups and downs over the years, yet Maker and the other Smiths
have thus far proved astonishingly loyal towards respecting Morrissey's
privacy – barring a courtroom outburst in December 1996 during the

infamous royalties battle which, had the judge not imposed a partial press embargo, might have made for some unsavoury tabloid headlines. More of which anon . . .

4

All This and Heaven Too

'I don't take to praise and fawning because I feel that if you accept that, you have to accept it when someone calls you a pile of shit, which I also don't accept. The moment is the performance, and when it's over the communication is over as well.'

– Morrissey

Several months before The Smiths' split, convinced that he and Johnny Marr would never iron out their differences – or at least feeling that a break might enable tempers to cool and allow for a recharging of batteries – Morrissey had engaged Stephen Street (who among other things had produced *Strangeways Here We Come*) as his personal producer and new songwriting partner.

Morrissey had doubtless entered the most apprehensive phase of his career so far. Having professionally only worked with Johnny Marr, whom he had not heard from since the previous May, Marr's company, support and above all his guiding hand must have been sorely missed. Even so, by the middle of September 1987, work on his first solo album was well underway at the Wool Hall Studios, near Bath. Augmenting the project was Vini Reilly, the guitarist with Durutti Column who had been worshipping Morrissey from afar for some time. Reilly knew Andrew Berry, a friend of Johnny Marr's from his X Clothes days and a former glam rock enthusiast turned celebrity hairdresser whom Marr had brought along to The Smiths' first Hacienda performance to act as DJ. It was Berry, also a friend of Stephen Street, who introduced Reilly to Morrissey.

At the time, Reilly was too gushing with admiration to be objective about working with an artiste renowned for being difficult, but he genuinely appears to have encountered few problems, and the glow was still there in March 1994, long after it was all over and he participated in a debate on Morrissey commissioned by the *Manchester Evening News*. Confessing that like everyone else he had been frightened of Morrissey on account of the reputation that preceded him, he recalled for Rosemary Barratt the pleasant surprise that had awaited him:

> I think he appreciated that someone actually spoke to him about real things. Too many people just try to be nice and please him. We talked about everything – sex, love, girls, music, politics. I found him to be one of the nicest, most genuine people I've ever worked with. I was more of a prima donna during these sessions than he ever was. Most musicians are pompous and self-important. He's quite the opposite, a very humble person . . . When I saw Morrissey on stage, I couldn't take my eyes off him. People describe it as a sort of psychiatric transference. It's like being in love, and real stars reflect it back at you. Whether you like him or not, he's a star.

For Reilly, the most trying aspect of his venture was getting used to Morrissey's unorthodox working methods – the fact that he rarely visited the studio during the early stages of putting a song together, more often than not constructing his songs around a set piece of music from the wealth of lyrics and ideas scribbled into the notebook he carried around with him. Technically, of course, neither Reilly nor Stephen Street were in the Johnny Marr league, but where they did succeed was in composing generally gentler music which, combined with Reilly's playing, brought out the melody in Morrissey's voice – the kind of approach that had made lower-range numbers such as 'Last Night I Dreamt That Somebody Loved Me' so memorable. Marr's often aggressive riffs had frequently forced Morrissey to overreach his limited vocal range – or when this was not possible, to remain flat, as had happened during The Smiths' concert at the Paris Eldorado. As for drama – this was intensified by his new drummer, Andrew Paresi, who was probably more effective than Mike Joyce had been because he too never went over the top, thereby allowing Morrissey to avoid straining his voice.

One of the first songs to emerge from the Wool Hall sessions was 'Suedehead', coupled with 'I Know Very Well How I Got My Name', which EMI released as a single in February 1988. And if there were scoffs from detractors that Morrissey would never make it on his own, this first solo release silenced them: the record peaked at number 5 in the charts, higher than any Smiths single. In fact, the situation was exactly the same as it had always been – there was no transition from frontman to solo artiste. Morrissey had simply found himself a new set of musicians.

'Suedehead' owes its title to one of the novels in the Richard Allen trilogy (*Skinhead, Suedehead, Suedehead Escapes* – 1971, 1972 and 1973 respectively), which follows the unpleasant adventures of anti-hero Joe Hawkins and his group of racist, anti-gay cronies – harrowing reading and absolutely nothing to do with the song, though Kris Kirk once suggested that this was Morrissey poking fun at Billy Mackenzie, who was just starting to lose his hair at the time. The lyric calls to mind Mackenzie's alleged visit to Morrissey's flat; it certainly refers to an intrusion of privacy along with the unwanted telephone calls and 'silly notes'. Morrissey confessed that the song was about someone, but would not elaborate – and with a shrug of the shoulder ends the piece by declaring, 'Still, it was a good lay,' suggesting that though the intrusion might have been unwelcome, the outcome had certainly proved worthwhile.

'I would like to go to Indiana and mess with James Dean's soil,' Morrissey once told *Sounds*, 'But so many others have done it. They have taken away the monument and the grass. What's left for me?' He would achieve his ambition in February 1988 when filming the 'travelogue' video for 'Suedehead'. Brilliantly directed by Tim Broad, the iconography packed into this little gem (none of which has anything to do with the song's lyrics) is more potent than that of any other Morrissey video. It begins at the singer's home, where he is reclining in his bath, dreamlike, surveyed by a huge but unflattering picture of the bespectacled Dean. Next to the typewriter on the table spanning the bath are: a volume of Byron (also the actor's middle name); a handwritten sheet containing Dean's thoughts and signed 'Jim Brando Clift Dean'; and a copy of the *Fairmount News* announcing his death. The bathmat, a gift from an American fan, is inscribed THERE IS A LIGHT THAT NEVER GOES OUT; the title of The Smiths' song itself comes from a Hoosier work by Indiana poet laureate James Whitcomb Riley, whose book Morrissey is espied reading in the film. Next we see a photograph of Richard Davalos, the actor who played Jimmy's brother in *East Of Eden*, before Morrissey's nephew shows up with a parcel – containing Antoine de Saint-Exupery's allegorical fable, *Le Petit Prince*, said to have been Jimmy's favourite read. Morrissey is next seen poring over this in the streets of Fairmount – Tim Broad had anticipated him kicking through the puddles and emulating Jimmy in Gottfried Helnwein's famous study *Boulevard Of Broken Dreams*, but on 7 February 1988, the eve of what would have been Jimmy's 57th birthday, the town was snowbound.

All the familiar sights are taken in, less commercial than Graceland and as such affecting an air of genuine, heartfelt sadness: the café where Jimmy hung out as a boy, the drugstore, the high school where he first trod the boards, the Winslow farm, the handprint and initials in the cement. Morrissey poses on Jimmy's motor-scooter, plays his bongos in the paddock, and is even permitted to drive the old red tractor, aided by a little off-screen instruction. In the icy barn, Broad borrows from Valentino's *The Four Horsemen Of The Apocalypse* by having Morrissey snort steam down his nostrils like a stud stallion on a frosty morning. Then he heads for the cemetery where there are two graves – that of the fictitious Cal Dean (Cal Trask was Jimmy's character in *East of Eden*) and the real grave, where Morrissey reverently kneels amongst the snow-capped floral tributes. And again Tim Broad borrows from the Valentino film (a scene also used to close Elvis Presley's *Love Me Tender*) when, as the picture fades, James Dean's image materialises, ghost-like, to take over the screen, one sad young man surveying another in what has been a four-minute masterpiece of cinematography.

Astonishingly, the 'Suedehead' film – which was approved by James Dean's surviving relatives, Marcus and Ortense Winslow – attracted severe criticism from the tabloids. The 'exclusive' in the *Daily Mirror* read, WEIRD: MORRISSEY SITS ON JAMES DEAN'S GRAVE! –

which, of course, he had not done. The reporter, Gill Pringle, added that the singer had 'wept at the graveside', which was true, though Tim Broad had respectfully not captured this on camera. Broad himself only exacerbated the detractors' scoffs by boasting, 'Morrissey is a genius and a poet. In some ways I think James Dean is his spiritual guide.' Morrissey hit back below the belt by accusing Gill Pringle of lying.

The classic camp cover stars had died out with The Smiths. Now, it was Morrissey's turn! He was, and always had been, immensely photogenic. There was no such thing as a bad angle for him, and the photograph of the bare-chested singer that adorned the sleeve of this single release – snapped by a fan the previous year at the London Palladium – set a precedent for some very beautiful, almost always homoerotic images. Some fans were known to have bought two of each release so that one could be framed! An unnamed *NME* journalist, recalling the Leo Ford picture on the first Smiths single, asked Morrissey if he would like to pose naked for one of his covers – bringing the response, 'Well, it might detract from record sales. I don't want to enter the charts at number 92.' Such a record, of course, would doubtless have proved a smash hit.

The photograph gracing the cover of Morrissey's debut album, *Viva Hate* – a shadowy profile by Anton Corbijn – was even better, eliciting the comment from *The Face*'s Nick Kent, 'His solo career will see him becoming the Montgomery Clift of the Nineties.' A few years previously, when asked what his life would be like, should The Smiths ever disband, Morrissey had said, 'Misery, despair. I'll probably end up in a room somewhere, bearded and with a beer-belly, surrounded by books and a cat.' Upon reading the comment, Johnny Marr had responded, 'Sometimes I think he's in need of a good humping.' On the back of the album was a shot of clouds – which made little sense until the full photograph from which this segment had been taken appeared in the press: it was a shot of the tomb of George Formby Sr, in Warrington Cemetery.

Viva Hate was released in a blaze of publicity and zoomed straight to the top of the charts. Accompanying it were several self-deprecating philosophies that could just as easily have been penned by Oscar Wilde himself:

'I don't blame anyone for bringing me into the world, but I do feel that life is excessively over-rated.'

'I find hate omnipresent and love very difficult to find. Hate makes the world go around.'

'I often pass a mirror, and when I glance into it slightly I don't recognise myself at all. You look into a mirror and wonder, "Where have I seen that person before?" Then you remember. It was at a neighbour's funeral, and it was the corpse.'

The album was stunning, each of the dozen songs firmly, faithfully adhering to the *réaliste* tradition, and just as good as anything Morrissey had produced with Johnny Marr, who kept his opinions about his erstwhile partner's solo releases to himself until the spring of 1991. Then, speaking to *NME*'s Danny Kelly, the sour taste was clearly still in his mouth when he said, sarcastically, 'I thought *Viva Hate* was very good. I listened to it in its entirety, and I haven't heard it since.'

Stephen Street audaciously told *NME* at the time of the album's release, having confessed that he had not been overly fond of The Smiths, 'It's only since I've heard this new material that I've realised how major a talent he is. Where it's sad and emotional, it's really heart-breaking stuff.' Writing for the same publication on 19 March, Alan Jackson also hailed Morrissey's Johnny Marr-less success:

Viva Hate finds Narcissus poking a stick into the murky waters of his private pond, disturbing and distorting his reflection and seeming not to care if he detracts from his appearance. It's a brave record, and sometimes beautiful – honest, angry and vulnerable, mercifully free of commercial restraints.

The American magazine *The Advocate* devoted an entire page of its 10 May 1988 issue to singing Morrissey's praises. Sire Records had despatched the album with a topless promo shot of the singer, one arm raised suggestively. Under the heading, MORRISSEY'S REVENGE: Homo Hymns For Misfits & Outcasts, reviewer Adam Block enthused:

Well, we have a *shaved* armpit, Mr Morrissey. Isn't that special? I wonder: when did we last do drag? *Viva Hate* is the vinyl equivalent of that shaved armpit flashed at the pop public: nervy, outrageous, and wickedly blasé . . . 'Pity Me Because I Am Too Sensitive For This World, And Everyone Is Wrong Except Me.' When Morrissey penned that chapter title for his brief fan bio *James Dean Is Not Dead* – published before the heyday of The Smiths – he could have been reciting his own mantra. Morrissey's dry extravagance, devotion to misfits and outcasts, homo lyricism and vicious wit are all deliciously queer and shimmer against lush, ragged and playful melodies on *Viva Hate* . . . This LP by Morrissey, the self-professed gay, celibate, militant vegetarian and British pop's most beguiling brat – is a masterpiece. The Smiths are dead. Viva Morrissey!

The album kicks off with a roisterous 'Alsatian Cousin', whose title (nothing to do with the song) comes from *Forty Years On*, the 1968 play by Alan Bennett, who later became a friend. The song deals with the old chestnut of age-gap sex, to which is added a touch of voyeurism. The narrator has watched a pair of lovers in the forecourt, then later at a campsite where the tent-flap is deliberately left wide open. But there is a problem: the fact that, al fresco, sex is unsatisfactory because the older lover with the leather elbow patches has always been accustomed to doing it on his desk.

'Little Man, What Now?' is a slant on the old Judy Garland song, 'I'm Just An In-Between' – here, the 'too old for toys, too young for boys' theme is transcribed as 'too old to be a child-star, too young to play leads', though the title comes from a 1932 novel of German social problems (*Kleiner Man, Was Nun?*) by Hans Fallada. There have been numerous suggestions as to the identity of the song's subject, a nervous juvenile axed from a television soap because of his lamentable acting – the most likely candidate being Roger Tonge, who played the wheelchair-bound Sandy Richardson in the original *Crossroads*.

Without any doubt, the most accomplished song on the album is 'Everyday Is Like Sunday', backed with a luscious, six-piece string section headed by virtuoso violinist Fenella Barton. One is instinctively reminded of the similarly self-deprecating poet laureate John Betjeman, a great social observer and loather of modernity – notably in the bleakness of 'Death In Leamington', or the inspiration here, the condemnation of modern architecture: 'Come, friendly bombs, and fall on Slough/It isn't fit for humans now.' In Morrissey's case, the attack is against 'the seaside town . . . they forgot to bomb', and one instinctively thinks of the grotesque ugliness of Blackpool with its overblown, addictive commercialism. Who has not experienced the misery of such a place, out of season, where there is nothing to do but play bingo and slot-machines, quaff 'greased tea' and generally wish one were some place else? The song, released as a single in June 1988, reached number 9 in the charts. There have been a number of cover versions since, none worthy of mention.

The video for 'Everyday Is Like Sunday' was filmed by Tim Broad at the much more pleasantly located Southend-on-Sea, and was supposedly based on the film *Jacques Brel Is Alive And Well And Living In Paris*, in which Brel makes cameo appearances between performances of his songs by others – in Morrissey's case as a cyclist, a café patron, shop assistant, etc. However, following a row with yet another short-lived manager, Gail Colson, he failed to turn up for the shoot, and Broad carried on without him. Image-wise, it is almost as important as the video for 'Suedehead'. A trio of women (Billie Whitelaw, ex-*Coronation Street* actress Cheryl Murray and Lucette Henderson in an I DON'T EAT MY FRIENDS T-shirt and inscribing 'Meat Is Murder/Cruelty Without Beauty' on postcards) are out shopping. Morrissey is everywhere. In the record store, surrounded by posters of him, everybody has the 12-inch version of the single being promoted tucked under their arm; on the television he is seen at home, sitting in his bath; he appears half-naked on hoardings. He is seen in the 'flesh' just once (filmed in London and added to the video later) when the ladies return home to spy on him through the television. And on the television in the lounge is *Carry On Camping*, Charles Hawtrey's last film – save that here, his 'Morning everybody!' has been overdubbed by Tallulah Bankhead.

Of the other songs on *Viva Hate*, 'Bengali In Platforms' is mentioned elsewhere. The subjects of 'The Ordinary Boys' are so institutionalised by their mundane, backstreet lives that they never want to change. 'Dial-A-Cliché', one of the weaker songs, links this theme with the 'do-as-I-do' tactics of Northern parenthood, and asks whether one should follow in the footsteps of one's elders with one's own offspring. 'Angel, Angel, Down We Go Together' has the singer offering his strength and support to dissuade a friend, who has fallen in with the wrong crowd, from suicide. 'Late Night, Maudlin Street', a very long, morose pastiche but brilliant nonetheless, recalls the tough Manchester suburb Morrissey grew up in, juxtaposing this with the name of the problem-hit school in *Carry On Teacher*. From personal experience, one has sensed the feeling of immense relief to be finally saying goodbye to the source of one's unhappiness, the place where generations have forcibly lived in misery and hardship – 'Where the world's ugliest boy became . . . the world's ugliest man' – afraid of breaking away from drudgery and tradition because this is how life has always been. The narrator recalls the dramas in his youth: the picture he kept at the side of the bed of the lover he never meant to hurt; the time he drove the lover home after the last bus had gone; the first time they saw each other naked – 'Me – without clothes? Well a nation turns its back and gags.' In similar vein, though much more optimistic, is 'Break Up The Family', with its reference to 'There Is A Light That Never Goes Out' – the fact that the young man, tough and gung-ho, is so happy to be getting out of a rut for the first time that he will not mind if the brakes fail on his lover's car. And again the lover is a man. Then, almost in the next breath, Morrissey declares, 'I Don't Mind If You Forget Me' – words spoken to a lover whose hope of a possible reunion is dashed by the stark put-down, 'Rejection is one thing, but rejection from a fool is cruel.'

Originally intended for the album *The Queen Is Dead*, but subsequently shelved, 'Margaret On The Guillotine' resurfaced on *Viva*

Hate. Adam Block of *The Advocate* aptly applauded the piece as, 'A chilling dollop of Ortonesque deadpan that makes The Sex Pistols' "God Save The Queen" sound like an infantile temper tantrum.' For a number of years, Morrissey's hatred of prime minister Margaret Thatcher appeared to be bordering on the pathological. On 12 October 1984 – the very day The Smiths had begun a tour of Northern Ireland – an IRA bomb exploded at Brighton's Grand Hotel, killing three people and badly injuring some twenty more, including the wife of Norman Tebbit, the then Secretary of State for Trade and Industry. Morrissey was quick to comment: 'The only sorrow of the Brighton bombing is that Thatcher escaped unscathed'. It was an opinion shared by others who were, like himself, not supporters of terrorism but were weary of Conservative rule. The tabloids were full of such remarks; jokes about the tragedy were cracked on radio and television programmes. A working-men's club in South Yorkshire seriously considered a whip-round 'to pay for the bomber to have another go'.

The tabloids, some of whose members shared Morrissey's sentiments but who, of course, would never have dared make this public, singled him out by re-publishing some of the earlier attacks he had made on the Tories and the royals – not that this dissuaded him in the least. When asked by one reporter, tongue-in-cheek, what he would do if one of his fans shot Mrs Thatcher, Morrissey replied seriously, 'Well, I'd obviously marry that person!' In 'Margaret On The Guillotine', he politely requests of the Iron Lady, 'Please die . . . make the dream real'! The song was revered by his massive gay following, virulently opposed to the Tories' notorious Clause 28, the law that banned councils and schools in England and Wales from intentionally promoting homosexuality. In March 1988, Morrissey told Shaun Phillips of *Sounds*,

I find the Thatcher syndrome very stressful and evil. The most perfect example is Clause 28. I think that embodies Thatcher's very nature and her quite natural hatred. I think that's been the story throughout her reign, so I don't see the point of wandering about Marble Arch in a pink T-shirt carrying books by Andrea Dworkin.

In France, Morrissey's near-contemporary, Renaud, was impressed enough by Morrissey's song to compose 'Miss Maggie', lyrically a better piece, which caused a storm when he introduced it on stage at the pantheon of French entertainment, the Paris Olympia. Slipping filthy epithets into the propagandist stanzas, he ended the piece by doing something Morrissey would never have done: turning his back on the audience, he feigned urination against a portrait of Mrs Thatcher. The song topped the French charts for two months, but although it was poetically better constructed than Morrissey's offering, the latter's was the more romantic of the two – for even the swish of the guillotine at the end sounds erotic. José Artur, the French broadcaster who played both songs on his cult evening show on French Inter-radio, said of Morrissey, 'He has fashioned the most dramatic ending to a song since the shattered glass of Edith Piaf's "Les Amants D'un Jour".'

Morrissey had hit the headlines in 1984 with what was ultimately a perfectly logical condemnation of Band Aid, Bob Geldof's brainchild, which raised millions for the victims of the Ethiopian famine – and which, like the celebrity reality programmes of today, also revived the flagging careers of many artists involved, who might otherwise not have bothered participating without pay. Morrissey's theory, by no means a racist view, was that England should first of all put its own house in order, particularly when the Ethiopian problem almost solely lay with Ethiopia itself – due to ignorance of birth control and too much of its resources being spent on weapons and warfare. His subsequent press statement – 'People like Thatcher and the royals could solve the Ethiopian situation within ten seconds, but Band Aid was almost directly aimed at unemployed people' – went down like the proverbial lead balloon, particularly when added to his earlier anti-Conservative comment, 'One can have a great concern for the people of Ethiopia, but it's another thing to inflict daily torture on the people of England.'

Morrissey's attacks on Margaret Thatcher only intensified with the passing of time, and repeated attempts to gag him always failed – such as on the occasion of The Smiths' first visit to Dublin early in 1986, when the *Sunday Correspondent*'s George Byrne asked him if he really had meant all the 'mean things' he had said about Mrs Thatcher. 'Every word,' he replied. 'When people who are intelligent come along, they want to get rid of them or gag them . . . It's not because I'm a vile person, but because I have views.' He was however treading on thin ice when, having referred to his family background, Byrne asked him for his views on the Anglo-Irish agreement:

> You can turn on the news and hear that six innocent people have been shot dead in Belfast, and it doesn't warrant comment, which I say with massive regret because death and murder are part of a situation which is obviously unbridgeable. I certainly don't think that in England there's any desire, politically, to make life any easier in Belfast. Distance gives great comfort to the politicians who have to deal with it.

It would take almost another decade for Morrissey to address the Anglo-Irish problem in song. 'This Is Not Your Country', written with Alain Whyte, was on the B-side of 'Satan Rejected My Soul', released in 1997, and commemorated the thirtieth anniversary of the Northern Ireland Civil Rights Association. This long, obscure but stirring piece tells of the Irishman who feels he is no longer welcome in the country of his birth when all he sees are road-blocks and barbed wire. He cannot go out without being questioned and harassed: 'British soldier pointing a gun, and I'm only trying to post a letter!' He does not know why his son was shot – he has just laid him in a three-foot box, and no one cares. 'Home Sweet Fortress,' he says sarcastically to the soldier, 'We hate your kind' – only to be told, 'Zip up your mouth!'

In the same interview, Morrissey took another swipe at Band Aid, and again, 'distance' was the operative word – 'It confronted a problem that wasn't actually in our land. Distance made it remotely glamorous. I wonder, if Bob Geldof had been concerned with certain domestic problems, would the idea have been so warmly embraced by the music industry?'

In the wake of his attacks on Margaret Thatcher, the *Star* had run the headline, MAD MORRISSEY IN 'KILL MAGGIE' FURY, and this ultimately led to one of several brushes with Geoffrey Dickens, the Conservative MP for Littleborough & Saddleworth who had been out to get Morrissey for some time – not just on account of his political views, but because of what Dickens referred to as his involvement with 'witchcraft' ('Ouija Board, Ouija Board') and 'the child sex issue' (The Smiths' 'Reel Around The Fountain', for example). As a founder member of the Conservative Family Campaign, Dickens had petitioned for the recriminalisation of homosexuality, and advocated the obligatory tagging of 'well-known' gay men and lesbians 'to keep AIDS under control'. Despite the gravity of the matter, Morrissey must have howled along with thousands of others to hear Dickens announce, in a speech during the Clause 28 debate, 'The homosexual fraternity are only likely to get support from us if they stop flaunting their homosexuality and thrusting it down our throats.'

Dickens now accused Morrissey of being actively involved with a terrorist network! As a matter of course, officers from Special Branch were therefore ordered to search his Manchester home. Nothing untoward was found, and whether he was actually cautioned or had his fingerprints and a mugshot taken is not known – but it's extremely unlikely, as the visit is known to have ended with police officers asking Morrissey for his autograph. As for Geoffrey Dickens, it seemed that he did not practise what he was fond of preaching where family values were concerned – he was to hit the headlines himself when it emerged that he had left his wife for a woman he had met at a tea-dance. When he died, Terry Sanderson of *Gay Times* observed, 'Perhaps his gravestone should be etched with the epitaph, "Here lies a man who talked bollocks" – and let's hope that the witches he so feared don't have the urge to dig him up again.'

Whether Morrissey really wanted to see Margaret Thatcher assassinated is a matter for conjecture; certainly there were many like him who would have shed no tears over her demise from natural causes. Even so, he did not submit lightly to being taken to task by a hypocrite MP in what was supposed to be a democratic society, though it should be said that, as a public figure whose every last word was adhered to by many impressionable young people, Morrissey should surely have kept some comments to himself. No one can deny that, as with any great artiste, his fanbase contained a tiny element who might have done anything to please him.

There was a coda of sorts a few years later with 'He Knows I'd Love To See Him', from the *Bona Drag* album. The 'He' of the title is widely regarded as Morrissey's semi-estranged father, and the song ponders what Peter Morrissey might have had to say about his son's being accused by the police as 'Just another fool with radical views' – hence the line, 'My name still conjures up deadly deeds and a bad taste in the mouth', suggesting that even as a child he had been opinionated. In interviews, Morrissey has always spoken of his mother with great affection, often regretting being unable to spend as much time with her and his sister, Jacqueline, as he would like. About his father, he appears indifferent. In April 2003, when Andrew Harrison of *Word* asked Morrissey what his father did, the response was a sharpish, 'He does . . . certain things. Let's leave it at that.'

Margaret Thatcher resigned as prime minister in November 1990 and her successor, John Major, received no sympathy from Morrissey. Speaking in the spring of 1994 to Stuart Maconie for *Q*, he proclaimed, 'John Major is no one's idea of a Prime Minister, and is a terrible human mistake . . . If we focused on Clare Short or even Harriet Harman, here are people with some personality . . . John Smith [then Labour leader, who died soon afterwards] . . . would be better suited to selling bread and no-one would buy it. It makes one long for Communism.'

In the same interview, Maconie brought up the topic of assailant David Kang firing blank shots at Prince Charles during his recent visit to Australia, and asked if Morrissey wished the bullets had been real. 'I think it would have really shaken British politics up . . . I think it would have made the world a more interesting place,' he replied. 'But one of them is bound to get it soon . . . Could be me!' Observers might have posed the question: was Morrissey referring to himself as the proposed victim, aka 'the 18th pale descendant of some old queen or other' – or as the would-be assassin?

Morrissey did not have a great deal to say about the first Gulf War, other than that he was not interested. He was vocal about its successor, however. 'Who do you hate?' Andrew Harrison asked him:

In the wider world, George W and Tony Bland are insufferable, egotistical insane despots. It is unforgivable of them to send people to Iraq, and certain death. In this country [by this time Morrissey was a resident of Los Angeles] American error is unthinkable . . . I was here on September 11 and you could see clearly that it has given America another opportunity to bully people . . . In this country the police have absolute power – they can shoot you in the street and the courts will always side with them. So it is a very fascist country.

The singer's sly reference to Tony Blair as 'Tony Bland' was no slip of the tongue – as anarchic as ever, he was linking the British prime minister to the young coma victim from Derbyshire who in the nineties had been at the centre of a very heated public debate, as had Karen Quinlan before him, over whether he should be allowed to remain on a life-support machine when doctors at a Sheffield hospital had pronounced him clinically dead.

The irreverence continued in June 2003 when, in an interview with Manchester's *City Life* magazine, Morrissey made comparisons between Blair and one of Britain's best-loved camp comedians:

More dangerously [than the Americans being unable to find Saddam Hussein – at the time of the interview – and Osama bin Laden] has anyone noticed the facial and physical similarity between Tony Blair and Larry Grayson? And is it not a coincidence that Larry Grayson 'died' as soon as Blair became Prime Minister? Am I the only one who suspects that this country is being run by Larry Grayson?

Most of Morrissey's fans and detractors had read these comments in print and, probably like myself, imagined some sort of dictatorial figure standing upon a soapbox, waving his arms about in a foul-tempered frenzy. No so! In *The Importance Of Being Morrissey*, billed as his first television interview in sixteen years (in fact, it was his first major screen interview, period) and broadcast on Channel 4 during the late spring of 2003, it is astonishing to witness just how laid-back he is while delivering these withering attacks. His sore points, aside from the omnipresent barbs against the British music press, were still meat-eaters, the royals and politicians. Linking the first two he said, 'It's all just abuse and it's human evil, which is why I think the Royal Family is evil because they enjoy fox-hunting. These are despicable people – and Charles above all has no intelligence whatsoever.' Alluding to his own declining interest in English football, he added, 'If it was a politician they were kicking around, if it was Tony Blair instead of a round object, I'd be captivated!'

To tie in with *Viva Hate*'s release, Morrissey granted interviews to three very different journalists: Paul Morley, one-time marketing executive of Frankie Goes To Hollywood; Shaun Phillips of *Sounds*; and *NME*'s Len Brown. A fourth interview, with *Gay Times*' Kris Kirk, was allegedly turned down: Morrissey had gone a long way since his interview with Catherine Miles, Kris said, and would not have relished 'being backed into a corner by one of his own'.

Of the three, Morley's was the most literate, his questions bordering between the witty and the downright audacious, though Morrissey started this particular ball rolling by greeting his fellow Mancunian with, 'The last time we met, we romped naked together at playschool.' What ensued was a high-camp Louella Parsons-versus-Hedda Hopper debate, with Morley asking his subject, 'How did you move from being the village idiot to being the gangleader?' A little more such bantering, and it was down to the more serious stuff. Morrissey spoke of his shyness, of how he still had to go into another room when the window-cleaner called. He let slip a couple of one-liners: 'Being selfish is the first step towards maturity' and, 'If I hadn't found my social position when I was a teenager so amusing, I would have strangled myself.' He spoke of his horror of flying: 'I always feel that I have to be racked by physical fear, and if I am I'll arrive safe. I feel if I relax, drink a whisky, converse, the plane will crash. I have to be in total turmoil, or the plane won't make it.'

Sex, of course, was an obligatory topic, but when asked if there was any sex in Morrissey, he replied philosophically, 'None whatsoever, which in itself is quite sexy. In a particular sense, I'm a virgin . . . I've always felt above sex and love because all the emotions I need to impress come from within myself.' This was a far cry from the interview given at around the same time to Kris Kirk by his former soulmate, James Maker, who claimed his own most recent enterprise had been feature roles in two gay porno-flicks, *Bike Boys Go Ape* and *Well-Hung Studs*. Speaking of his fondness for the casting-couch, Maker told Kris, 'Begin with your managers and screw your way up the hierarchy.' Another friend, Pete Burns, had told the story of how he preferred sharing hotel rooms with his wife and one of his male musicians. 'That way,' he added, 'I can give it or take it, depending on the mood I'm in. It was always my ambition to form a homo band.' Kris was unmoved by such boasts and observed, 'In a world where stars are too often pigeon-holed, my candidate for sainthood is Morrissey, who artistically and morally is streets ahead of these people. He sets out to be a decent man, and he succeeds because this is what he is.'

Shaun Phillips' interview took place at London's Hyde Park Corner, and did not get off to a brilliant start when, observing Morrissey's inflamed eye – he was breaking in new contact lenses – Phillips suggested a 'corrective visit' to a nearby public toilet renowned for importuning, hardly a welcome comment after the Frank Owen piece in *Melody Maker*, which still rankled, though the singer reacted only by arching an eyebrow. It also seems portentously ironic that the subject of George Michael cropped up several times during the ensuing conversation, with Morrissey stating categorically, 'I don't feel institutionalised. I don't feel faintly akin to George Michael or his world, for that matter. If he had to live my life for five minutes, he'd strangle himself with the nearest piece of cord.'

Another sore point was Morrissey's recent Peel session for Radio One. This had been recorded but not broadcast – he claimed that he had not given of his best because the Maida Vale technicians had been rude, insensitive and disrespectful. 'It was really awful, horrible,' he told Phillips. 'They're quite accustomed to treat everyone like they were some insignificant, unsigned group from Poole. That's how I felt . . . as though I'd never seen a record, let alone made one.'

Locationally perhaps, Morrissey's most important interview – albeit that the printed result was no great shakes – took place at Chelsea's

Cadogan Hotel, in the very room where Oscar Wilde had been arrested in April 1895. Morrissey appears to have been in a doleful mood, largely because various refurbishments over the years had left no trace of his hero. 'I thought the aura of the room would create some interesting physical vibrations,' he told *NME*'s Len Brown in February 1988, 'but they seem to have painted over even the energy.' Aside from 'Suedehead', there was no mention in Brown's piece of any Morrissey work extant of The Smiths, whose demise he now reflected upon with genuine sadness: 'The Smiths were almost like a painting. Every month you'd add a little bit here and a little bit there . . . but it wasn't quite complete and it was whipped away.'

Morrissey's first two solo singles had zoomed into the Top Ten with virtually no airplay and little publicity. His first solo concert, however, was a frenzy of emotion and reminiscent of Dorothy Squires' December 1970 comeback at the London Palladium when, unable to find backing despite one of her records ('My Way') staying in the charts for fifty weeks, she had hired the place herself. For his comeback on 22 December 1988 – though like Squires he had never truthfully been away – Morrissey hired the unlikeliest of venues: the Civic Hall in Wolverhampton. Then he filled some fans with dread by announcing, 'This is me saying goodbye', while others, upon hearing that he would be accompanied by Andy Rourke, Mike Joyce and Craig Gannon, believed that what he was effectively saying was that he was abandoning his solo career and re-forming The Smiths, but without Johnny Marr.

This rumour was the topic of conversation among the long line of apostles gathered outside the theatre, ones who had made the pilgrimage from all over the country. Some of these had lived and slept rough for several days and nights – in the backs of trucks, in bus shelters and shop doorways, heedless of the cold and police harassment. Nothing had been too much trouble for what might have been their last glimpse of the man they loved.

The reason for the concert was twofold: the crowd scenes before and after the event, as well as part of the show itself, were to be filmed for inclusion in a showcase video, directed and edited by Tim Broad:

Hulmerist, which would also contain the promotional videos for six Morrissey singles, including 'The Last Of The Famous International Playboys', scheduled for release in February 1989.

NME's James Brown would observe the following week, 'The excitement and atmosphere inside the hall was like nothing I have ever experienced at any public event. Sensible and intelligent fans were transformed into screaming Mozettes (male and female) at the return of their beloved rebel boy.' The fervour, however, had begun long before Morrissey stepped on to the stage. Because the show was to be filmed, the organisers were not allowed to charge for tickets. Under normal circumstances, this would have meant dispensing complimentary tickets to local advertisers and businesses, civic dignitaries and such who were rarely interested in who was on the bill so long as they were getting a free night out – and with the residue being offered to the public on a first-come-first-served basis. Morrissey was having none of this, and because it was his baby, so to speak, he had decided that tickets would only be allotted to fans who turned up wearing Smiths or Morrissey T-shirts. Wolverhampton town centre had to be cordoned off when 5,000 fans besieged the box office for the 1,700 tickets on offer – smashing down barriers and trying to get into the theatre via side doors and windows. When some of these were broken, the police brought in dogs, though there was no trouble to speak of.

The scenario was reminiscent of one of the *Carry Ons*. Adjacent to the Civic Hall there stood a blood transfusion van, and a compound housing several pit donkeys – said to have been Morrissey's belated tribute to the 1984 strike. The spirit of Christmas was evoked by strategically placed ghetto-blasters playing seasonal songs by Bing Crosby and Ruby Murray – and adding to the general bonhomie of the atmosphere were jugglers, Morrissey lookalikes, and one young man who entertained the crowd by eating the bunch of daffodils he had brought! Morrissey himself arrived in a 1950s cream-and-green Vista school bus that had been used in one of the *St Trinian's* films. 'The bus was the wrong choice because it broke down twice,' he told James Brown, 'I had a driver, he also broke down twice. It was very typical of Old England to let me down.'

The thunderous applause that greeted Morrissey when he strode on to the stage lasted almost ten minutes – to the artiste, an eternity. He was wearing a black diaphanous shirt, through which was revealed a markedly hunkier torso than hitherto: since his last appearance he had obviously worked out, though he has always denied doing such things. (In January 1994 The Smiths' PR man/chauffeur, Dave Harper, told *Q*'s David Cavanagh that though Morrissey had never appeared to eat anything but cake while with the group, he had been immensely strong. Recalling the day he helped Morrissey to move out of his Kensington flat, Harper admitted he had been unable to lift his iron dumbbells off the floor, while Morrissey had effortlessly picked them up with one hand!)

Watching from the gallery, the *Observer*'s Simon Reynolds had described the singer as, 'A paradigm of a certain ethereal, inhibited masculinity which would rather live in dreams than risk being disappointed by reality.' Effectively, though, this was a dream come true. The concert was fairly short, just seven songs beginning with The Smiths' 'Stop Me If You've Heard This One Before', but each one represented a histrionic event. A precedent was set too in that Morrissey performed in front of a massive canvas stage backdrop – this one featuring the uncredited Italian child actor from a sixties Anna Magnani film, the same image that had appeared on the sleeve of 'That Joke Isn't Funny Anymore'.

The live song that ended up on the *Hulmerist* video was 'Sister I'm A Poet', for which there was the obligatory exposing of pectorals – though it could also be said that Morrissey was offering them his heart. 'Sweet And Tender Hooligan' was an invitation to scores of stage invaders: the security men who had rough-frisked youngsters on their way into the theatre had been instructed to go easy on these once the performance began, and this show of affection is endlessly touching. Not surprisingly there was hardly a dry eye in the house, and at times Morrissey too was on the verge of tears. It must also have been an emotional time for Stephen Street, witnessing for the first time the overwhelming response to his compositions – though his stay within the Morrissey court would be brief and prove far from satisfactory. As for Morrissey, he was so carried away by it all that at times he seemed oblivious to his surroundings. Vocally, he was not at his best on account of the non-stop hugging and kissing. But who cared? 'It would have been nice to complete a song without interruption,' he said afterwards, 'but for some reason it just didn't matter. The night went for me beyond performing. It was something else.' After 'Interesting Drug', he wallowed in Strangeways nostalgia with 'Death At One's Elbow', and closed with 'Disappointed' – which ended portentously with the line, 'This is the last song I will ever sing' . . . then raised an almighty cheer by adding another, 'No, I've changed my mind!'

NME's James Brown, obviously as enthralled by and attracted to the spectacle as everyone else at Wolverhampton, summed him up as, 'The sweet and tender, untouchable topless Adonis, always ready to reveal his inner thoughts and passions, yet just as eager to veil them in lyrical and sexual ambiguity.'

In retrospect, it seems an entirely logical progression after this otherwise softly spoken man's exploration of teenage thuggery and murder, after his championing of shoplifting and violent death and suicide, that Morrissey should turn to gang rivalry. He even went so far as to form a 'gang' of his own (albeit one comprising only his rockabilly musicians), paying a kind of homage to the two most notorious such outfits in recent memory – the Kray and Richardson gangs who, by the time he began to adopt an interest in gangster iconography, had already passed into East End legend and the realms of hero worship.

Just as there are regular Smiths sightseeing trips around the band's native Manchester, so one of the essential stopping-off points of 'Morrissey's London' is the area associated with its most famous villains. Twins Ronnie and Reggie Kray, born in 1933, had resided at 179 Vallance Road in Bethnal Green – though the house they grew up in has long since been demolished. Throughout the sixties they had led a regal existence almost rivalling Hollywood's elite, making a fortune from illegal drinking-gambling clubs, and extortion and collection rackets, simultaneously gaining both fear and respect among the community. Boxing enthusiasts (like Morrissey himself), they sparred at Repton Boys Club, and held 'Firm' meetings at several local pubs including the Lion, the Carpenters Arms and – more notoriously – the Blind Beggar, where in February 1966 Ronnie Kray shot dead George Cornell, a member of the rival Charlie Richardson gang – one of the few who had not been rounded up by the police and put away. Arrested, both Krays were sentenced to a minimum of thirty years in prison, and never saw freedom again. Ronnie died in 1995, Reggie five years later. Morrissey is known to have sent flowers to Reggie Kray's funeral.

'The Last Of The Famous International Playboys', Morrissey's magnificent anthem to hero-worship of the corrupt, revolves around the Krays. Not that he necessarily condoned their actions, as he explained on New York's WDRE Radio in November 1991:

I think a lot of people, in order to be seen, in order to be famous and in order to be acknowledged, do something destructive or commit murder. In America, the perfect example is serial killers who quite obviously don't mind being caught and don't mind being known as mass-murderers. They want their element of fame, and they get it always.

In January 1989, speaking to NME's James Brown and confessing that he was interested in the infamy attached to grisly crimes that perversely created celebrities out of murderers, Morrissey had accused tabloid journalists of 'furthering the male hetero-sexist fantasy' by the way they had reported some of these crimes. In particular he denounced them for 'glamorising' a serial-attacker of female students in Manchester by labelling him 'The Fox'. 'It's always done in relation to men who attack women,' he told Brown. 'When men attack men they're never ever given glamorous names.'

A gay theme persists throughout Tim Broad's stunning video for 'The Last Of The Famous International Playboys', which opens with a nipple-flashing singer, Craig Gannon, Stephen Street, Andy Rourke and Mike Joyce playing against an unlucky green background, and it is this which alternates with the vignette of the terrified youth, perceived as the 'dear hero imprisoned' – not in jail, but in his bedroom whose walls are plastered with macho Elvis/Jack Nicholson/George Best posters. The hunky actor is Jason Rush, a blond bombshell who had appeared in the hard-hitting gay acceptance TV drama *The Two Of Us*, a role he later extended to the character he played in *EastEnders*. Indeed, in Broad's film he is wearing an *EastEnders* T-shirt. We see him sparring and punching the air, psyching himself up for an excursion into the dark, dangerous streets of Bermondsey that sees him sprinting as if pursued past a Prince's Trust hoarding – depicting a skinhead and the slogan, HELP US TO ENCOURAGE HIM TO CREATE WEALTH, NOT AGGRO. Then, having achieved nothing and seen no one, we see the youth back in his room, where he feels safe once more.

Surprisingly, the song brought no media condemnation for eulogising the Krays twice, but instead unexpected quibbles over the North/South divide. In February 1989 a journalist from *Record Mirror* sarcastically asked Morrissey why he, a Northerner, should be singing about 'an obviously Southern hero'. Never short of a cutting response, Morrissey replied, 'They are known in the North . . . we do have televisions now, though there's a slight shadow on the commercials.'

For thousands of fans, wishful thinking took over. There was only one playboy and Morrissey played straight into their hands – and hormones – by telling James Brown of *NME*, 'The Last of the Famous International Playboys are Bowie, Bolan, Devoto and me!' Many would have argued that he was better-looking, and certainly more charismatic if not more tongue-in-cheek arrogant, than the other three added together. But there was more. In 1923, *Variety* had asked Rudolph Valentino who, male or female, had been in his opinion the most beautiful person in Hollywood and he had responded, quite seriously, 'Myself.' Morrissey had also witnessed mass adulation close at hand, and one can imagine the fans applauding – and the detractors cringing – upon reading what he told James Brown next, confirming that of all the heroes and villains he worshipped, one stood out from the rest:

> I think I must be, absolutely, a total sex object in every sense of the word. A lot of men and a lot of women find me unmistakably attractive. It amuses me. I sit down and wonder why, and then someone writes me a beautiful letter and tells me why . . . And a lot

of the male followers who are as far as the eye can see natural specimens have very anguished rabid desires in my direction. I find that quite histrionic. Even though an equal proportion of female followers do too, perhaps that's less remarkable than having a vast army of male followers. They're not multi-sexual beings or urban Warholian creatures, they're just your very, very natural living breathing boys.

'The Last Of The Famous International Playboys' entered the charts with such gusto that the music press were sure it would give Morrissey his first number 1. It stalled at number 6, not that this prevented it from becoming an immediate standard, a set piece of his shows, and a song that may only rightfully be performed by him without attracting severe criticism.

The song was coupled with 'Lucky Lisp', a pun on 'Lucky Lips', a big hit for American singer Gale Storm (who recorded it the week of Morrissey's birth) and subsequently revived by Cliff Richard. When Morrissey pronounces, 'When your talent becomes apparent, I will roar from the stalls . . . The Saints smile shyly down on you . . . Jesus made this all for you, love,' one is hard put to determine (as Cliff does have a slight lisp, and considering his religious stance) whether he is praising or mocking him.

No sooner had '. . . Playboys' dropped out of the charts than EMI released its successor, 'Interesting Drug', which reached number 9 in the charts. This bouncy piece had backing vocals by Kirsty MacColl. On the flipside was 'Such A Little Thing Makes A Big Difference', a hopeless plea to the bicycle-chain-wielding thug to shape up and be nicer, and which contains the classic Morrissey observation, 'Most people keep their brains between their legs.' The 12-inch included 'Sweet And Tender Hooligan' from the Wolverhampton concert, and there was a supplementary 12-inch etched with the words, 'MotorCycle Au Pair Boy' (thought by some to be a sly reference to James Maker and his porn-star practices), and featuring a portrait, drawn by Morrissey himself, of Oscar Wilde clutching a sunflower.

Tim Broad's film vignette for 'Interesting Drug', also included on *Hulmerist*, caused a stir with its juxtaposition of anti-Conservative

propaganda and *Carry On* humour. The fictitious Hawtrey High School
For Boys becomes a base not just for Animal Rights activists, but for the
then unemployment crisis and Norman Tebbit's controversial statement
to state benefits dependants, 'Get on your bike and find yourself a job!'
The busty actress Diane Alton is seen chaining her bicycle to the school
railings, as the camera zooms in on the manufacturer's logo: CHOPPER.
Her badge is inscribed, 'I've Never Had A Job Because I've Never Wanted
One' – a line from The Smiths' 'You've Got Everything Now'.

Within the school, the hunkier-than-usual sixth formers (average age
twenty) lounge around reading *NME*, cover courtesy of Diana Dors.
Some wear women's high-heels and chalk slogans on toilet walls. A shot
of the graffiti, THERE ARE SOME BAD PEOPLE ON THE RISE, precedes the
pupils rushing out into the playground where Morrissey is handing out
Animal Rights leaflets. Led by Diane Alton, weary of campaigning and
now dressed as a bunny girl, the pupils raid the laboratory and set the
animals free. A much more disturbing message follows with scenes of
seal-clubbing and anti-fur posters.

These final images, coupled with the wording of the graffiti, brought
about a national outcry, which led to the film being banned by the BBC.
For once, *NME*'s Danny Kelly supported Morrissey, albeit in a
lampooning way, urging fans, 'Whip out your STREET IS MURDER
promotional quill now, dash off a series of letters to EMI and all the TV
companies and demand to see it TODAY!' The film was eventually
shown on *Top Of The Pops*, but only after the word 'rise' had been
changed to 'right', which made little sense to the press until Morrissey
enlightened them ('The bad people on the rise are the willing students
of Tebbit') and the seal-culling scene removed.

For the time being, Morrissey's massive success in Britain meant that
he did not seek to try his chances overseas, despite the flood of offers.
The almighty dollar, he declared, was of secondary importance to
patriotism. And once more he hit out at the de-Anglification of the
country of his birth, telling James Brown of *NME* in March 1989:

> The generations of people who made England such a fascinating,
> interesting and artistically gentle place are slipping away. That

generation is almost all but gone. We're almost at a stage when there won't be anyone living who can remember the Second World War . . . Even the English language, I find, has been hopelessly mucked about with and everything is American or Australian. It's not that I dislike America. America is fine on the other side of the Atlantic. It works quite well and it's interesting. If Margaret Thatcher was a strong person, which she isn't, she wouldn't allow this Americanisation to happen.

With his apparent dislike of travelling, neither did Morrissey seem in any particular hurry to visit Europe again. 'I'm not going to pop up in some greasy Greek festival or at some waterlogged field in Belgium,' he told James Brown, 'I'm not going to be photographed in the Greek Amphitheatre with Yoko Ono and Art Garfunkel.' This innocuous comment brought complaints from aggrieved Greek and Belgian fans. Morrissey found an irate letter from one of the latter, Christophe Devos, sufficiently amusing to warrant a reply, which concluded, in large letters, 'BELGIUM IS SO FAR AWAY!' Devos told me, 'It did not make my day – but it made my whole life!'

Neither did Morrissey appear to have any plans for performing on home territory. Much of the first half of 1989 was spent writing songs. No longer keen on working with Stephen Street, he had a new production team: Clive Langer and Alan Winstanley, who had previously worked with Blue Rondo A La Turk, Madness and Elvis Costello. The pair owned the Hook End Manor Studios near Reading, in Berkshire, which had formerly been a Tudor monastery: importantly for Morrissey, it was within easy driving distance of the jail where his hero Oscar Wilde had been incarcerated. Even so, due to unforeseen problems, there would be more leftover songs produced or co-written on the new, as yet untitled album, than anything else. One was 'Ouija Board, Ouija Board', released as a single in November 1989. On the B-side was 'Yes, I Am Blind' with music by Andy Rourke and the 12-inch featured a very neat cover of the old Herman's Hermits hit, 'East West', far superior to the original.

The record reached number 18 in the charts, and like its predecessor was condemned by the tabloids, who should by now have learned how to recognise Morrissey's fate-orientated cynicism: the narrator lamenting the death of a friend who has left 'the unhappy planet with all the carnivores and destructors on it' – but whose attempts to reach her on the other side backfire when the board spells out his name and tells him, 'P-U-S-H O-Double F!'

Morrissey engaged comedienne Joan Sims for his 'Ouija Board, Ouija Board' video of 1989. Shot in the garden of his then home in the Manchester suburb of Bowden, it featured Sims as a deranged medium. At the shoot for the video, the two got along like a house on fire: 'He treated me like a princess all day,' Sims recalled, 'he had such a ripe sense of humour. And if ever you want a CV of my *Carry Ons*, he knows them better than I do. He's a very brainy chap. I hate to call him a pop star because it's such a horrible word. He's a very nice gentleman.' Of Sims, Morrissey observed, 'Standing next to her was my greatest moment of the year. She was so enormously gifted. And here was I, a silly sausage from somewhere near Manchester.'

Astonishingly, the song was attacked by the Church who, without listening to the lyrics and supported by tabloid hacks, accused Morrissey of inciting fans to become involved with the occult. His biting response, when asked to comment on the rag that had branded him 'devil worshipper', was, 'The only contact I ever made with the dead was when I spoke to a journalist from the *Sun*.' In November 1991, the subject would be brought up in an interview with New York's WDRE Radio. When asked if he believed in the afterlife, he said that he did and enlightened listeners as to the practice known as 'Twelve O'Clock Handle':

If you stare into a mirror at midnight in a completely darkened room with a candle below your face, your face supposedly changes into the face of somebody who has died and who wants to reach you, or somebody who has died and doesn't want to reach you. I find that incredibly effective. Have you tried it? It's extremely frightening because most people's faces do change automatically . . . It's a very, very private thing, and I think it depends on how open or sensitive you are. If you're closed, nothing comes to you.

Nick Kent, mistrusted by Morrissey, but handy to have on side because he was still one of the most widely read journalists on the music scene, had been invited to Hook End Manor in November 1989. As had happened during the recording of *Strangeways Here We Come*, Morrissey also taped the interview, though with his propensity towards evading personal questions one might also have expected him to choose his responses more carefully. Kent confessed to liking 'Ouija Board, Ouija Board', though by the time the feature finally appeared in *The Face* in March 1990, he had demoted it to 'numbingly bad'. Neither did Kent do himself any favours by revealing that Clive Langer had referred to Morrissey as, 'Someone who comes up with the best song titles in the world, only somewhere along the line he seems to forget the song', before adding, 'It looks as if Langer is about to join Stephen Street in Morrissey's out-tray.' Hardly surprising, one might feel, if Langer had really said this.

The interview had begun badly, with Kent addressing him as 'Mozz' – bringing a snappy, 'It makes me sound like a racehorse.' One also gets the impression that Kent was deliberately trying to wind him up – or catch him off his guard, particularly when he proceeded with, 'Don't you feel you have to come out in some way to face the Nineties?' Again, the response was a grandiose, 'I believe my position in this coming decade is perhaps one of the most challenging and interesting things that's ever happened in British pop-music.' His interrogator, however, was insistent:

KENT: You write a lot about the homosexual experience . . .
MORRISSEY: Well . . . not a lot.
KENT: Okay, you write a lot about homosexual longing.
MORRISSEY: I've always said that I leave things very open and that I sing about people. Without limitation. And I don't think that automatically makes me a homosexual.
KENT: What about . . . sexual relationships?
MORRISSEY: I don't have relationships at all. It's out of the question.
KENT: Why?
MORRISSEY: Partly because I was always attracted to men or women

who were never attracted to me. And I was never attracted to women or men who were attracted to me. So that's the problem. I've never met the right person.

It seemed that Kent, the music world and the fans had their answer: by his own admission, it appeared that Morrissey was currently – for want of a better description – a non-practising bisexual. The 'news' delighted *Gay Times*' Kris Kirk. 'Did you see the photograph in *The Face*?' he asked me, 'Morrissey's wearing a wedding ring . . . I mean, who could do something like [1990 single] 'November Spawned A Monster' – all that prick-teasing and exposing of flesh, and *not* be a Friend of Dorothy?'

Kris Kirk had attended The Smiths' very first performance in London, and in his stunning joint-feature ('Morrissey: Saint Or Sinner') with Richard Smith for *Gay Times* in August 1990, in the wake of Nick Kent's *Face* interview, Kris coined the gay Smithdom quip of the year, 'Here was a young shaver whose oxters I'd dearly love to sniff close up!' Even so, he was not sycophantic toward his idol, criticising Morrissey for his comments about Margaret Thatcher, for what he considered had been careless remarks about black music, and for his romanticising of suicide. Moreover, he took him to task for his extreme arrogance.

The second part of the *Gay Times* feature, Richard Smith's 'The God That Failed', picked up on Morrissey's obsession, in his early Smiths songs, with males, and explained why he thought this had in recent times been changed to more of a sexual ambiguity. His conclusion was spot-on, and hardly surprising:

He never believed he'd be anywhere near as successful as he went on to become. Once it became clear that The Smiths were destined not for the originally intended Indie cultdom, but for stardom, a large lyrical retreat and rethink was swiftly undertaken. None-the-less, whilst his songs then became non-gender specific to a man, they still only stood up to a homosexual reading.

Linking his analysis with the long line of Smiths 'Camp Hall Of Fame' covers, Smith concluded, 'Like anyone reasonably well-raised in gay culture, I could pick up the references, allusions and signs . . . The message couldn't have been any clearer if he'd put Jeff Stryker or Judy Garland on them.'

In September 2003, in the issue of *Gay Times* feting what would have been The Smiths' twentieth anniversary, Richard Smith could safely observe, 'Looking at the man, jumping to the conclusion that Morrissey was gay as a goose was as easy as sliding off a butter mountain.' Now, he pleaded, 'If you are gay then please, please, please wake up [to] the fact that it's the Nineties and some sort of stand is expected.'

The feature brought in a flood of letters from irate fans who claimed they had 'proof' of Morrissey's sexuality: some from heterosexual women (sent to a gay magazine!) claiming he could not possibly be gay because they had shared intimate moments with him, others from gay men declaring the opposite. 'The tone of every letter was that of wishful thinking,' Kris said. The next issue of *Gay Times* published a 'defence', penned by a fan named David Semple, part of which read:

It's a good story. Cultish singer writes songs with a clear gay message, then when he becomes successful he hushes down that message, disregarding all the gay people who put him where he was. The problem is, it isn't true. Morrissey's lyrics have never been more explicitly homosexual than on his most recent album, *Viva Hate* . . . but like Julian Clary [he] prefers double-entendres to direct statements. Morrissey couldn't sing 'Glad To Be Gay' or 'There's More To Love Than Boy Meets Girl' because he writes in the persona of a shy, unloved loner, closeted not so much about his sexuality as about his whole being. Tabloid readers would love to believe that homosexuals are an alien tribe appearing on earth from elsewhere, not their children or their brothers and sisters, but Morrissey rejects such a simplistic and repressive view and writes about a world of uncertain, awakening sexuality.

For the time being, if not for ever, Morrissey was keeping quiet: he had said too much already to Nick Kent, and would never speak to him again. As for Richard Smith, he would never stop singing Morrissey's praises in his highly individual no-nonsense way, and in August 1993 he wrote a feature for *Gay Times* entitled 'Cock Rock', which detailed 23 of 'the most noted penii in pop'. Morrissey appeared in eleventh position, behind Bowie and Lennon but ahead of Prince and Elvis Presley. Morrissey's photograph was captioned, 'Included here as one of only two pop stars who claim not to use their naughty bits for anything naughty. The other is, of course, Cliff Richard. You can draw your own conclusions.'

Meanwhile, on 9 February 1990, Morrissey flew to Los Angeles for a brief visit that began with an appearance at KROQ, the city's most important 'alternative' radio station. There had been little publicity, yet he was still greeted by over a thousand screaming fans, and at one stage of the proceedings was photographed with tears in his eyes. The interview itself was unrevealing. The American public in general knew little or nothing about him as yet, other than that he seemed to cause a big fuss wherever he went, and the questions were centred around a potted biography and a list of his likes and dislikes made available to the DJ. Only one caused him hassle: when he was asked if, in the world of pop music, there was any place for Madonna or Janet Jackson. Morrissey had revised his opinion of the Material Girl, who had been elevated from 'the nearest thing to organised prostitution' to 'quite an independent individual person'. Of the other singer he stated, 'Janet Jackson, as far as I'm concerned, has no talent at all.' This brought in dozens of complaints – though many others would argue he was simply speaking the truth.

Even so, the officials at KROQ knew that they were on to a good thing, and adopted Morrissey as a 'foundation artiste' – an honour almost equating to one being given Freedom of the City, promoting subsequent record releases with receptions, posters, car-stickers, calendars and other memorabilia. The move also led to a Smiths boom – bearing in mind that to the Americans, as to everyone else, Morrissey and The Smiths were one and the same. Over the next few months, six of their albums would go gold, selling in excess of 500,000 copies each.

And, while the British music press were still busy insulting him, an anonymous journalist observed in a syndicated column, 'When words aren't enough to describe the way someone else's words set to music make you feel, you know you are dealing with a genius.'

Morrissey returned to England, where for the first time ever he was forced to consider taking legal action against a fan. In March 1990 a feature entitled 'Morrissey's Manchester' appeared in the *Independent*, in which Jim White escorted readers on an exhaustive tour of the city – the usual Smiths spots, along with Boddington's Brewery, Strangeways Prison and some of the seedier sides of Hulme. For his piece White had been assisted by a fan named Robert Graham, who in 1989 had written a play about The Smiths (Morrissey had ignored his invitation to attend the premiere at the Contact Theatre) and Eliot Marks, another fan who had been organising Smiths conventions since the band's demise. The first, in August 1988, had attracted 1,200 visitors from around the world, and there had since been successful conventions in Tokyo, Los Angeles and latterly at Le Locomotif, a gay club in Paris's Pigalle-Blanche district.

Morrissey was indifferent towards these events, but he saw red when he learned of Marks' proclamation, read out in Paris, 'All monies raised by conventions past and present will go to the charity of Morrissey's choice.' Morrissey's press office threatened Marks with prosecution, and in turn was sent a petition, part of which read, 'Discos around the country laugh when we request your music, so we need somewhere where we can all come together away from the music that's destroying our country. Please give us your blessing to hold further events. Life is not worth living without the music to cling to.' The response was that such profiteering under someone else's name would not be tolerated, and Morrissey's blessing was denied.

Robert Graham would exact a revenge of sorts, later telling the *Independent* that in his opinion, Morrissey was a conman, adding, 'He encourages longing in his fans that he knows is empty and destructive. He was a fan himself, he should know better.'

Morrissey, meanwhile, returned to Hook End Manor where work resumed on the new album, now titled *Bona Drag*. Several new songs were cut: 'He Knows I'd Love To See Him', 'Striptease With A

Difference' (which tells of manipulating a game of strip poker so that one loses) and 'Get Off The Stage'. The latter was Morrissey's comment on the so-called 'geriatric content' of the *Billboard* charts, which had appalled him during his last visit to America: The Grateful Dead, Bob Dylan, The Rolling Stones and Eric Clapton were all considered by him to be way beyond their sell-by date. 'Oh, you silly old man, you're making a fool of yourself,' he expostulates, declaring that all the songs sound the same. Then the piece delightfully almost turns into an old-time French-Canadian reel as the musicians join in with the chorus and he concludes, 'When we get our money back, I'd like to see your back in plaster!' Very nice, but because of 'difficulties' that were never made public, it soon emerged that the album would never see the light of day as Morrissey had intended: instead, it became a collection of singles, B-sides and oddments.

Morrissey was besieged by journalists wanting interviews, but was in no mood for pleasantries. He was also still seething about Nick Kent's feature in *The Face*. 'He's more obsessed with me than he is with his own mother,' he told Jean-Daniel Beauvallet, 'but I take that as a compliment.' 'I could tell you things about Nick Kent that would take the frizz out of your Afro,' he told Len Brown, writing a profile for the November issue of *Vox*, to coincide with the album's belated release – though truthfully he only had himself to blame for speaking about his sexuality in the first place.

Only six songs were salvaged from the proposed album. 'November Spawned A Monster' was a tremendously bold, beautiful, moving pastiche that wrenched every last fibre of emotion from the Morrissey frame. Coupled with 'He Knows I'd Love To See Him' and 'The Girl Least Likely To', it reached number 12 in the charts. For backing vocals, Morrissey had hired Canadian singer Mary Margaret O'Hara, who had recently toured Britain and released an album, *Miss America*. 'I haven't in a decade heard someone singing because of a deep-set personal neurosis, absolute need and desperation,' he said of her at the time. 'You'd think she might fall apart at any second and become a pile of rags and bones on stage.' O'Hara's singing is certainly an acquired taste, though in this particular song it works astonishingly well.

The song (though otherwise unconnected with its title) does fit into the category known by the French as 'Les enfants de novembre' – collectively, the oppressed peoples of the world, whether this be by way of creed, colour, sexuality, war, or in this instance disability. As so often in his work, Morrissey helps us to comprehend her plight by climbing inside the skin of the 'poor twisted' child who must suffer life not just a 'frame of twisted limbs', but the object of everyone's pity, which is the last thing she wants. It rails against the limitations imposed upon a wheelchair-bound young woman whose only ambition in life is to walk down the street, wearing the clothes she has bought for herself. As usual, the critics donned their blinkers to attack the song, particularly the line, 'If the lights were out, could you even bear to kiss her on the mouth?' – to their way of thinking, this was Morrissey mocking the afflicted.

The promotional video for the song, filmed by Tim Broad at Mushroom Rock, in the remote, sun-scorched Death Valley, remains the finest piece of Morrissey's work ever captured on celluloid. Wearing a black, diaphanous top, neither shirt nor blouse, he is the epitome of narcissism, homoeroticism, pain, anguish, and muscular male beauty – yet despite his writhing and preening never seems to go over the top. On the Continent, favourable comparisons were made between this vignette of vignettes and the death throes of the young Resistance fighter in the famous Wajda film of 1958, *Ashes And Diamonds* – no little wonder, for its star Zbigniev Cybulsky was regarded as 'The Polish James Dean'. Indeed, when the Morrissey film was premiered on Warsaw television in the autumn of 1990, he was introduced as 'The English Cybulsky'.

According to Morrissey's record company, there was no promotional video for his next single – 'Piccadilly Palare', released in November 1990 and peaking at number 18 in the charts – because they considered it 'insufficiently commercial', which begs the question: why release it in the first place? The statement was, of course, untrue: though Morrissey's videos usually have little if anything to do with the subject of the song, EMI were worried that there would always be a first time, and felt that the topic of rent boys would prove too much for mainstream television. The song was backed with 'Get Off The Stage', and Stephen

Street's 'At Amber' which, because the critics were too busy deciphering and attacking the A-side, got off more lightly than it otherwise might have done. In this one the narrator, staying at a seedy hotel where 'the clime and the grime gel' and compel him to sleep in his clothes, calls his disabled friend to say how much he envies him for not being able to walk so that he doesn't have to put up with what the narrator is having to endure.

Modern rent boys – the ones who were legally underage, as opposed to those of Wilde's day – had been brought to the attention of the uninitiated general public during the late sixties, courtesy of television drama-documentaries such as *Johnny Go Home*. Watching this enables one to appreciate Morrissey's song all the more. The 'rails' he refers to are the black iron railings separating the terraced buildings from the pavements – from here, or from 'The Rack' (the notorious Meat Rack amusement arcade, which turned up again in the television's *The Vice* in 2003) the Dilly Boys plied their trade, calling out to well-heeled gentlemen (the 'belted coats') who, of course, ignored or insulted them if they were not interested in paying for their 'easy meat'.

Polari – derived from *palavrear*, Portuguese mariners' argot for 'to chatter to locals' – was a popular form of communication among the gay community of late 19th-century London, a nonsensical-sounding collection of phrases and buzzwords that enabled one to size up a potential client without attracting attention from bystanders. Of course, if the man under scrutiny was not interested in having sex, he would have had no idea what was being said. The parlance came back in a big way during the sixties, courtesy of the Light Programme's (a predecessor of Radio 2) Sunday afternoon cult comedy radio show, *Round The Horne*. This featured Julian and Sandy, the first openly gay characters to appear on British national radio, portrayed by Kenneth Williams and Hugh Paddick. The Polari term for homosexual, *omme poloni* ('man-woman'), frequently appears in biographies of Oscar Wilde. My good friend Peter Burton, for over thirty years the peerless keystone of gay journalism, explained the gist of Polari in his fascinating personal memoir, *Parallel Lives*:

As *freely ommes* (young men) . . . we would *zhoosh* (style) our *riah* (hair), powder our *eeks* (faces), climb into our *bona* (fabulous) new *drag* (clothes) don our *batts* (shoes) and *troll* off to some bona *bijou* (little) bar. In the bar we would stand around with our *sisters*, *varda* (look at) the bona *cartes* (genitals) on the butch omme *ajax* (nearby) who, if we fluttered our *ogle riahs* (eyelashes) at him sweetly, might just troll over to offer a light for the unlit *vogue* (cigarette) clenched between our teeth.

Other choice Polari phrases included *dolly basket, naff lucoddi* (nice crotch, shame about the body), but in the recorded version of his song (several verses had to be deleted to keep it to an acceptable length) Morrissey sticks to just a few of the regular words. Also, by the time he wrote it, some of these had taken on new meanings, as has happened in other areas of the English language – examples being *bona* (hard-on) and *troll* (cruise). One also has to remember that the majority of men who spoke Polari were adults heading towards middle age. The critics, therefore, were both ignorant and wrong to accuse Morrissey of encouraging underage sex in the song.

Surprisingly, it was the gay press leading the attack this time. In his excellent combined feature with Kris Kirk for *Gay Times*, 'Morrissey: Saint Or Sinner', Richard Smith took exception to 'Piccadilly Palare' and demanded, 'If you're not gay, then get your hands off our history. You can't steal the very words from our lips just so you can embellish your songs with (pardon the pun) a bit of rough.'

The publicity that 'Piccadilly Palare' attracted resurrected once again the question of Morrissey's sexuality. He had intimated at a non-practising AC/DC status to Nick Kent, though few people genuinely believed that no one had ever found one of the handsomest men in British show business attractive, no matter how picky he might have been. In fact, he could have made the situation a whole lot easier on himself by telling journalists to mind their own business. As things stood, with his appetite for certain elements of gay culture, he had allowed himself to be forced into an awkward corner. And *Gay Times*' Richard Smith had a valid point: if he was gay, the gay press wanted him to come out properly and offer strength and support to all those fans who had shut themselves up in bedrooms – seeking solace in his music to help them come to terms with being gay. And if he was not totally gay, then they wanted him to say so, leave off their culture and stop flaunting it in their faces. 'Being gay isn't for making money out of unless you're a fully paid-up member of the company,' Kris Kirk admonished. 'Otherwise you get out of the theatre and find yourself another job.'

While interviewing Morrissey for *Vox*, Len Brown wisely steered clear of the issue of sexuality, and focused instead on the recent insurgence of Mancunian groups: The Happy Mondays, 808 State (who, according to one unfounded story, Morrissey had thought of joining), The Stone Roses and Northside, to name but a few. Then there were the 'old guard': New Order, James and the like. Morrissey was unimpressed. 'If I was herded in with those groups,' he told Brown, 'believe me, I'd emigrate to Norway. I'm not the enemy of those groups, but I still have a boring, old-fashioned notion of talent.'

The gist of the interview was that, despite being an established artiste with one of the biggest labels in the UK, and with millions of record sales behind him, he was now actually selling less records than some of these acts. For Morrissey, though, it was quality that counted, not quantity. 'I never believed that sitting on top of the pop arena was a nice place to be,' he told Brown, before confessing one of the secrets of his success, 'I think there's always a danger in trying to give an audience what it wants. I think it's more interesting to give an audience something it might not want.' The audience certainly wanted the rehashed *Bona Drag*: it went to number 9 in the charts.

The album's release coincided with yet another reshuffling of the Morrissey cabinet, in preparation for the recording of his next album. Again, this displayed the difficulties he so frequently encountered when working with others, but at least it was a process that kept everyone on their toes and ensured the freshness of his work. The latest manager was Fachtna O'Ceallaigh, who had worked with The Boomtown Rats and Sinead O'Connor. Tom Verlaine, the American guitarist formerly with Television, was approached to work with Morrissey as a songwriter, but declined, throwing away a potential fortune, declaring that Morrissey's working methods – adding lyrics to taped, prepared tunes – were unacceptable. The problem was solved when Clive Langer brought in Bristol-born songwriter-musician Mark Nevin, a glam-rock enthusiast who had formed Fairground Attraction with Eddi Reader and topped the charts with 'Perfect'. He told me:

> Fachtna O'Ceallaigh promised me that Morrissey would call me at home, but that never happened. I just sent him some tapes through the post, and waited for his response, which seemed to take for ever. Then suddenly I received a postcard. It was the first of hundreds, and he'd scrawled across it just one word – 'PERFECT!' I was thrilled. Our first song together was 'Tony The Pony', though I doubt anyone remembers it now.

The line-up was completed by Andrew Paresi (the drummer who had worked on *Viva Hate*), keyboard players Seamus Behan and Steve Hart and Madness' bass player Mark Bedford, raga-violinist Ali Khan adding a touch of the exotic. The new album, recorded at Hook End Manor, was given the title *Kill Uncle*, and as a taster in February 1991 EMI released the single 'Our Frank' (coupled with 'Journalists Who Lie'/'Tony The Pony'), a cynical ballad not quite up to Morrissey's usual standards and which barely scraped into the Top 30. Neither did the song impart any particular obvious message, though the line 'Give me a cigarette' was taken literally by some fans – in future concert performances, cigarettes would be flung on to the stage along with the customary flowers, mindless of the fact that Morrissey had never smoked!

Kill Uncle was released in March 1991, and reached number 8 in the charts. Despite much adverse criticism it is a good album, not as intense as its successors would be, but enjoyable all the same – its only fault being that, including only ten songs and running to just 33 minutes, it is too short. And because of its lack of drama, it is one of those 'mood' albums best listened to late at night when the lights are low.

The album opens with 'Our Frank', while 'Asian Rut' is discussed in the next chapter. The third song on the album, 'Sing Your Life', was released as a single in April and reached a disappointing number 33 in the charts – hardly surprising, for despite its catchy tune it received virtually no airplay. It was coupled with 'The Loop' (which certainly ought to have been on the album) and Paul Weller's 'That's Entertainment', of which more later. To whom, in the song, Morrissey is urging, 'Just walk up to the microphone and sing . . . now's your chance to shine' is not known.

There were two collaborations with Clive Langer. 'Mute Witness' tackles once more the topic of disability: the story of the deaf and dumb thalidomide victim who is hopelessly trying to describe an event that has distressed her – and to complicate matters, Morrissey has allowed this to happen in the notorious gay cruising area of Clapham Common. The second Langer contribution was 'Found, Found, Found', an ode to Morrissey's friendship with Michael Stipe, the gifted, frail-looking singer from REM, who was slightly younger than himself.

As with many of his early friendships, this too had started off on a pen-pal basis, with Stipe writing to Morrissey first; recently the pair had met, 'to walk in huge circles through Hyde Park'. Stipe, in those days, was as famed for his intense privacy as for his searingly lachrymose vocal technique. Since then, the singer has emerged from the closet and lost few if any of his fans, chiefly because they had always suspected him of being gay in the first place. Looking back, one therefore re-examines the question of why he would have been platonically drawn to Morrissey: both were eccentrics, admirers of off-beats such as Patti Smith and The New York Dolls; both were vegetarian; both were loners infatuated with realism, homoeroticism and death; both claimed when tongues inevitably started wagging that their lyrics were specifically genderless – though while Morrissey was hedging to explain the boast, 'Still, it was a good lay', Stipe was cutting to the chase by pronouncing, 'I'm in your possession/Nothing's free, so fuck me kitten.'

In 'Found, Found, Found', Morrissey steps into the shoes of the réaliste, or torch singer, to emphasise, 'The more you offer trust, the more you chase, the more you cry, the more you're bound to lose.' He told Select's Mark Kemp in March 1991,

Michael is a very kind, generous person. The whole joy of the friendship is that music doesn't come into it. We don't ever talk about REM or whatever it is I do. There are other things to discuss . . . and who knows, we may even get a cover on *Hello!*

Morrissey was referring to the time-honoured superstition that couples snapped for the famous glossy celebrity weekly rarely stay together once they have appeared in it. What Stipe had to say about such an albeit tongue-in-cheek statement, or whether their friendship progressed beyond the platonic, is not known. That Morrissey was the more forceful partner in the friendship was suggested when Kemp asked him if he would like to work professionally with Stipe: 'It isn't decided yet what we'll do, but it would be nice to do something unusual, some Righteous Brothers type thing. I'd like to lead the way. It would be one of those funny, historic bits of television that's so rare these days, especially in England.' One finds it hard even envisaging such a project between the immaculately turned out Stretford bard and the rather more raggedy REM frontman. 'It'd be like teaming Donny Osmond with Albert Steptoe,' Kris Kirk observed.

The lyrics of *Bona Drag*'s 'The Harsh Truth Of The Camera Lie' could almost be autobiographical, were it not for the fact that the friendly photographer who is the narrator shares the humiliation of his subject's compulsion to put on an act in public life – coupled with his/her aversion towards facing unfriendly photographers who seek out tell-all blemishes. It was almost an allegory of how, in the not too distant future, some sections of the media would be applying the 'warts-and-all' technique to Morrissey himself – particularly the closing stanza, 'I don't want to be judged any more . . . I would sooner be just blindly loved.' And with 'The Last Of The Family Line', the 'I-will-never-marry' theme resurfaces when Morrissey dons the proverbial hairshirt to avow that, after fifteen generations of 'honouring nature', this last family survivor is at least 'spared the pain of ever saying goodbye'.

Two of the weaker songs on the album (weaker by Morrissey's standards, anyway) are 'Driving Your Girlfriend Home', with Linder on backing vocals, and 'King Leer'. In the former, Morrissey assumes the mantle of the kindly agony uncle who explains to a friend's boyfriend the despondency in the relationship she is trying hard to avoid. He tells him, 'She's laughing to stop crying.' In 'King Leer', the plight of the long-suffering girlfriend resurfaces, when rescue from the money-grabbing boyfriend is attempted by the temptation of bribery: 'vodka and Tizer', 'a homeless Chihuahua', and finally the narrator's body – though as usual with the self-deprecating Morrissey, nothing much happens in this department, and in any case his caring efforts are not appreciated by the ungrateful, spoilt little rich girl.

Few songs better sum up Morrissey's life than the closing track of the album, 'There's A Place In Hell For Me And My Friends', later adapted into French by this author for Barbara, who sadly did not live long enough to record it:

> Nous espèrons qu'autour du fourneau
> La peau et l'sang et les os
> Ne nous empêch'rons de pleurer
> Pleurer comme quand on était vivant

The truly dazzling, unadorned studio version of this song, enriched by Mark Nevin's solitary piano accompaniment (far more poignant than the arrangements for the subsequent concert and KROQ versions) becomes a graceful, tender hymn to malignity, an early epitaph – the fact that death, in common with nakedness, removes social boundaries and enables all mankind to become equal. Not surprisingly, it became his most requested song in France, and when *Les Inrockuptibles'* Jean-Daniel Beauvallet asked him in February 1991 if he merited such a place, he replied seriously, 'There's no other alternative. Some of us have to end up in hell and I'm ready to suffer the flames. In any case, there won't be enough room for all of us in heaven!'

At least one of the *Kill Uncle* songs is thought to have been pencilled in for the soundtrack of the gay road-movie *The Living End*, directed by Greg Araki and released in 1993. This tells the story of two HIV-positive lovers who, while not knowing when the end will come, blaze a trail of destruction across America. Why permission to use the song(s) was denied is not known – Kris Kirk believed that it might have had something to do with video director Tim Broad's recently discovered HIV status – but the actor Craig Gilmore was allowed to wear a Morrissey T-shirt in one scene, a shot from which was used for the playbills, and the film became a big favourite with gay Morrissey fans.

Meanwhile, wary of the difficulties posed by an ever-changing line-up, and also aware that his fans had been starved of live performances for far too long, Morrissey had begun his search for a reliable backing group long before the release of *Kill Uncle*. He wanted Mark Nevin, but Nevin had contractual obligations elsewhere that prevented him from going on the road. First up was Boz (Martin) Boorer, a 27-year-old guitarist who had worked with Sinead O'Connor, the offbeat Irish singer Morrissey had always admired. Morrissey was entering his rockabilly phase; in 1978 Boorer had joined The Polecats, average age fifteen, hailed as a 'genuine rockabilly band'. Morrissey had admired their 'Rockabilly Rebel'/'Chicken Shack' single, released on the Nervous label. The Polecats had successfully played New York and toured Europe, disbanding around the end of 1990 – coinciding with Boorer's meeting with Morrissey in a Holland Park restaurant. Another short-lived rockabilly outfit that Morrissey liked was The Memphis Sinners, comprising Alain Whyte and Spencer Cobrin – respectively lead guitar/backing vocals and drummer – and a multi-tattooed bassist named Gary Day. All were in their mid-to-late twenties. Their first 'assignment' with Morrissey had been backing him in the 'Sing Your Life' video, an audition of sorts filmed at the Camden Workers Social Club (with cameos from Mark Nevin and Chrissie Hynde), which they had passed with flying colours.

Neither Whyte nor Cobrin had been big Smiths fans, which Whyte figured would work in his favour. 'That's why we've always got on so well,' he told me in 1995, 'Moz had rid himself of all that excess baggage before we came along. He likes the way we've always taken him at face value. He's a good bloke to work for.' Spencer Cobrin was more direct: 'I was raised on Jimi Hendrix and The Who. Whenever The Smiths came on the radio, I'd switch the bloody thing off!' By far the smallest of the ensemble, but solidly built, Cobrin made up for any lack of stature with his ferocious playing, rivalling Mike Joyce at his best and even purloining one of his statements – 'Balls-out is my only speed!'

In amassing his quartet of rebels, Morrissey was saying goodbye to The Smiths for ever. Indeed, rather than being left behind in a sparkling blaze of regret, his best years were in many ways still to come.

5

Hail, Hail, the Gang's All Here!

He is a living link between Victorian literary ideals and modern-day bedsit drama . . . the uncrowned, undisputed champion of some of the more complex aspects of the human condition, and as such quite possibly the most influential entertainer of his generation.

David Bret

The gathering of The Morrissey Gang coincided with his 'black phase' with the British music press, when seemingly everyone was out for the jugular, attacking his every move and utterance. Even the simple question on one edition of the BBC's *University Challenge*, 'Who was the singer with The Smiths?' brought scornful remarks. Mark Nevin told me,

I remember asking myself, why did these people have to be ugly? It just shows how wicked some people can be when you give them a pen and an opportunity to write something in a newspaper. That's why I feel Morrissey enjoys touring so much. Because of the way the press has turned against him, he likes to be where he's more appreciated, like in America where they're more positive about him. The British press live in this journalists' Never-Never World where people do all these weird things that only make sense in a newspaper.

Even Tony Parsons, the respected scribe who subsequently defended the singer against his fiercest critics, was unable to resist taking a dig in the *Independent*, though he did confess to liking some of the songs:

> Morrissey documents the hot passions that stir the hearts of old English boys; he is the embodiment of pimply angst that seethes behind polite lace curtains. He is a music-hall Hamlet, a stand-up depressive, the revenge of the nerds . . . but, three solo albums down the line, the patron saint of miserable little buggers is still waiting for solo greatness to come along . . . Let's hope he hasn't lost Johnny Marr's number.

This latter comment was but one of many waspish remarks that Morrissey was starting to find irksome, but the *Kill Uncle* tour must have restored his faith in humanity. When, in November 1989, Nick Kent had asked him about touring, and particularly about touring America, he had replied – very assuredly, as if gazing into a crystal ball – 'The way I feel about America now is, if I had a strong body of people and went to America, I would be an absolutely suffocatingly enormous figure. But until I find that body of people, I'm not going to do it.' Now, he seemingly had found the right people, certainly the right musicians, but he was still not interested in visiting America – or England, for that matter. It was *NME* who announced that he would be playing Dublin, Paris, Deinze in Belgium, Utrecht in Holland, Cologne, Berlin and Hamburg – and that hopefully he would be playing a few Scottish dates, and maybe some English ones at the end of the year. The fans, particularly those who had flocked to the pilgrimage at Wolverhampton, were far from pleased.

Next, there was the question of who would be supporting him; more importantly, bearing in mind that 90 per cent of Morrissey concert-goers are interested only in him, there was the stage backdrop. For the former, several Morrissey-friendly acts are thought to have been proposed, some of whom had supported The Smiths: James, Easterhouse, The Woodentops, Lloyd Cole. Morrissey told *Les Inrockuptibles*' Jean-Daniel Beauvallet, 'I wanted to give them a helping hand, but not one of them offered me any gratitude – and Lloyd Cole was a very good friend until he started saying nasty things about me behind my back.' He therefore chose Phranc, an American folk singer who billed herself 'The first all-out Jewish lesbian poet'. As for the backdrop, Morrissey announced that the *Kill Uncle* tour mascot would be Edith Sitwell, the Scarborough-born poet-eccentric extraordinaire who had once publicly declared that her immense wisdom had been born of a long, unrequited love affair with the Russian painter, Pavel Tchelitchew – unrequited on account of his homosexuality.

The Sitwells – Edith and her younger brother, Osbert and Sacheverell – were almost the Warhols of their day, publishing between them a mountain of essays and poems covering every aspect of the arts. Like Morrissey, they championed many 'human interest' causes; like him they were revered without question, or loathed like pariahs. James Agate, the most influential American critic of his day, called them 'artists pretending to be asses'. Edith Sitwell's shock-tactic poem 'Façade', set to music by William Walton, had outraged 1920s London society; in the poem 'Gold Coast Customs', she had expressed her 'horror of all civilisation'. Her poems had become even more daring after World War II, and had been set to jazz and dance rhythms. Like Morrissey, Sitwell also had a knack of putting her foot in it, pontificating at one of her world famous Bayswater tea-parties, 'I have been brought up on Rhythm as other children are brought up on Glaxo!' – and at another, when a coach load of noisy children were arriving, 'It almost makes one wish for another King Herod!'

Also like Morrissey, Edith Sitwell nurtured a fondness for hats: turbans, pompadours, hideous creations with plumes and stuffed birds, but in her case these had rarely suited her bony, heavy-lidded features. She also favoured dressing in black, telling journalists in her resonant contralto tones, 'I'm in mourning for the world!' In the en profile by Cecil Beaton – which, as well as the on-stage backdrop, appeared on *Kill Uncle* posters, passes and laminates – Sitwell wears white, looks birdlike in her high toque, and clasps her lizardous, multi-ringed hands to her breast. Printed on to a massive sheet of canvas and illuminated by a spotlight, the image looks awesome.

Even so, due to a technicians' hitch, Edith Sitwell did not make her debut at Dublin's National Stadium on 27 April 1991 – Morrissey's first full-length concert as a solo performer. The 2,000-plus tickets had sold within an hour of the shutters going up. As at Wolverhampton, hundreds of fans had camped out overnight (albeit in better weather conditions than for Wolverhampton), to be assured of access to the standing area in front of the stage. Word soon got around that upon Morrissey's instruction there would be no protection barrier: he needed those hugs just as much as the flowers the fans had brought. Phranc managed to get through her whole 40-minute support slot without being heckled. Then the house-lights dipped as the speakers shook to the aria 'Death', by Klaus Nomi . . .

The fact that the venue was actually a boxing stadium (in retrospect, perhaps an indication that Morrissey had shrugged off his 'angst' years and was heading towards a tougher image) informed the turn of phrase in the review of the evening by *NME*'s Stuart Maconie: 'Rabbit-punched by his former friends, declared out for the count by a score of Harry Carpenters, the old champ is coaxed out of retirement for another shot at the crown.' Maconie also observed that the audience was much younger than the crowd of former Smiths fans he had anticipated: 'The only way they could have bought *Meat Is Murder* is by being wheeled into the store in a pram.'

Morrissey's entrance was stupendous, like that of a national hero returning from the front, save that this hero had eschewed his trenchcoat for tight-fitting Levi's and a baggy gold lurex chemise. He had made a statement that had appeared in syndicated columns earlier that week: 'If I were knocked down by a passing train tomorrow, I would be considered the most important artist ever in the history of English pop music. I'm a one-off. Every word I speak is cherished. It's a terrible curse, and sometimes I wish I could just blend in and go to the pub.' The boast rang true when for two whole minutes he stood, cruciform, in the spotlight as the flashlights popped and the screams and yells of the fans seriously threatened the foundations. The Garda, having watched footage of Wolverhampton and fearful of a riot, had placed supplementary chairs in the pit – these were now passed, hand-to-hand, to the back of the auditorium. Only then were the fans permitted to surge forwards and pelt Morrissey with thousands of flowers.

His opening number, 'Interesting Drug', was virtually inaudible on account of the fans' excitement. One of these grabbed the microphone from him to yell, 'I love you, Steven!'; Morrissey grabbed it back and growled, 'Thank you, but I don't know who Steven is!' By the time he had worked through a tremulous 'Mute Witness', the stage invasions, with fans skidding on the carpet of mushy flowers, were getting risky. 'This is all very touching,' he announced, 'but if you stay off the stage, we'll be able to play better!' This of course was like inviting a child into a sweetshop and expecting him to keep his hands in his pockets. During the 'birthing' section of 'November Spawned A Monster', Morrissey doubled up as if in agony – causing the Garda to think he had been genuinely injured – until he just as suddenly sprang to his feet. He certainly was not expecting the rugger tackle that brought him down halfway through 'Our Frank' – he hit the deck with a heavy thud, but decided against breaking off the song – and, like an astute thespian, at exactly the right moment spat out the appropriate line, 'Give it a rest, won't you?' The audience went wild!

Two songs were premiered in Dublin: 'Pregnant For The Last Time', and the delectable 'I've Changed My Plea To Guilty' (this author's second-favourite Morrissey song), one of the most emotive numbers he ever performed and which later would be criminally relegated to a B-side. The fact that this song was being delivered in a country devoured for decades by political strife – and was this *really* about the tragically heroic Bobby Sands, as some suggested? – only made the song doubly moving. Bravo, Morrissey!

By this time, not wishing to ruin his beautiful top, Morrissey had changed into an already-shredded shirt, which would not survive the rest of the evening. The New York Dolls' 'Trash', a quickly rehearsed late addition to the programme, was introduced as a tribute to Johnny Thunders who had died earlier that week. For many, though, one of the evening's highlights was Morrissey's and Alain Whyte's mind-blowing adaptation of Paul Weller's *revenchard* anthem, 'That's Entertainment', which one eye-witness described as 'orgasmic'. The piece was a modern, acerbic response to the Irving Berlin standard of the same title, belted out in the 1950s by Judy Garland and Ethel Merman – save that in the Weller version of events the 'entertainment' culminates with 'lights going out and a kick in the balls'.

The reviews were ecstatic. Friend Michael Bracewell paraphrased Oscar Wilde, writing in the *Guardian* that, 'He has nothing to declare but his genius.' *Melody Maker*'s Everett True, having seemingly witnessed a different performance to everyone else, customarily attacked Morrissey in a lengthy feature, but came right in the end by cryptically pronouncing him, 'The most charismatic performer this side of an Oliver Stone movie.' A perspiring, still bare-chested Morrissey afforded Cathy Dillon of *Hot Press* a few minutes of his time in the wings. 'He's an interviewer's dream – Woody Allen's mind in Montgomery Clift's body,' she enthused. To prove this latter point, as if proof were needed, the photo-graph accompanying Dillon's lament for Smithdom was airbrushed from the waist down, giving every impression that Morrissey had posed naked, which he had not.

Two evenings after Dublin, Morrissey played L'Elysée Montmartre in Paris – like the earlier Eldorado a prejudiced establishment frequently out of bounds to pop stars, though in the eyes of the French he had ascended the *chansonnier* ladder since then; he would never reach the very top, but he was held in much higher esteem than any of his contemporaries. The concert was taped by Bernard Lemoin, and relayed later in the week by France Inter on José Artur's *Pop-Club*. Subsequently it appeared on a bootleg CD, *Posing In Paris*. Although Morrissey never spoke a word of French – not even a *merci* between songs – the people had taken him to their hearts. *France-Dimanche* reported how, when he had announced, 'I *still* cannot speak French,' a dozen Japanese girls standing next to the stage had begun sobbing hysterically. The newspaper feature compared him not with any French male singer but with Barbara – the greatest of all the modern *chanteuses* since Piaf and a close friend of this author's. The comparison was neither con-descending nor bizarre. Barbara was an intensely private woman who conducted an equally private love affair with her public for close on forty years: concert seasons, chart-topping albums (her last, in 1996, sold two million copies in a week), divided by lengthy, crippling periods of solitude at her country retreat. And, as with Morrissey, her lyrics focused on subjects frowned upon by the 'brush-it-under-the-carpet' Anglo-Saxon world: AIDS, the drugs-related death of a teenager, the death and roadside burial of her errant father in 'Nantes', her first million-selling single. Like Morrissey, Barbara placed the love of her public before that of any partner. Like him too, her best work was in front of an audience. Unlike him, on the other hand, she never risked sabotaging her career by persistent deliberation or attacking others.

Such qualities were not overlooked by Jean-Daniel Beauvallet, who for the April 1991 issue of *Les Inrockuptibles* asked Morrissey the same question he would subsequently put to Barbara. Was he afraid of the prospect of growing old alone? To a British journalist, the response might have been flippant. To a trusted, sensible foreigner it was rather sad:

Whatever happens to me, my situation couldn't be worse than when I was seventeen. Do you remember a poem 'At Seventeen' by Janis Ian? [Sings a verse of this] What more can I add? Age doesn't frighten me. I could say that having money makes life easier the older I get . . . The truth is, as I get older, I'm better able to understand myself, to tame my terrible depressions. I can't eliminate them completely, but I have learned how to confront them head-on. When you've endured such an atrocious childhood, you have to make the best of what's left. The only certain companion for me is myself . . . The only way of escaping my own particular world would be by letting someone else into it, to *drag* me out of it. Otherwise I find it best to make do with waiting, with dreaming.

After sell-out concerts in Deinze and Utrecht, The Morrissey Gang moved on to Germany, by which time their number had been augmented by Wigan-born journalist Stuart Maconie, commissioned to write a piece for *NME*. Morrissey was made aware of Maconie's alleged abhorrence of the prejudiced treatment the singer was getting from his music press colleagues and, warming to his Lancashire twang, he invited

Maconie to tag along with himself and the musicians for a night on the town. Describing him as, 'An enormous, capricious talent who's come through a hail of slings and arrows of outrageous fortune with the stoic optimism of a Captain Mainwaring', Maconie told me:

> Morrissey was in his element in Berlin, laughing all the time and cracking jokes. He's a very witty man. Somebody wanted him to pose for a photograph so he lay down in the middle of the road and got hit by a bicycle. He just stood up and said, 'I don't know whether to throw the bike into the Rhine, or whatever the river's called here, or act like a perfect gentleman, which is something I'm good at!' Later on, myself, Morrissey, the lads from the band and a few others had a couple of drinks in the hotel bar, and I suggested going walkabout. That surprised him a bit, being treated like a mate. So we set off around Berlin looking for things to do. We went into a couple of clubs, but none of them were brilliant, so we all talked. He told me that he was frighteningly happy, and he seemed to enjoy being treated like a normal person, which is what he is. Morrissey's at his most relaxed when he's with other Northerners. I'm also very proud that one of the best interviews he ever did was with me. Us Northerners have to stick together!

Maconie's interview with Morrissey, the last time he afforded *NME* the time of day, was inspiring – due to the absolute absence of misinterpretation, the fact that Maconie published his comments verbatim ('On the grounds that you'd prefer to listen to him than me!') without attempting to draw attention to himself, as too often happens with the music press. At a time when the tabloids were into their 'outing' phase, the headline itself was an attack on the system: MORRISSEY COMES OUT! (FOR A DRINK). And as was to be expected, Morrissey's observations were rich with gritty, razor-sharp humour. First and foremost, he was fed up of talking about his old group, and felt that a rational man such as Maconie might help him convince everyone else of this:

How they met: 'Johnny came up and pressed his nose against the window.'
Morrissey and Marr, England's finest songwriting partnership, pictured in 1985.

The Smiths in 1987, shortly before their split.

Speaking of Oscar Wilde in 1989, Morrissey said, 'In a way he became my companion, and as I get older the adoration increases.' Stills Press Agency/Rex

Pictured after Belfort, France, 1992 — by now Europe had awarded him the prestigious *chansonnier* tag.

Dirk Van Gils

In Minneapolis, USA, 1992.

Fawn

At JFK airport in 1992, Morrissey said of America, 'It seems that people like me here more than anywhere else in the world.'

Sandy Lee

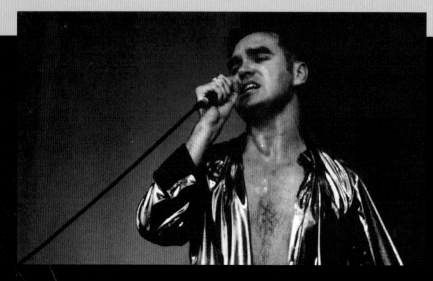

'I think there's always a danger in trying to give an audience what it wants. I think it's more interesting to give an audience something it might not want.'

Above and below: During the *Your Arsenal* tour, 1992. Mark Nicholson; Annette Wikander

'I'm in a dialogue with my audience and that's something I need.'

Above and right: The warrior and his battle scars during the Boxers tour, 1995.

Manuel Rios

Above: Morrissey tells his audience: 'We're fully grown adults. If you want to stay in your seats that's okay with me — but you don't have to!'

Manuel Rios

Right: 'I am human and I want to be loved.' Taking a moment to bathe in his fans' adulation, the Boxers tour, 1995.

Manuel Rios

Morrissey, on the eve of his mighty
comeback, promoting *You Are The
Quarry* in (*above*) Las Vegas and (*left*)
New York, April/May 2004.

Reuters/Ethan Miller; Dara Kushner/Famous

At the moment I look on The Smiths as a dead cat that must be buried in a shoebox at the bottom of the garden. And that is not to spit upon anyone who might walk in here wearing a Smiths T-shirt. I would never do that. But my past is almost denying me a future. So as for The Smiths, I have my tin hat on, and I'm bringing down the blackout.

On the subject of idolatry, he commented, 'It's drastically simple. At the risk of sounding more pompous than I am, I was always more loved than adored. Eric Clapton is admired. But who could love him – his own mother, perhaps?' And on the subject of solo success and his new band of brothers:

What amazes me is the number of people who say my solo records aren't as good as The Smiths'. It's a logic that they don't apply to any other ex-Smith. So what they're in effect saying is, 'Morrissey, we consider you to have *been* The Smiths.' I've been pinching myself so much that my legs are brown. Everything I've worked for these past twenty-four months has come right, and the core of that is the four individuals I'm working with. They are central to everything I do. They are the best musicians I've had the joy of working with. I do hope people will not constantly want to write about The Smiths and the Good Old Days, the days when we got bad reviews and we didn't play so well sometimes. These musicians are *better*. I don't want people to wait until I'm hit by a milk-float to realise what a great group this is.

And, of his despondency with the music scene, Morrissey pronounced, 'Given the competition, it's easy to shine, or at least to shine in a reasonably buffed manner. The rock press is currently having to create personalities out of a dull herd of new groups. You're kidding if you think The Manic Street Preachers mean anything to anybody. Watching *Top Of The Pops* and, I shudder to say it, MTV, is like watching a road accident.'

Maconie wanted to know if Morrissey was still contemptuous of journalists, and of British journalists in particular. He replied that he was not, adding, 'This will seem an unreadably bloated remark but, as time goes by, my individuality is affirmed by those writers who can't stand my guts. They are constantly handing me back-handed compliments . . . I must mean more to them than their own mothers.' And finally, referring to Morrissey's stalwart patriotism, would come a remark that his music press enemies would recall in years to come, made after Maconie indicated the purple varnish on his thumbnails, and asked what this stood for: 'Skinheads in nail-varnish represent the Britain I love. The skinhead was an entirely British invention. If ever I was asked for an autograph by someone wearing some of those awful Cure baseball boots, I'd take it as a sign from hell that the curtain was coming down!'

Tim Broad took advantage of the sojourn in Berlin, using it as a backdrop for the promotional video for Morrissey's next single, 'Pregnant For The Last Time'. He and the musicians were seen on stage in the spartan-looking Metropole Theatre with the obligatory flaunting of flesh to reveal messages scrawled across Morrissey's chest: first the word SINGER in capital letters, then VOICE – pretty tame compared with the invitation INITIATE ME, a photograph of which had graced the front page of *NME* and which now appeared on bootleg posters on sale outside the theatre. The bequiffed quintet were also seen out in the city streets – playing Frisbee and visiting the Brandenburg Gate. There was an impromptu appearance by Eva Busch, the veteran actress-singer who had been Marlene Dietrich's rival at the time of the Weimar Republic – and the late Jobriath, who featured courtesy of an album cover brandished by the singer. What the German fans made of the new, argot-laden song, even those fluent in English, is anybody's guess – particularly the phrase, 'corned-beef legs', a term coined during World War II to describe the blotches pregnant women suffered through sitting too close to the coal-fire for too long. It was a fine, bouncy companion-piece to the earlier 'End Of The Family Line', dealing as it does with traditional expectations of ordinary working-class folk who are too stuck in their ways to ever do anything different than ordinary. Released in July, the record only reached number 25 in the charts. On the B-side was 'Skin Storm', while the 12-inch featured 'Disappointed' and Marc Bolan's 'Cosmic Dancer', both recorded on stage in Utrecht.

The brief European tour ended a few days later in Copenhagen, leaving a week's gap before Morrissey's three Scottish dates. These did not go so well as anticipated. In Aberdeen on 14 May he complained of feeling unwell, and by the next morning had developed a severe throat infection and high temperature. He managed to get halfway through that evening's concert at Dundee's Caird Hall, but the next one at Glasgow's impressive Concert Hall had to be cancelled. Some fans reacted badly, causing pandemonium outside the venue until informed by an EMI spokesman that Morrissey would make amends by returning to Glasgow immediately after his American tour, scheduled to open at San Diego's Sports Arena on 30 May.

On the eve of his biggest venture, the British music tabloids announced that Morrissey and support act Phranc would soon be entering the studio to record a cover version of the 1975 Elton John–Kiki Dee hit, 'Don't Go Breaking My Heart'. This was supported by a statement, supposedly from Morrissey, 'Our song will help break the ice at discos and stop the boys huddling in corners and make them ask the girls to go for a twirl around the tiles.' According to EMI, no duet had ever been planned and there was no statement – Morrissey's enemies were attempting to discredit him again, by the fact that if yet another promised project never got underway, he would be seen to be letting the fans down once more. That such an undertaking had never even been discussed should have been evident from Morrissey's outburst to Select's Mark Kemp earlier in the year, 'I could never ever begin to explain the utter loathing I feel for dance music. That two people can sit in their bedroom in Detroit with a little bit of machinery and come out with this huge wall of sound is sterility at its utmost. I want to see real people on stage, playing real instruments.' And in any case, Phranc had to drop out of the tour owing to the death of her brother.

In his interview, Kemp had asked Morrissey what he would do if it all ended suddenly. He had replied almost with abject indifference,

I would absolutely mind my own business. I'd live in a crumbling cottage somewhere in Somerset, out of the way. I would not try to re-invent a pop persona. I'm too saddled with dignity to do such a thing. I'm persecuted by a sense of pride and dogged by cunning foresight.

If American ticket sales were anything to go by, this rural retreat was a long way off. British bands such as EMF and Jesus Jones who had done well in the US charts had recently been criticised for their inability to fill 3,000-seater venues. Morrissey, who had enjoyed no chart success at all in America since turning solo, staggered everyone by selling the 18,000 tickets for the Los Angeles Forum concert of 2 June in just fifteen minutes, and the 20,000 tickets for his opening concert in San Diego in less than an hour – faster than any predecessor, including Michael Jackson and Madonna, though why the press should have made an issue of this (and demoted the Forum's capacity to 14,000 in print) when he was just as big in his field as they were is baffling.

Fans at the Forum were given a surprise when, toward the end of the concert, David Bowie walked on to the stage and joined Morrissey in a somewhat tremulous duet of 'Cosmic Dancer'. Kristine McKenna of the *Los Angeles Times*, astonished to have seen so many young men clambering on to the stage to kiss Morrissey, was just as surprised when he confessed to having a feminine side – and when he drew comparisons between himself and the biggest gay icon of them all:

Take women singers. They're allowed to say intimate things and be fragile, whereas men aren't. Singers like Judy Garland had enormous strength, yet they were on the edge and you know that they simply couldn't end the song and walk away. The song went with them. They carried that burden throughout their lives. Singers attract fans who have aspects of their own personality. I think people think I'm very passionate and obsessive, and they know this isn't a profession for me – it's a vocation.

The remaining 25 venues also sold out in record time: only the Sacramento Exposition Center failed him, with a third of its tickets remaining unsold due to poor advertising. Television newsreels even broadcast footage of tearful, disappointed fans at freeway exits –

waving Edith Sitwell posters and flagging down similarly recognisable fans with $100 bills.

As in England, there were the detractors, albeit on a smaller scale. Warlock Pinchers, a Colorado-based group, had recorded their attack on the singer, 'Morrissey Rides A Cock Horse', two years previously and this had gone virtually unnoticed. Now, hoping to ride as such on the immense publicity surrounding the tour, Tupelo Records re-released it in a cover adorned by a very attractive photograph of Morrissey. Many of his fans bought it just for this, only to be horrified when they took out the record itself, the inner label of which depicted a drawing of Morrissey, chanting 'Ouija Board, Ouija Board', whilst simulating anal sex with a skeleton over James Dean's grave. And if this was not enough, the lyrics included the line, 'Crybaby son-of-bitch no-talent motherfucker.'

Morrissey was understandably furious, but took no action against the group or their record company, declaring rightly that this would only bolster their publicity. Suffice to say, they very quickly faded into obscurity. He also rejected innumerable requests for 'in-depth' interviews, though he did allow media admittance to a soundcheck at the Orange County Amphitheater on 1 June where, in Edith Sitwell T-shirt, shades and a large hat, he was filmed rehearsing 'Sing Your Life'. There should have been an appearance on a local television show, *Request Video*, hosted by Gia Desantis, but Morrissey backed out at the last minute, which was perhaps just as well. Permitted to interview his musicians but specifically instructed not to ask personal questions about Morrissey, Desantis giggled her way through the proceedings, and asked such silly questions as, 'What's the funniest thing Morrissey's done whilst he's been here?' The replies were mostly monosyllabic; Spencer Cobrin, bored by it all, fell asleep.

The American fans differed from their British counterparts. Robert Sandall of *Q* observed, 'There is no typical American Mozzaphile: androgynous teenagers, Latino gangsters, booted skinheads, suited thirtysomethings, a few stray gays and a handful of senior citizens have all been sighted.' Jo Slee, Morrissey's long-time personal assistant-factotum-temporary manager, told the press, 'He attracts this gentle adoration from everybody, but you'd need a degree in sociology to work him out.'

At some venues, audiences were restrained from 'stepping out of line' and from throwing 'missiles' – in other words, stage invasions and flowers were forbidden. Considering the fact that these were key components of a Morrissey recital, most of his performances were muted and lacking in spontaneity. KROQ Radio had scheduled a return visit, but rather than risk the ballyhoo of having him show up at the station, his three songs were recorded live at the Capital Studios. Later, they were released on a CD: the version of 'There Is A Place In Hell For Me And My Friends' is in a class of its own.

At Berkeley's Greek Theater on 8 June, one official, thinking he was acting in everyone's interest, placed large cardboard boxes outside the venue labelled GIFTS FOR MORRISSEY. These were quickly filled with all manner of paraphernalia: volumes of Oscar Wilde, greetings cards, red ('Our Frank') pullovers, flowers, nude snaps of fans – along with dozens of packets of pork scratchings, underwear to which were attached the donors' names and addresses in the hope that Morrissey would wear the items and send them back – and condoms, presumably with the same thought in mind!

In Phoenix on 11 June, Tim Broad shot the promotional video for 'My Love Life', though as yet this had only been penciled in for Morrissey's next single. In it, he is seen driving the gang through the streets of the city in a hired 1970s Rolls-Royce Corniche, the top down and the breeze blowing through his hair – welcome relief in the 104-degree temperatures. The combination of dreamy music and monochrome imagery gives the piece a relaxed David Lynch-like effect. The single was released in the UK the following October, but only just edged into the Top 30. The song was coupled with the superb 'I've Changed My Plea To Guilty' – almost certainly the record would have done better with this on the A-side – and the KROQ live version of 'There's A Place In Hell For Me And My Friends'. And in Britain, for the first time, a Morrissey sleeve was given the thumbs-down by many allegedly 'copycat celibate' fans because it contained a sunbathing shot by Linder Sterling of the singer's shapely lower half encased in tight-fitting boxer shorts bearing the logo,

'Campus Oscar Wilde'. Obviously, the thought of their hero having a little fun every once in a while was too much for some.

Morrissey, meanwhile, irked by the enforced lack of contact with his fans this side of the Atlantic, according to the promoter 'threw a wobbly' and demanded that security should be relaxed for his concert at the Dallas Starplex on 11 June: this was to be filmed by Tim Broad, and 'put into storage' for future release as a commercial video. It was released the following year on 26 July, the date Oscar Wilde had visited Dallas during his trip to the USA.

Live In Dallas brought an unexpected attack in *Select* from Stuart Maconie, the reporter Morrissey had got along with so well in Berlin, and who would interview him again a few years hence – suggestive that Morrissey cannot have seen what Maconie wrote in *Select*, otherwise he might have given him a wide berth. Referring to him as 'an emotional cripple with a cruel streak', and 'an old tart', Maconie criticised the singer for spending so much of his time on stage with his shirt off, and added of Morrissey's 'dead cat buried at the bottom of the garden', 'If The Smiths had never existed it would be possible to watch videos like this without rocking back and forth and sobbing quietly.'

Why Morrissey had his video filmed at a venue where the acoustics were below average is not known; it may well be that this was the only venue prepared to submit to his relaxed security demands and give the fans free rein to their emotions. To most of these American establishments he was an unknown quantity, and as with some of the older Parisian theatres, their proprietors did not want the places wrecked. They were yet to find out that Morrissey fans were not hooligans. Even so, the stage invasions became increasingly difficult for the staff at the Starplex to tolerate, and the final straw came after a stupid, unwarranted guitar-smashing sequence following 'That's Entertainment'. 'There were so many kids milling around the stage, looking like they were in a trance but that they might explode any minute,' an official said later. 'The fans had had their money's worth, but if anybody was to blame for the fiasco it was the idiot on the guitar.'

News of the guitar-smashing episode spread like wildfire. In Detroit, DO NOT CROSS signs were posted in front of the barrier: three fans, invited on to the stage by Morrissey to join in with the chorus of 'Sing Your Life', were dragged off by bouncers, handed over to armed police, and subsequently fined for 'civil violation'. There was a similar incident at Chicago's World Theater, capacity 30,000. Afterwards, accusing his American record company, Sire, of attempting to spice up his shows by feeding the media with false rumours of his 'prima donna tactics, mood-swings and tantrums' unless he was given all of his own way, Morrissey told the *Chicago Tribune*'s Greg Kot:

> It's all lies. It's disheartening, but I would never, to coin that delightful American expression, kiss ass. I don't *want* to become a commodity, a dishrag, and [regarding the future] I'm completely fatalistic in that I believe whatever happens is meant to happen for the eventual good, if not the immediate good. Though I can go through moments that are quite depressing, I secretly know that I'll profit from them. I just have to wait and see why things happen.

Philadelphia was something of a family affair, with Morrissey's mother, sister and his two nephews turning up for the show. The whole glamorous shebang – or at least the first leg of it – ended on 13 July with a triumphant recital at New York's Madison Square Garden, after which he was felicitated by Michael Stipe, Matt Dillon, and Lloyd Cole, the latter obviously forgiven for what he is supposed to have said. 'That was Morrissey through and through,' Kirsty MacColl told me. 'He would be all over a person one minute, then kick them out of his life the next, often never explaining why. I was one of the lucky ones . . . I'm really surprised that his love-life didn't make the tabloids, especially the way he treated some people whose only crime had been to care about him unconditionally one way or the other.'

One week later, Morrissey played his first London date in five years, at the Wembley Arena – an event that was preceded by chaos when trains to the venue were terminated several miles from their destination. Unaware of this, Morrissey inadvertently made matters worse when he brought the starting time of the show forward by half an hour. Phranc had returned to the fold for the British leg of the tour, but on account of the mad dash the fans missed not just her, but some of Morrissey's performance too. The Sitwell backdrop had been replaced by a less effective one of Harvey Keitel – the 'Bigmouth Strikes Again' pose from the 1968 film *Who's That Knocking At My Door*, which Morrissey had been after for years. There was further drama when the microphone failed during his opening song, 'Interesting Drug'. Even so, everything else he did was exemplary, as determined by the quality of the bootleg CD that appeared soon afterwards.

The reviews in the British music press were mostly vacuous, vulgar and lacking wholly in professional integrity. *NME* managed a little decorum for once by publishing a sensational picture spread by Kevin Cummins. One, of the singer draped upside down over a monitor – captioned 'The Arched Back-Deacon of Wembley' – remains definitive. Their reporter David Quantick observed, 'This is so impressive that Mozzer's other stage actions – tearing his clothes up, baring a breast to the audience, and good old waving his arms about – seem mundane and workaday.' Another photograph, with Morrissey looking slightly menacing, later graced the cover of this author's *Morrissey: Landscapes Of The Mind*. The reviews in the broadsheets were generally better penned and more respectful. David Sinclair of *The Times* called it 'one of the most gripping spectacles likely to be seen this year'. *Select* drew attention to Morrissey's delivery of 'Mute Witness' – on his back, feet pointing to the rafters and executing 'a mating ritual originally meant for some species of parrot.' Various publications reported the moment when a bear-hug from a burly fan went wrong – Morrissey grabbed him, effortlessly raised him inches from the floor, and swung him around in such fashion that those nearest the stage found themselves ducking in case he let go! 'So many people underestimate him,' Linder Sterling told me. 'They don't even begin to realise how phenomenally strong he is.'

After Wembley it was the Brixton Academy, the scene of The Smiths' very last British concert in December 1986. Many fans expected him to mark the occasion with at least one Smiths song, but he did not. From London he moved on to Brighton, Liverpool, Doncaster, Blackpool and Glasgow's Concert Hall – where admirers were still miffed about the May cancellation. Here, the bouncers were worse than they had been in

America. Three youngsters were hospitalised after falling foul of their over-zealous security.

The Japanese have always been wildly receptive of drama queens, *chanteuses-réalistes*, and generally over-the-top performers: Barbara, Freddie Mercury, the great French *tragedienne* Damia who specialised in songs about death, Jacqueline Danno (this author's godmother) – Japanese fans could never get enough of them. Morrissey was already well known here. Smiths and Morrissey memorabilia could be found in shop windows in the Ginza, Tokyo's liveliest thoroughfare, almost a Japanese Soho or Pigalle: geisha boys in the classy *kage-me-jaya* ('tea-houses amongst the shadows') sported Morrissey quiffs. The country's most famous female impersonator, Miwa (Akihiro Maruyama) – 55 but still very glamorous and known as 'The Japanese Piaf' – was not averse to adding the odd Morrissey song to his impressive repertoire.

The announcement of Morrissey's impending visit was of sufficient importance to warrant a feature on the front page of the anti-show-business *Nihon Keizai Shinbun*, Japan's equivalent of the *Financial Times*, on 23 August 1991. The tabloids followed this up with resumés of his career, though there were no bare-chested photographs in a country that frowned upon such things. His fan base was strongest among the gay community, where he had joined the ranks of *gaijin*, as welcome foreigners are called – because Western men are frequently bigger, better endowed and more hirsute than their Oriental counterparts – and comparisons were made with Freddie Mercury, a massive star in Japan, by the ones who heeded the rumours (very wrong!) that Morrissey enjoyed a similar lifestyle. Obviously, they would be in for a big surprise: unlike Mercury, Morrissey would not be painting the town red each night after the show; neither would he be taking to the stage at the (albeit highly respectable) Miwa Club, a gay Lido-style nightspot much favoured by tourists, which had nevertheless added his portrait to its famous Stars Gallery.

The first concert took place on 27 August at the recently built Fukuoka Sun Palace, a smallish venue where the security, like every-where else on the tour, was atrocious. Because the Japanese authorities had never heard of Morrissey, and because of the comparisons with

Freddie Mercury, they expected a Queen-sized throng to turn up for the 1,500 tickets on sale. Subsequently the building was surrounded by police with batons, and the starting time of the concert (again, as everywhere else) – at 6.30 p.m. already early by European standards – was brought forward by two hours! This was only the beginning. Fans were searched on their way into the auditorium: all flowers were confiscated, checked for hidden devices and drugs, labelled with the sender's name, and taken backstage to be given to Morrissey after the show – defeating the objective, of course. Additionally, the tannoys blasted out police warnings: anyone trying to get on to the stage would be arrested. Morrissey accused the authorities of meanness, encouraged fans to make a move on him, and was delighted when one over-enthusiastic handshake led to him being relieved of a shirtsleeve. The spoils were squabbled over by a group of completely hysterical girls, one of whom appeared to go into a fit. The repercussions would be severe, however.

Preferring not to spend the night in Fukuoka, seeing as the show had finished two hours earlier than expected, Morrissey and his entourage boarded the bullet train to Osaka – followed by two dozen admirers 'chaperoned' by a charming young lady named Kanako Ishikawa who, through her sheer politeness, very soon earned Morrissey's respect and later founded the *Lucky Lisp* fanzine. During the journey he actually made the effort to visit their carriage, where he chatted, posed for photographs and signed autographs. These youngsters were certainly more fortunate than their peers, for Morrissey had flatly refused to give any press interviews, and neither would there be any radio/television appearances. Against his wishes, EMI-Toshiba had released a Japan-only six-track CD that the authorities had banned from the airwaves because, they declared, one of the songs (Paul Weller's 'That's Entertainment') had been responsible for 'inciting eruptions' between bouncers and fans.

Such problems, aggravated by an acute lack of communication, brought out the riot police in Osaka long before fans began arriving at the 8,000-seater County Hall. These ordered barriers to be erected not just in front of the stage, but in the aisles. Because of the impeccable acoustics, plans had been made to record the performance in its entirety for commercial release, but these were shelved because of Morrissey's refusal to meet the Toshiba executives. The result was an otherwise excellent bootleg CD, *Nothing To Declare But My Jeans*.

The security staff continued their hounding of the fans at Nagoya's Century Hall on 1 September – for the innocuous throwing of cigarettes on to the stage during 'Our Frank'. Matters came to a head the next day at the 10,000-seater Budokan, Tokyo's most prestigious concert hall. Here, each block of seats had been fenced in, as Kanako Ishikawa explained:

> Morrissey spent part of the morning walking around the animal market. That evening, we were the ones in cages. Fans who committed the crime of standing up in their seats were grabbed by bouncers and dragged, by their clothes or hair, and thrown into the street. The flowers which we had taken for him were on the stage, still in their wrappings like in a florist's shop. He threw these back through the bars after his first encore, then took off his shirt and threw this. One fan did manage to get past the security, and when he hugged Morrissey, Morrissey was terrified of letting him go. It was such a cold, horrible atmosphere.

During his walkabout, trailed by some of the most timid fans he had ever seen, Morrissey felt wholly at ease, not in the least threatened. Kevin Cummins had tagged along to photograph him for *NME*, though there would be no interview: headed ANNOYING NAGOYA, there would be just a clutch of exceptional pictures, captioned by Morrissey himself under the pseudonym Alf Button. A group of very ecstatic concert-goers were labelled, 'a good lay, a-ha!'; one of him about to board the bullet-train was inscribed, 'It's Hiroshima That We're Nearing'. Above a stage-shot in front of the backdrop he had written, 'On A Clear Day You Can See Edith Sitwell.' More controversially, a snap of him holding up a T-shirt depicting a snarling skinhead was captioned, 'Bury My Heart At Broadwater Farm' – a reference to the site of the murder of PC Keith Blakelock. Other gems included an adaptation of a line from Noël

Coward's *Private Lives* – 'Excuse me, but have you seen a biscuit tin by Moonlight?' – penned by Tallulah Bankhead in her famous send-up when she had toured with the play for several years back in the forties amidst scenes of gay hysteria. And finally there was a photograph of Morrissey posed next to the slogan, PENIS [sic] MIGHTIER THAN THE SWORD, and captioned, 'Bring Me Home And Stab Me.' More reverently, he visited the Hie Ginja Shinto shrine at Akasaka. Many shoppers and tourists paused to watch this posturing and to take photographs themselves, aware that someone important was in town, but far too polite to ask who he was. Aware of this, he began handing out scraps of paper upon which he had scrawled not his autograph, but MISTAKEN FOR JOBRIATH YET AGAIN! The Jobriath quip referred to the Japanese CD, the cover of which featured a photograph of Alain Whyte and Gary Day poring over Jobriath's first album, and it later emerged that attempts to track down the singer for a support slot in a future tour had failed. Astonishingly, no one appears to have found out that he had been dead for seven years. Meanwhile, that evening and the next, 'Will Never Marry' was dropped from Morrissey's set and replaced with 'Cosmic Dancer'.

Morrissey's final concert in Japan, on 3 September, was at the huge 15,000-seater Yokohama Arena. Here, he growled at the bullying bouncers and actually smashed his microphone against one of the barriers in protest. Early the next morning, he took the train to Narita airport, no doubt relieved that it was all over. 'A few of us accompanied him,' Kanako said. 'He looked sad to be leaving, and I know that part of his sadness was over the way we had been treated. I half expected him to announce that he would never come here again. That wouldn't have surprised me at all. But he just waved, and left.'

It would take him a long time to set foot in Japan again.

In 1992, Shinko, a Japanese publishing house, encouraged by folksinger-journalist Goroh Nakagawa, attempted to right the wrongs of the recent past – and of course made a great deal of money in the process – by issuing what was promoted as a 'tribute anthology': a 335-page tome containing translations of all 112 Smiths songs, and around 90 per cent of Morrissey's output – 'Piccadilly Palare' and the other vernacular numbers were given up as a bad job. Some of the translations were by Yuji Sakamoto, who would have acted as interpreter should Morrissey have given any interviews to the Japanese press. Given some of the interpretations in this book, one may only express relief that their paths never crossed: the relative innocence of 'This Charming Man' is transformed into an ode to male prostitution, with the observation, 'The charming man is seized and captured . . . and a man says, "To stay beautiful, you need money!" ' Dreadful or not, the fans still rushed out to buy the book in their thousands.

Though he looked fit and well, the long hours travelling and the stressful concerts in Japan had taken their toll, and when Morrissey arrived in New Zealand for the start of what should have been a ten-date Australasian tour, the press reported that he was suffering from 'excessive fatigue'. The concert at Auckland's Campbell Centre on 7 September went well. There were no problems with security, and he seemed relaxed in his backstage interview with the *New Zealand Herald*'s Jill Graham, one of the country's most respected journalists. Morrissey used Graham as a sounding-board for an attack on the British music press, not that this would have much effect thousands of miles away from the root of the problem. 'The only good pop-writer now is someone creased with cynicism, who despises everything,' he said. 'I've been scarred too often. Nowadays I only speak to people who like and understand me. I feel I don't have to curtsy to anyone.' Graham also wanted to know why he did not converse with the audience between songs, though she should have known that with any *chansonnier*, dialogue only robs the performance of emotion and continuity.

In Wellington, Morrissey was in fine form, but three days later when he walked on to the stage in Brisbane, he looked gaunt and found himself making a Herculean effort to get through his set. A doctor was summoned to his dressing room; the singer had a temperature of 102 degrees and was diagnosed with viral flu aggravated by acute sinusitis – the worst malady that can befall a singer, particularly in hot countries. There was no question of the tour continuing, and he flew home at once – leaving disappointed Australian fans with only a brief spot on a chat show in which he performed 'King Leer' to savour.

On 29 September, back to full health, Morrissey embarked on a brief British tour: seven dates, beginning with the Dublin Point, and with Phranc supporting once more. By now, the music press had sunk to an all-time low in their treatment of him. The hacks were no longer content with attacking his performances, which were better than they had ever been – they started a lynching campaign against the man himself. One criticism *was* justified, the fact that at the Brixton Academy there was yet another senseless, premeditated smashing of guitars. 'To see someone who at one time purported to be a "sensitive person" actively involved in it is absolutely incredible and appalling,' one fan complained to *NME*'s letters column. In fact, it was all a cleverly arranged publicity stunt thought up by EMI – to get Morrissey into the newspapers and hopefully push his new single, 'Pregnant For The Last Time', further up the charts than its predecessors. There was, however, no excuse for journalists to pass extremely vitriolic remarks about his persona. Barbara Ellen's comments in *Melody Maker*, following Morrissey's Hanley concert, were more of a personal attack than a musical review and it is no small wonder he did not sue her, as Cliff Richard once had.

Morrissey's 4 October performance at London's Hammersmith Odeon was filmed by Fuji of Japan, for transmission on their WOWOW satellite channel (more dreadful subtitles, Kanako said!), but not released commercially as originally planned – a shame, for the quality is better than that of *Live In Dallas*. It did end up on the bootleg market, though, and is well worth searching for. What fans do not see here is the unpleasant incident halfway through when, during 'Driving Your Girlfriend Home', Morrissey invited a young man on to the stage – only to have him set upon by four burly bouncers who drag him off the stage and into the aisle. Morrissey ordered the band to stop playing, begged the audience to excuse him while he sorted out 'this sham of security' – and disappeared for fifteen minutes. The offending bouncer was himself removed from the theatre after a very heated argument in the wings, and the recital allowed to continue.

The second and final leg of Morrissey's seventeen-date North American tour opened in Vancouver on 28 October. With Phranc now having left the 'company' for good, he was supported by The Planet Rockers, a not-so-good rockabilly outfit from Nashville. The backdrop was a still of a weeping Diana Dors, as the condemned murderess in *Yield To The Night* (1956, US title: *Blonde Sinner*). As before, tickets for every venue had sold out in record time, with very little advertising. At San Francisco's Shoreline Amphitheater, on Halloween, many fans turned up wearing fancy dress – there was a coach load of Teenage Mutant Ninja Turtles, another of vampires. Even guitarist Boz Boorer entered into the fun of it all, dressing up as a 'tart' in a spangled dress!

There were severe security problems at Westwood's Pauley Pavilion, on the UCLA campus. The venue, a hockey stadium, was staging its first major concert since 1981 when The Pretenders had taken it by storm, and the authorities – having been told of Morrissey's 'difference of opinion' with the bouncer in the wings at the Hammersmith Odeon – anticipated trouble when 11,500 tickets moved in just sixteen minutes. The shutters were brought down, leaving several hundred tickets unsold: instructions had been given that the pit should remain empty, and that everyone should stay seated throughout the performance. Morrissey must have been reminded of his Japanese concerts, when there had frequently been a thirty-foot void between himself and the front row, and to an artist for whom personal contact was vital, this was tantamount to damming his life-blood. He tossed his tambourine into the crowd during his fourth song, 'The Loop', hoping to coax them into moving forwards. When this failed to work he announced, 'We're fully grown adults. If you want to stay in your seats, that's okay with me – but you don't have to!'

What Morrissey did not know was that the first ten rows of seats were unsecured folding chairs. During 'Sister I'm A Poet', the 'invasion' song from Wolverhampton, pandemonium ensued when the upturned chairs acted as caltrops, entangling hundreds of pairs of legs and sending fans careering in all directions. Many of the more sensible fans helped some two hundred security staff to aid the injured, whilst the lunatic fringe took advantage of those on the floor, using them as bridges to get to the stage, while Morrissey yelled down the microphone, 'Please don't tread on anybody's toes!' Then his 'phenomenal strength' referred to by

Linder Sterling was put to the test when a hefty fan, tripping over a cable and grabbing hold of Morrissey's thigh, found himself being dragged from one end of the stage to the other – with Morrissey still singing and not once going off key!

Clearly, the situation had got out of control, and could not be allowed to continue: halfway through his ninth song, 'We Hate It When Our Friends Become Successful', two huge bouncers stormtrooped the stage and escorted him into the wings for his own safety. The musicians followed, and while the debris was being cleared from the pit, Morrissey chatted to the casualties in the makeshift first-aid room – fifty or so, none of them badly hurt. He was all for resuming the concert, but this was considered too risky, and when the ones out front heard the announcement over the tannoy that the building would have to be evacuated, there was a frantic smashing of seats and setting off of fire alarms. A merchandising stall was ransacked and its till looted. To top it all, the whole sorry saga – including the arrival of the riot police, who were seen beating fans, willy-nilly, with batons – was filmed by a television news crew who happened to be in the neighbourhood. Damage was estimated at around $2,000. Morrissey did offer to pick up the tab, and may even have done so. 'He looked so very, very sad,' observed a Reuters columnist, 'but he behaved like the perfect English gentleman right until the very end. It was our own people, notably the cops, whose behaviour was objectionable.'

A warning was issued prior to Morrissey's show at San Diego's Starlight Bowl that anyone leaving their seats, for any reason, would be ejected from the stadium. A hundred people were allowed into the pit – winners of a local radio competition – which only slightly took the chill off the atmosphere. In Santa Monica on 4 November, a television crew was actually on standby to film a hoped-for riot. The best they got, according to Jo Slee, was 'footage of a bunch of sweaty teenagers fainting'. From a personal stance the evening was perhaps the most important in Morrissey's current calendar: amongst those ushered into the dressing room after the show were The New York Dolls' guitarist Sylvain Sylvain, and their bassist, Arthur Kane. He must have been very flattered to be told that they considered his version of 'Trash' better than their own.

When Morrissey arrived in Minneapolis on 7 November the city was under three feet of snow and recovering from days of sub-zero blizzards. It was equally cold in Chicago the next day, and adding to the dilemma was the last-minute change of venue. Many tickets for the UIC Pavilion had been snapped up by scalpers, and resold for several times their value. These were deemed acceptable by the Aragon Ballroom like any others, but only after they had been exchanged for general admission tickets. As many fans liked to hang on to their ticket stubs (and often frame them, along with the receipts, so that they could boast how much they had paid to get in!) this caused a great deal of dissension amongst a small group of fans. These publicly accused Morrissey of ripping them off, when it had been their fault in the first place for paying over the odds. Before long, this small but vitriolic band of dissidents would be thirsting for revenge.

On 11 November, shortly before his concert at the Nassau Coliseum, Long Island, Morrissey was interviewed by New York's WDRE Radio. He sounded weary, and as had happened in Australia was reported to be under the weather: the dramatic changes in temperature between indoor and outdoor arenas, the merciless American winter, the non-stop stream of personal appearances, the long hours on the road – all these had taken their toll. Even so, he admitted that he loved touring, and that surprisingly he was not homesick. Referring to the mindless violence of the security staff at the Pauley Stadium, he defended the fans – and himself:

> It only becomes disturbing when security *assumes* that it's violence and not passion. It's *always* passion, never *ever* violence, and the people who get to the stage and on to the stage are very gentle people, but unfortunately they're dragged off by their hair and in some cases get beaten up. It's a shame. I don't imagine that some-body would go through all the trouble of scrambling towards the stage and getting past security, climbing up. They wouldn't go through that trouble for anybody, so they must mean it.

After the show, Morrissey was driven away from the venue in a state of near exhaustion: later that night he collapsed in his hotel room. As in Australia, a doctor was summoned who advised him not to continue with the tour. Therefore the remaining eleven dates on the circuit were cancelled. Most of the fans were sympathetic, despite being distressed over not being able to see him, and many of these would have been seeing him for the first time. As for the so-called 'Chicago-turncoats', who had seen Morrissey dozens of times and often prevented the former from getting tickets by way of their sheer greed, these lodged an 'official' complaint with an influential fanzine: Morrissey was now accused of having such an ego in allowing this to interfere with his professional integrity – unable to fill large venues, they claimed, and unwilling to be relegated to smaller ones – that he had taken the coward's way out and abandoned his tour. Such fans, of course, he did not need. Even those who professed to being his most fervent admirers – the ones producing the *Sing Your Life* fanzine, its pages filled mostly with vacuous, long-winded 'The Time I Met Morrissey' stories – went out of their way to discredit him, though these had long since been demoted by him to the ranks of the nuisance fans.

Such accusations, entirely false and aimed at a performer for whom there had hardly ever been such a thing as emotional or physical compromise – who had put on 68 highly charged concerts in six months, putting up with all manner of discomfort and despite an almost paranoid fear of flying – were nothing short of spiteful. Again, he did not need to be associated with such selfish, grasping individuals – for this was the man who, not so long before, had told an American reporter, with the utmost sincerity, 'It seems that people like me here more than anywhere else in the world.'

'I always maintain that I'm very rarely interviewed, but persistently cross-examined,' Morrissey told *Rage*'s Dermott Hayes towards the close of this most extraordinary year. 'Most pop personalities are literally so plain and dull, that anyone who appears to have a vaguely working brain comes across as conniving. Therefore I'm drilled.'

He was becoming increasingly reticent about speaking to the British music press, though by and large the troublesome element was with the weeklies – the magazines were generally less vituperative. Even reporters alternating between one discipline and another changed tactics to suit the editor's agenda, but so far as the weeklies were concerned, Morrissey's face simply did not fit – save on their front covers to boost flagging circulation figures. *Rage* seemed to fit into neither category and in his piece, 'Mistletoe And Whine', Hayes made a point of professing his surprise that the 'nutty recluse' was still around, and even went as far as asking him why he was – bringing the caustic response, 'I can't think of being a postman.' Robert Sandall, writing for *Q*, audaciously adorned the subtitle of his account of Morrissey's American tour with the pun, 'He's The Biggest Cult That Ever Was'. Little wonder then, that the singer began turning his back on these people.

A formidable component of the American adventure had been 'We Hate It When Our Friends Become Successful', one of Morrissey's first collaborations with Alain Whyte, though one doubts many of his admirers Stateside grasping its theme of the North/South divide. In England, it was performed for the first time at the 30th Amnesty International show, televised on 28 December 1991, and bringing to a close Morrissey's most successful year so far as a solo artiste.

Oscar Wilde had famously opined, 'Your friends will sympathise with everything but your success.' Few British songs have so significantly linked their authors with a topic: the fact that a Northern upbringing does not equate to coalmines, ferrets, pigeon fanciers and hotpot. 'I've never worn a flat cap, and I don't smoke Senior Service,' Morrissey made a point of saying. And, like every other Morrissey song, this one tells a story: the fact that he was starting to find life in a Manchester suburb, albeit an opulent one, increasingly intolerable now that he was famous, with pestering fans hammering on his door day and night, with the locals envious of his success and persistently looking down their noses at him. He told Adrian Deevoy of *Q*, 'There's the most vicious sense of competition in Manchester – so many jealous, vile creatures. That's what "We Hate It When Our Friends Become Successful" is all about. In Manchester you're accepted so long as you're scrambling and on your knees. If you have any success, they hate your guts.'

The single was released in April 1992, coupled with three of the songs from the Hammersmith Odeon, and reached a modest number 17 in the charts. There was a promotional video, filmed in a disused mid-19th-century schoolhouse and its incumbent wasteland, off Wapping High Street. The clean, smart clothes of the Morrissey gang (he wears blue satin, they Lonsdale T-shirts in different colours) contrast sharply and shockingly with the ramshackle buildings. Looking at them, one finds it hard to discern if they are out in search of trouble, or kicks. Gary Day toys with his flick-knife (the scene was cut when the video was televised) while Spencer Cobrin sizes up Morrissey as one might approach a sex-for-sale stud – he leans against him suggestively, but all he wants is to offer Morrissey a lick of his ice-cream cone, which gives him a fit of the giggles. The video ends with them all wandering off, and a close-up of the graffiti-daubed REARDON STREET sign, featuring slogans such as 'I Never Wanted To Kill, I'm Not Naturally Evil' and 'I Will Live My Life As I Will Undoubtedly Die, Alone'.

The song, and the subsequent *Your Arsenal* album, was the brainchild of Hull-born Mick Ronson, possibly the best producer Morrissey worked with, the man who helped him reach unsurpassed heights in his career. Theirs was also an extremely cordial working relationship, attributed by both of them to their geographical connection. 'It affects the way you look at the world, the way you deal with people. It affects everything,' Ronson told Tony Parsons of his Northern upbringing.

Ronson had been a pioneer of British glam rock, playing in a local group, The Rats, before a momentous meeting with David Bowie in 1970 that had transformed The Rats into The Spiders From Mars and resulted in five million-selling albums: *The Man Who Sold The World*, *Hunky Dory*, *Ziggy Stardust*, *Aladdin Sane* and *Pin-Ups*. Ronson had also very successfully worked with Mott The Hoople and Lou Reed (arranging the controversial 'Walk On The Wild Side'). What particularly enabled Morrissey to place Ronson on a pedestal was that he had worked with ex-New York Doll, David Johansen. In the summer of 1992, Morrissey told Jean-Daniel Beauvallet of *Les Inrockuptibles*, 'Mick was responsible for Bowie's best work, of that there's no doubt. He's a very underestimated talent who combines showmanship with great humility. Working with him on my new album has been the greatest privilege of my life.' Sadly, *Your Arsenal* would also prove Ronson's swansong: he had recently been diagnosed terminally ill with cancer.

The album was released in July 1992, and reached number 4 in the charts. It was universally acclaimed as Morrissey's best since *Viva Hate*, and equalled anything he had ever done with The Smiths. The sleeve bore two thought-provoking photographs by Linder Sterling, snapped on stage at the Nassau Coliseum, of the singer suggestively brandishing his microphone at crotch height. Morrissey's 'stomach scar' (his navel), we were reminded, appeared courtesy of Davyhulme Hospital! There was no lyric sheet with this one – just an inner shot of the Krays' rival, Charlie Richardson, taken during a trip to the seaside with his toddler daughter circa 1960. The reason for the missing lyrics, Morrissey declared, was because this time he wanted the fans to listen to the album for its overall value, with equal emphasis on his musicians and the melodies as opposed to just the words – which in the past many fans were said to have studied for days before actually putting the album into the machine. Detractors from the music press would argue that Morrissey had purposely omitted the lyrics because some of them were so contentious that, had the fans read them first, they would have given the album a wide berth. Not, one would imagine, very likely.

Leading the plaudits was *The Times*' David Sinclair, who called the album 'concise, dramatic and artful' and praised the musicians' ability to 'weld the motor of Morrissey's erratic inspiration to the golden chassis'. An anonymous reviewer in *Q*, still in mourning for The Smiths, called it 'a kind of "Kenneth-Williams-Meets-Laurence-Olivier-Down-On-The-Rainy-Pier-For-Pie-And-Mash" that captured our hearts way back when.' And whereas the usually offensive remarks made by the tabloids are not worthy of repetition, *Select* published a lengthy feature headed THE FEAST OF STEVEN – within which the album was in turn reviewed and reviled by '15 top pop celebrities' who by and large did not have a clue what they were talking about, and many of whom are forgotten today. A couple of exceptions were Siobhan Fahey of Shakespears Sister – who spoke for the fans when she said, 'He's my complete idol, like a cosy blanket you pull over you when you're feeling down' – and Linder Sterling, who observed:

Your Arsenal has Morrissey riding bare-backed on rich, feisty guitars, glistening as he rises with the audacity to still believe in the enduring embrace of a simple song. In his quieter moments he dives deep into our ventricles, wistfully celebrating his search for the domain of the heart.

Your Arsenal was Morrissey's all-embracing, symbolic lament for the decline of the British culture he had been passionate about all his life. No song better represented his feelings about this than 'Glamorous Glue'. 'We won't vote Conservative because we never have,' he opines, a phrase pronounced by many obstinate Northerners when election day comes around: no matter who the Labour candidate is, they will always vote for him or her because this is a matter of identity. Then he reminds us of what we already know: 'We look to Los Angeles for the language we use . . . London is dead!' When asked by Jean-Daniel Beauvallet what, in his opinion, was dead in the England of today, he replied, 'England itself. Everything is influenced by American culture – everyone under fifty speaks American, and that's sad. We once had a strong identity and now it's gone completely.'

In the same vein as 'Glamorous Glue', but perhaps more controversial, was 'We'll Let You Know', Morrissey's take on the depiction of an unwanted member of our society: the football hooligan. It is a sad state of affairs that the archetypal Briton in the eyes of many Europeans is the thug who attends football matches solely in order to make life a misery for genuine fans. The song, a lilting ballad embellished with the creaking of turnstiles and muted stadium screams, is a direct contrast to the raucous chanting one hears at these events – Morrissey is mocking the hooligans much as he ridicules the National Front for attending a disco. And likewise it was misrepresented by the media, for the narrators are the hooligans themselves, the otherwise self-confessed 'nice boys' who offer the paltry excuse that it is the *turnstiles* that make them hostile, before finally boasting, 'We are the last truly British people you will ever know.'

'Glamorous Glue' should have been released as a single in America, for the purpose of which a video was shot in a Chicago blues club where there is only one customer – black musician Al Lewis, here to listen to a group of English lads lamenting, 'England is dead!' 'Tomorrow', the replacement release, had a video shot in and around Nice (by Zach Snyder). This is almost a monochrome re-enactment of the scenario of 'We Hate It When Our Friends Become Successful' – The Morrissey Gang, looking like they are on the prowl again, acting laddishly as they wander through alleyways of crumbling brickwork towards the Old Town, and its unsuspecting al fresco diners. The single, like the earlier 'My Love Life', was housed in a sleeve that some fans found outré: Morrissey, in tight-fitting swimtrunks, reclining next to Gary Day on a sunlounger! The song, which topped the University charts, tells the familiar tale of the prevarication experienced during the quest for lasting love – the fact that the narrator, Morrissey, begs the object of his desire to put their arms around him and reassure him that he really is loved, only to dampen the proceedings by declaring, before this happens, 'I know you don't mean it!'

The song that was to prove Morrissey's most controversial, 'The National Front Disco' is an outsider's observation of recruitment techniques once employed by the National Front – the movement had at one time blatantly distributed leaflets outside schools. In this song he steps not just into the shoes of the oppressor, but into those of his bewildered parents who lament, 'Where is our boy? We've lost our boy!' – bringing the response from the well-raised, led-astray young man, 'England for the English!'

The song was to attract criticism from the usual quarters, but what most detractors failed to see was that Morrissey was poking fun at the National Front by suggesting that its supposedly hard-bitten recruits would attend something so 'wimpish' as a disco. 'The *phenomenon* of the National Front interests me,' he told Robert Chalmers of the *Observer Magazine*. 'It interests me like it interests everyone, just as all manner of sexuality interests everyone. But that doesn't mean that you necessarily want to take part.' Morrissey himself had said more or less the same thing to *Q* magazine's Adrian Deevoy, linking 'The National Front Disco' with the earlier 'November Spawned A Monster':

Whether you choose to write about wheelchair-bound people or the subject of racism, the context of the song is often overlooked. People look at the title and shudder and say whatever is in that song shouldn't exist because the subject, to millions of people, is so awful.

In other words, Morrissey was saying that in criticising him, these people were only revealing their own prejudices.

Of the remaining songs the opening number, 'You're Gonna Need Someone On Your Side', is a perfect example of Morrissey's promise that this was going to be a 'physical' album: a mass of unfettered glam-rock guitars, crowd noises, ticking clocks, snatches of radio/television dialogue. The lyrics are so fresh and innovative that one might assume Morrissey has assigned himself to total seclusion and soul-searching to come up with them. In fact, he and Alain Whyte had worked on some of them during the maelstrom of pressure that had constituted the previous American tour. Indeed, the line, 'Give yourself a break, before you break down' ought to have been the singer's advice to himself back then, in view of the way he had almost worked himself into the ground.

'Certain People I Know' and 'You're The One For Me, Fatty' were released as singles in Britain (respectively charting at numbers 34 and 19). The former, coupled with 'Jack The Ripper', had a Linder Sterling cover photograph taken at Hoxton Market in London's East End, close to where the Krays had been born. The video was filmed in South Chicago on the shore of Lake Michigan, and is a feast of homo-eroticism, with the gang giving the impression yet again that they are on the 'pull', save that it was filmed at a very unromantic 5 a.m. when there was no one around to pull, and everyone looks half-frozen to death! Because Tim Broad was by this time too ill to travel, it was filmed by George Tiffin. Morrissey, barefoot and bare-chested under his jacket, wanders along the beach, ever sure of himself. 'And when I swing it so it catches his eye,' he sings, and one wonders whether this is gay locker-room parlance as a topless Spencer Cobrin strolls up to him, swinging a branding iron. It all seems like harmless fun, though it very nearly ended up with Morrissey losing one of his musicians for good when he tried to order them to wear contoured Speedos. Jo Slee includes the instruction in *Peepholism*, part of which reads, 'So: Are you Gazzo, Spenno and Ringo Whyte prepared to risk real mannish trunks as opposed to the usual sexless plywood shorts that you usually wear?' The offended musician later told me, 'This time he'd gone too far. Mozza wouldn't walk around at the crack of dawn getting his nuts frozen, so why should we?'

Margaret Thatcher, politicians, the royals, one or two writers, music journalists in general – these were only dastardly villains in Morrissey's eyes. Then there were the *real* villains: criminals such as Hindley and Brady, who were deservedly loathed. Additionally there were the so-called villains of yore, the ones who had moved into folklore with the passing of time: 'Troubled Joe' of the mid-19th-century Anglo-Irish troubles, referred to in 'A Rush And A Push And This Land Is Ours' – and Jack the Ripper – the subject and title of a fascinating but very much underrated Morrissey song.

In this darkly amusing piece, Morrissey acts as *agent provocateur*, meeting up with the killer, telling him how tired he looks, how his face is as mean as his life has been. He adds that he wants him – 'Crash into my arms!' – even if it is the last thing he will ever do, which of course is what could happen in a real-life situation and for some would make the sex doubly exciting – though the Ripper does not realise that this is, in fact, a trap.

The inspiration behind the song was actually Walter Satterthwait's avant-garde novel *Wilde West* (Collins Crime Club, 1992). This is a fictional recreation of Oscar Wilde's 1882 lecture tour of the American West, during which he had infamously opined at a customs house that he had nothing to declare but his genius. In Satterthwait's rewriting of history, in each city Wilde visits a Ripper-style killer is at work. The police begin to suspect various members of Oscar's weird and wonderful entourage, whereupon the great man himself sets about tracking down and unmasking the killer.

Morrissey's lyric also inadvertently links the 19th-century killer of Whitechapel prostitutes to the Yorkshire Ripper, Peter Sutcliffe – several policemen are known to have disguised themselves as whores in an attempt to trap him. In France the song was compared with *Lily Passion*, an extraordinary musical drama starring Barbara and Gérard Depardieu, which had packed out Le Zénith in Paris in 1986. In 1998, Morrissey included the song on an excellent American album, *My Early Burglary Years*, housed in a sleeve featuring his cover shot from the August 1990 issue of *Gay Times* – and which contained the most astonishing dissection of angst imaginable.

In 'You're The One For Me, Fatty', Morrissey champions obesity, the fact that big can really mean beautiful. The song was coupled with 'There Speaks A True Friend' and 'Pashernate Love' (a take on 'Mad Passionate Love', a hit in 1958 for *Carry On* star Bernard Bresslaw). In Morrissey's reading of this the plum line is, 'Pashernate love could make your sister erupt into wild blisters and boils.' The video, Tim Broad's last, featured celebrity ex-convict Joe Blair and Megan Siller, who later appeared in several episodes of BBC Television's *Casualty*. It centres around the latter's love of food – she even scoffs the flowers he has brought her when they go on a picnic! The actual inspiration for the song came from one of Morrissey's favourite comediennes, Victoria Wood, and her declaration of love for her heavyweight magician husband, Geoffrey Durham. It is a catchy, up-tempo number with strains of Buddy Holly, albeit that the setting is dreary Battersea with its 'hope and despair'. It became one of that summer's most hummable anthems – and was given an absolutely vile review in *NME*, whose anonymous scribe suggested that this 'one-trick pony helpless without its trainer' might be better off exiting pop for good. 'If he's very clever,' he or she concluded, 'he could do a Quentin Crisp and get a gimmick, like refusing to wash his cutlery or his groin for a decade.' What made such remarks unforgivable and hypocritical was that they appeared on page 16 of the publication – while on page 15 there was an expensive, full-page advertisement for the single. 'They took the money,' Morrissey's EMI spokesman said, 'and even then they rubbished him. How shameless can you get?'

Lyrically, one of the best songs on the album, and one of the most moving, is 'Seasick, Yet Still Docked', an allegory of sorts for Morrissey's mistreatment by the press: the fact that he was all too frequently attacked for doing something *before* he did it. He said at the time, 'You can sit in your room for months on end and see nobody, and cry quite bitterly into your pillow because the phone never rings – then you think of those recent weeks, and of your situation, and you burst out laughing at the absolute absurdity of life and expectation.' The song, a long one, links Morrissey with the legendary Belgian singer-songwriter Jacques Brel. In Mort Shuman's adaptation of Brel's 'Amsterdam', poorly covered by David Bowie and brilliantly so by Ute Lemper, Brel says of his sailor, 'He so wants to belch, but he's too full to try.' Morrissey politely declares, 'Tonight I've consumed much more than I can hold,' which may also be interpreted, regarding the detractors, to mean that he is reaching the end of his tether. Moreover, the overall theme of the piece with its ticking clock – time slowly but surely ebbing away – is reminiscent of Brel's 'Les Vieux', with the despondency of unrequited love transferred from the elderly couple waiting to die, to the plight of the sad young man. Morrissey told *Les Inrockuptibles*,

> All of us are working against the clock in our own way. I tend to have a cheese butty, sit back and relax. Everything eventuates. The day will arrive when you and I are not on this earth. People who have a sense of time and therefore urgency are quite fascinating! I've been accused of paying too much attention to death, but what's wrong with that? It's a pretty serious matter, especially when you're lying under the wheels of a double-decker bus!

All is not, however, doom and gloom, and the precognitive dream – that all will turn out well if this is what one wishes for – holds good with the penultimate song on the album, 'I Know It's Gonna Happen Someday', a work of considerable strength and emotion – and, like the earlier Brel song, subsequently covered by David Bowie.

On 25 May, Morrissey arrived in Los Angeles and checked in at the Sunset Marquis Hotel. With him was thirty-something Peter Hogg who, Morrissey claimed tongue-in-cheek, he had acquired courtesy of 'Rent-A-Chap' – and who was later described by Gary Day in a *Guardian* interview as 'a real detested troublemaker'. The two-week sojourn should have been a private affair, though the fans and the press soon put paid to this. The pair were photographed cycling on Venice Beach, shopping in the San Bernadino mall, and dining at Johnny Rocket's restaurant in Westwood. On 30 May they showed up at Fashions Nightclub on the Redondo Beach Pier, where a Morrissey/Smiths evening was in progress. Hogg was asked to judge a T-shirt and Morrissey look-alike contest – the prize, five minutes of 'intimate conversation' with the singer in a backroom.

After his vacation, tired of the lack of airplay in Britain and holding EMI partly responsible for not 'pushing' him, Morrissey chose to promote the album in person elsewhere. On 4 July, three weeks before its release, he appeared on the bill of Les Eurockéenes, one of the most prestigious events in the French calendar, staged annually at Belfort. His *vedette-américaine*, as supports are called on the Continent, were an uninspiring Ned's Atomic Dustbin, whose late arrival on stage almost prompted a riot from fans who were interested only in Morrissey. To calm everyone down the promoters sent out for several vanloads of flowers – chrysanthemums, which in France are traditionally sent to funerals! These were handed around, ready to be thrown at Morrissey. He took to the stage at midnight, wrapped in a huge Union Jack, and opened wholly without controversy with 'Glamorous Glue'. He played the introduction to 'November Spawned A Monster' himself, tremulously, on a violin borrowed from rock-chanteuse Catherine Lara. He also sang his own arrangement of 'My Insatiable One', a song by a then little-known group called Suede, whose Morrisseyesque frontman, Brett Anderson, gave everyone the impression that his outfit would soon be hailed as the new Smiths. Not surprisingly, perhaps, Suede's reign would be brief. The lines, 'On the escalator/You shit Paracetamol as the ridiculous world goes by' were frowned upon by many French fans for not being in keeping with Morrissey's clean-cut image. Neither was it deemed appropriate for French admirers to applaud and scream, American-style, while a song was in progress. Even during high-spirited performances by Eurockéenes regulars Barbara, Johnny Hallyday, Jean Guidoni and Veronique Sanson there had to be decorum so that audiences could listen to the singers and the messages of their songs. Morrissey was reminded of this by *Les Inrockuptibles'* Emmanuel Tellier. 'At times,' he responded, 'I would love nothing more than to sit at the edge of the stage and sing to a respectful silence with the applause coming only at the end of my songs. Then the other side of me tells me that if this happened, I would probably feel that I had failed.'

A few days after Belfort, Morrissey participated in the equally prestigious Festival de Leysin, in Switzerland, where even the foul weather and an on-stage tumble failed to rob the evening of its magic. Afterwards, he and the musicians spent a few days in Paris, where at the Hotel Bristol he was interviewed by *Q*'s Adrian Deevoy. Afterwards, as had happened in Berlin, everyone went walkabout – around the Pigalle-Blanche red-light district, where photographer Hugh Dixon snapped him against a background of neon Durex signs and sex-shop windows. The actual interview, however, was not quite the light-hearted affair Deevoy had expected, as he explained:

> The general atmosphere, and perhaps a little too much booze, had made us all giddy. There was devilment in his eyes, so I tweaked his eyebrows and asked him if they were real. 'No,' he said, 'they're held on with Velcro!' Then, just acting the fool, I asked him what he would do if I reached my hand under the table and stroked his knee. He said, 'Why don't you do it and see what happens?' I decided to change the subject, and jumped out of the frying pan by mentioning Vic Reeves and asking for his opinion about the sketch ['The Morrissey Consumer Monkey'] which had offended him. He glared at me and said, 'It was meant to be hurtful. Vic Reeves is a person who can't shut his mouth for three seconds because he feels he'll disintegrate into a bowl of dust. He's completely loathsome!'

On 26 July 1992, the day before *Your Arsenal* was released in Britain, Morrissey embarked on a brief non-singing tour of the United States, promoting the album by radio appearances, in-store signings, walkabouts and by generally just being there. He was also paving the way for a forthcoming tour that would see a repeat of the mass hysteria of his previous visit. He and Peter Hogg booked into the Sunset Marquis, where he was extremely cagey about speaking to the press. He had agreed to be interviewed by David Thomas of *You* (the *Mail On Sunday* supplement), but certain conditions were imposed: Thomas must refrain from mentioning The Smiths, Johnny Rogan, or Morrissey's sexuality. Effectively, therefore, the interview covered very little ground, though the subsequent feature was accompanied by some rather nice photographs taken in and around the hotel pool by Eddie Sanderson. Thomas later observed of his subject:

> He seems incapable of trusting either himself of anyone else enough to form a satisfactory relationship. His emotional life is a self-fulfilling prophecy that parallels his complaints about professional publicity. He wants to be written and talked about, but makes it incredibly difficult for any journalists to get close to him. He wants to be loved but behaves in a way that makes it impossible. This would not matter in the slightest were it not for the fact that, underneath all the rock star flim-flam, Morrissey is actually a very nice chap, excellent company, perfectly willing and able to talk about any subject one cares to throw at him.

Where Peter Hogg was during the interview is not known, but if Morrissey had imposed a ban on personal questions, he was soon titillating and teasing again, by repeating how he had acquired Hogg through 'Rent-A-Chap'. There were also rumours about other men in Morrissey's life but whether they were just fans who had a crush on him or whether their adoration was reciprocated is not known. As always, no one said anything.

A midnight appearance at a record store on 28 July made the television news. President Bush was in Grand Rapids at the same time, but the press attention was diverted to the bequiffed British singer's arrival at The Vinyl Solution, where he was mobbed by 2,000 screaming fans. The excitement continued with a surprise tie-in party at a rock club across the way. Twelve hundred people turned up at Houston's Record Rack the next day, and there were other gatherings in Chicago, Los Angeles, San Diego and New York.

Morrissey also appeared in a radio phone-in show with Tom Calderone of Long Island's WDRE-FM. The questions, from giddy fans, were rarely less than silly. When a woman called Nancy asked, 'As a psychiatrist, I just wanted to know why you left the lyrics out of this album?' Morrissey glibly responded, 'Well, as a *psychiatrist*, why do *you* think I did?' Put in her place, Nancy hung up. The tour ended on 5 August, when Morrissey's musicians flew out to join him on New York's *Hangin' Live With MTV*, where he sang 'You're The One For Me, Fatty' and 'Certain People I Know'. Several hundred fans had camped outside the entrance for 48 hours to acquire tickets for the ten-minute event.

On Saturday 8 August 1992 took place the first of what should have been two concerts at London's Finsbury Park. Topping the bill were the recently re-formed Madness, whose many fans included a small but potentially troublesome element, while Morrissey had been added to the bill at the last moment.

During the afternoon, the National Front – the movement which had appropriated the Union Jack as its own symbol – had coincidentally organised a 'British Troops Out of Northern Ireland' rally through the streets of neighbouring Islington. Trouble was expected once skinhead extremists, the worse for drink, began mingling with the Madness crowd. The instant Morrissey and his musicians took to the stage, the skinheads began hurling whatever missiles came to hand. Hundreds of genuine fans were there too, but their cheers were drowned by heckling and hoots of derision from the mob. Morrissey now made his big mistake – it was an error of judgement, no more – draping a large Union Jack about him during his second song, 'Glamorous Glue', and parading in front of the huge Derek Ridgers backdrop depicting a pair of seventies suedehead girls. He had done this before, to a more civilised crowd, at the Eurockéens festival at Belfort on 4 July. The drunk and disorderly element at Finsbury Park, however, were unable to see beyond their own agenda.

Then Morrissey erred again by performing 'The National Front Disco'. Hoodlums began pelting the stage with sharpened coins – proving that the violence was premeditated and that exactly the same would have happened with any support act. Finally, following a half-hearted 'You're The One For Me, Fatty', Morrissey walked off the stage.

He immediately dropped out of the next evening's concert, realising that this would upset hundreds of fans, en route to Finsbury Park from all corners of the globe and unaware of what had happened. Murray Chalmers, the press officer at EMI, issued an official statement:

> Morrissey is extremely disappointed that Sunday's planned performance could not go ahead due to the abysmal behaviour of a small group of loathsome yobbos. His management have requested the promoters to refund fans' money. A Christmas show is being scheduled for those fans who really want to enjoy without the aid of stimulants.

But Morrissey's detractors now had enough ammunition to prepare their most vitriolic attack yet.

There had already been controversy over 'Bengali In Platforms' and 'Asian Rut'. The former was a reworking of a Smiths song taped before their split but not released. Morrissey had commissioned Stephen Street to compose a new melody, and included it on his *Viva Hate* album. Queen frontman Freddie Mercury adored the piece and was convinced that it was about him. Though he had been born in Zanzibar and raised in Bombay, he liked to think that Morrissey had based it on his 'glam rock piss-take' of Gary Glitter during his pre-Queen phase when he had been known as Larry Lurex. The song was a classic case of 'shooting the messenger', for one does not have to delve too deeply into the lyrics to work out that the narrator is *anti*-racist. 'Shelve your plans,' he tells his young immigrant friend, speaking from personal experience as the descendant of immigrants himself, 'Don't blame me, don't hate me because I'm the one to tell you that life is hard when you belong here.'

What he meant, of course, was that in his opinion, with its current political climate life in Britain was not easy, socially or financially, even for those who had been brought up here – let alone being expected to conform when one had been brought up in a completely different culture. Morrissey had attempted to debate the issue with *Sounds'* Shaun Phillips during the spring of 1988. When Phillips audaciously asked if the song was meant to have a double-edge, after a deliberate pun that had seen the anti-Band Aid Morrissey contemptuously referring to the song as 'Bob Geldof In Platforms', he replied, 'No, not at all. There are many people who are so obsessed with racism that one can't mention the word Bengali. It instantly becomes a racist song, even if you're saying, "Bengali, marry me." But I still can't see any silent racism there.' Phillips recalled the much-discussed, much-misinterpreted line, arguing that if this was implying that Bengalis did not belong here, then Morrissey was not really taking a global view of the world. He was of course baiting him and trying to put words into his mouth. Morrissey finally shut him up with, 'If you went to Yugoslavia tomorrow, you'd probably feel that you didn't belong there.'

'Asian Rut', from the *Kill Uncle* album, was a tender lament deliberately misinterpreted by the music press, whom by this time Morrissey had declared 'not massively equipped upstairs'. To the spellbinding accompaniment of a raga-violin, he champions the plight of the Asian boy who has turned up at school, toting a gun and so calm that he must be on drugs, to avenge the murder of his best friend – a mission that fails when he is run down by racist cowards who only have the guts to operate when they are in gangs. The lyrics could not have been clearer, yet *NME* still accused Morrissey of 'playing games, gently stoking the fires, dodging behind words and trying to get up noses'.

Mark Nevin who composed the music for eight of the *Kill Uncle* songs, told me,

The first time I heard Morrissey speak the words aloud, I came close to tears. How can anyone call the song racist when it's so blatantly *anti-racist*? Does that mean you aren't allowed to mention Asian people without being called racist? I thought it the best song on *Kill Uncle*, just as 'Bengali In Platforms' was my favourite song on *Viva Hate*. Life really is hard when you don't belong here. And what you said about Morrissey is right. He really does climb into the other person's skin.

Now, in the wake of Finsbury Park, and in what was the start of one of the most vitriolic smear campaigns against a show business personality since the AIDS-related deaths of Rock Hudson and Freddie Mercury, a spokesman for *NME* read out a statement on Radio One:

> Following more controversial lyrics on Morrissey's album, flirting as that song does with right-wing imagery, going on stage in front of a largely skinhead audience, waving a Union Jack – there are questions that need to be asked in the house, so to speak, and we've asked them. We are the People's Friend. He's flirting with danger.

Morrissey never submitted to this pressure, simply because he felt there was no need to. To his way of thinking, there was nothing wrong with being proud of one's country. *NME* reacted by publishing a photograph of the flag-enveloped Morrissey on the cover of its 22 August issue – which just happened to be the anniversary of the Battle of Bosworth Field, where another maligned individual, the last truly English king, Richard III, had died at the hands of his oppressors. The banner headline read: MORRISSEY: FLYING THE FLAG OR FLIRTING WITH DISASTER? Within, spread over five full pages, were the lesser headlines: CAUCASIAN RUT: THIS ALARMING MAN, accompanied by more 'evidence' – another flag-waving picture, one of Morrissey proudly showing off his England lapel badge, two more of him holding up a skinhead T-shirt.

The Jam, we were reminded, had also adopted the Union Jack some years earlier, but they were excused because at the time they had explained that they had been reclaiming it from the Far Right. Obviously, it had not crossed anyone's mind that Morrissey might have been reclaiming it for the England he loved.

In charge of the Inquisition were Dele Fadele, Danny Kelly, Andrew Collins and Gavin Martin. It was a piece of one-sided journalistic propaganda: making the accusations now in anticipation of the subject coming forward to explain his side of things, by which time of course ('There's no smoke without fire . . .') the damage would already have been done. Morrissey was approached, but rather than waste time speaking to people who had so obviously set out to destroy him come what may, he issued a brief statement: 'My lawyers are poised. *NME* have been trying to end my career for four years, and year after year they fail. This year they will also fail.'

An *NME* insider informed me that as a 'safety precaution', the whole exercise had been supervised by a Morrissey-friendly journalist with a sound knowledge of the legal system – without whose help there might well have been a lawsuit.

Even so, it was bad enough, peppered with 'Morrissey quotes' pulled from any number of publications over the previous decade – printed out of context of the original interviews and appearing harsher than Morrissey had originally intended. Referring to a gay-bashing incident with James Maker that, it was claimed, may have been carried out by National Front supporters, the journalists asked, 'Has he changed from the persecuted to the persecutor? Or is he fascinated by the idea of racism, by the look of violent skinheads, to the extent of being oppressed so much, he falls in love with his oppressors?'

Next, the editorial ran through a catalogue of 'dubious' or 'nationalistically pointed' songs, deliberately not pointing out that their contentious lines had been mostly in quotation marks, delivered by the songs' narrators and not by the singer himself. His detractors might have argued that, after all, he had supplied these words in the first place, but this would have been rather like holding William Shakespeare responsible for the horrors of *Titus Andronicus*, when all he had done was dramatise them. Also used as evidence, unfairly because it was yet to be published, was a quote from a forthcoming issue of *Q*: 'I don't want to sound horrible or pessimistic but I don't really think, for instance, black people and white people will ever really get on or like each other. The French will never like the English – that tunnel will collapse.'

Morrissey was expressing an opinion, and anyone should have seen that. Yet at the very end of this diatribe, providing the reader/fan has not ripped the paper to shreds by now, one finds the First Inquisitor opining, far too late, 'For what it's worth, I don't think Morrissey is a racist. He just likes the trappings and the culture that surround the outsider element' – which, of course, we already knew.

NME went on to attack Morrissey for letting down his fans, a reference to his cancelling of an appearance at Glastonbury and the final dates of his last American tour. *NME* themselves had announced that he would be participating in the Glastonbury Festival during the weekend of 26/28 June: a huge number of tickets had been sold, and only days before the event a further 'press announcement' had declared that, following a bust-up with one of his musicians, Morrissey had decided to pull out. Needless to say the fans had been disappointed, genuinely thinking that he had deliberately let them down – until they learned that he had never agreed to the event in the first place. Though, to be fair, *NME* may have been misinformed about Morrissey definitely being booked for the festival, their feature included a 'special section' detailing how much the regular Morrissey fan had spent over the last year for not seeing him twice – 'an astonishing £189.60 for nothing but disappointment'.

The backlash was not just obscene, but bordering on the defamatory. *NME* claimed to have received hundreds of letters of support, though the ones they published came from the very worst of the lunatic fringe detractors. There was an 'open letter' feigning support from the despised (by Morrissey, anyway) Johnny Rogan who soon afterwards collaborated with the Mancunian band Family Foundation on an offensive track entitled 'Red Hot'. This was little more than a 'musical interview' with the former presenter of Channel 4's *The Word*, Terry Christian, who claimed to have known Morrissey at school. The track sarcastically 'debated' the Finsbury Park debacle; to add insult to injury, Rogan and Christian roped in former 'wronged' part-time Smith Craig Gannon to help with the music. Rogan then challenged Morrissey by way of an interview in *Select*, 'Give me a ring and we'll talk it over.' He was, of course, ignored. More vitriol followed from a newly founded Morrissey fanzine, *Miserable Lies*, apparently only interested in filling its pages with derisory remarks and ignoring Morrissey's music.

Morrissey finally spoke out during the summer of 1993, when the commotion had died down somewhat. He stated for the record that the aftermath of Finsbury Park had not perturbed him at all because he had never been guilty in the first place. Opening up more freely to a foreign journalist he trusted – a common feature in these prejudiced later years – he told *Les Inrockuptibles*' Emmanuel Tellier:

Not all skinheads are racists. Skinheads and the National Front are two different things. Skinheads are emblematic of the British working classes. I have no ties whatsoever with racism. I do like boxing! Does that make me violent?

And on the subject of 'The National Front Disco', Tellier told me, Morrissey added in a 'low voice but with clenched fists':

Anybody who listens to the entire song the way I sing it, and the vocal expression, knows only too well that I'm no racist and glorifier of xenophobia. The phrase 'England for the English' is in quotes, so those who call the song racist are not listening. The song tells of the sadness and regret I feel for anyone joining such a movement. And how can the English flag upset anyone? The Union Jack belongs to *everyone*, not just to the extremist parties. *I am not guilty!*

He was absolutely right. The athlete Sally Gunnell had recently wrapped the flag about her shoulders after winning her Olympic gold medal; the officiating soprano at the Last Night of the Proms had done so before leading the audience in the most roisterous 'Rule Britannia' in years. Yet the only British journalist to defend Morrissey was Tony Parsons, writing in the *Daily Telegraph*:

Personally, I don't think Morrissey has a racist bone in him. I can't believe anyone who can write a song like 'Suffer Little Children' isn't on the side of the angels. My great fear is that Morrissey will become the Sarah Ferguson of pop, driven into exile by the cruel and uncaring media. Let us pray it doesn't happen. It would be a tragedy if the crown prince of pop suffered the same fate as the Sloane who fell from grace. Put down that flag, Morrissey. Your country needs you.

*

Morrissey rested but briefly at home before embarking on the American leg of the *Your Arsenal* tour, a gruelling 53-date schedule that would keep him busy until the end of the year, and which opened on 12

September at Minneapolis's Orpheum Theater. Supporting were Gallon Drunk, a rockabilly/electro-punk band fronted by James Johnson: they had recently signed with Sire, Morrissey's US record label, and their biggest hit so far, 'Some Fools Mess', had been named Single of the Month by *NME* the previous November. By and large they would prove unreliable, and towards the end of October attempts would be made to find a replacement support. Kirsty MacColl was approached, but declined. 'I'm used to people coming to see *me*, my own fans,' she told me. 'Much as I admired Morrissey, I would never submit to being an also-ran.' Buffy Sainte-Marie was also contacted, and not surprisingly would have nothing to do with the idea. Feelers were again put out for Jobriath – people still did not know that he was dead. Finally, he settled for a Los Angeles-based outfit, the grandly named but not so grandly talented Big Sandy And The Fly-Right Boys.

The Edith Sitwell backdrop had been dispensed with – over the coming weeks Morrissey would be alternatively surveyed by Diana Dors, Elvis, Charlie Richardson, and the suedehead girls featured at Finsbury Park. The first concert was memorable only in that it ended prematurely due to a stage invasion, and this was almost repeated three evenings later in Toronto when there was a recurrence of the problem that had happened last time around at the Pauley Pavilion – i.e., folding chairs, which should never have been there in the first place. During 'The Girl Least Likely To', Morrissey was rugby-tackled to the floor by five fans, one of whom ripped open his shirt to kiss his heart. These were dragged off him, taken to the wings and handed over to the police. Morrissey walked off the stage just in time to see the fans being charged with public order offences, which meant that they would have to spend the night in jail. He kindly signed their release documents, tore strips off the bouncers, ensured that they would be fired, and the show continued. Afterwards he was confronted by a reporter from *Entertainment Weekly*, 'shocked' over the way he had lost his temper. He told her, 'I don't like it when people think of me as a wimpy, poetic, easily-crushed softie. I'm quite the opposite. I'm a construction worker!' The reporter from the *Toronto Star*, also witness to the tantrum, observed, 'Morrissey sings like a choirboy – one who was abandoned at birth and raised by a family of bikers.'

At El Paso, Texas, a young man leapt on to the stage just as Morrissey was in the process of whipping off his shirt: the fan did likewise, the pair danced for a whole minute, flailing each other with their discarded shirts before swapping them, footballer-style, then walked off the stage arm-in-arm! Three evenings later in San Antonio, in a fairly relaxed atmosphere, Morrissey told the audience between songs, 'You know that no one can legally hurt you!' He then pointed at a mean-looking bouncer who had made a move as if to attack a fan, and sang louder than usual, 'I'd hate to be like certain people I know!' Then, when the bouncer did step out of line, he stopped the band and growled, 'Excuse me, Mr Security in the red T-shirt. Leave him alone!'

In Houston, Texas, several hours before performing at The Summit, a 5,000-seater basketball stadium, Morrissey was interviewed by Robert Chalmers of the *Observer*. Chalmers told me of how he had been vetted, that getting to speak to Morrissey was almost as difficult as meeting a senior member of the Royal Family, but doubly exciting: finally, after studying the journalist's credentials, Morrissey had given him less than a day's notice to fly the ten hours from London – and then cut their interview time by half! Again – once The Smiths' split, the Rogan book and the ongoing feud with Mike Joyce had been dispensed with – the key topic was Morrissey's sexuality. 'I'm not running ahead and leaving clues behind bus-stops, as it were,' he said. 'One of my physical encounters was with a man. That was ten years ago. It was just a very brief, absurd and amusing moment. It wasn't love. I've *never* experienced that!' Chalmers then grasped the bull by the horns and asked him ('Seeing as my time was up anyway, I felt I had nothing to lose!') if he had ever slept with a woman, half expecting to be shown the door as had happened all those years ago when Antonella Black had crossed the line. Surprisingly, he did not:

> Yes, I feel completely open. If I met somebody tomorrow, male or female, and they loved me and I loved them, I would openly proclaim that I loved them, regardless of what they were. I think people should be loved whatever their gender, whatever their age. I am open to everything. I accept that my experience is different from that of most

men, but I feel reasonably normal. I don't feel like a freak. My world is bigger. I never lived in a small town with small morals.

Throughout the tour, Morrissey's musicians maintained a 'toughie' image, which in some ways demonstrated that they were no better than some headbanger groups of a previous generation. In Gainsville, on 16 November, Gary Day went haywire and trashed his guitar after 'The National Front Disco'. In New York, Spencer Cobrin trashed his drumkit with a microphone stand. Obviously, besides inciting violence, these people had money to burn: Cobrin and Alain Whyte were denounced by one journalist as 'like a couple of juvenile delinquents looking for a purse to snatch'.

In Charlottesville, Virginia, on 20 November, Morrissey played to his smallest ever American audience – just five hundred high-school students at the Performing Arts Center – but the performance was no less restrained than in the bigger arenas. Neither were there problems with security. Not so in New York, four evenings later, where his concert at the Limelight Club was delayed by several hours and the support act failed to turn up. The 1,200-strong audience contained a large proportion of gay fans from Greenwich Village, and tension was running high between these and a contingent of hecklers when Morrissey tore off his shirt to reveal the words 'SLIP IN' scrawled across his chest. Halfway through his set the Fire Department arrived and halted the proceedings: the 'official' reason was overcrowding, and this time Gary Day smashed his guitar to bits in a fit of pique.

The New York concert attracted only the worst kind of publicity when Day's antics turned up in a television news report, which helped overshadow the highlight of the tour – the first of two performances at the 13,000-seater Hollywood Bowl, which had sold out in just 22 minutes, eight minutes faster than the record held by The Beatles. The concert in San Antonio a few evenings later started off well enough. When a fan yelled, 'Morrissey for president!' he shouted back, 'Me for president? Then who'll vote for Ross Perot?' Such good humour was short lived, however, when he was forced to stop the show and rebuke a group of bouncers for hitting fans. He told Loraine Ali of *Alternative Press*,

If I see somebody manhandled, I become infuriated. I go slightly out of control. They treat them very aggressively, and when I consider that *I* pay the wages of security, I don't think it's fair. The only aggression that ever occurs at my concerts is *purely* from security.

In the same interview, Morrissey hit out at the American press for their lack of support by declining to interview him – effectively biting the hand that fed by omitting to mention that he had repeatedly refused to speak to them:

They'd rather interview Yoko Ono or talk to Julian Lennon. That's what makes American music quite sad – this enormous capacity not to recognise anything until it's gone. That's the history of the American rock press. They're never quite there. They were never there for Patti Smith, or for The New York Dolls.

The tour ended at the Tower Theater, Philadelphia, on 28 November, and the next day Morrissey and his musicians flew home. One week later, the American gay/fashion magazine *Details* published an interview that had taken months to set up, and which had apparently been granted only on condition that it would appear after Morrissey had left the country – the reasoning behind this being that if he allowed one carefully vetted journalist access into his private sanctum, others would expect to follow suit. 'Life's a bitch, and then you interview Morrissey,' David Keeps began his feature, 'Homme Alone', the title itself smacking heavily of Polari. 'He is a journalist's nightmare: infinitely quotable, but endlessly press-wary.'

Keeps, apparently as fond of titillation as his subject, had successfully petitioned for an interview during Morrissey's last stay at the Sunset Marquis, but this had been cancelled by Peter Hogg at the last minute. A second meeting had been arranged to take place in London on 10 August – the theory being that, if the senior editor of *Details* was so interested in speaking to the singer, then crossing the Atlantic to do so would prove no stumbling block. In the wake of Finsbury Park, this too had been cancelled. Anyone else would have given up, and rightly so, but on the morning of 18 September Keeps had received a call from Jo Slee: he was to report to Morrissey's hotel suite at once.

Reading the transcript of the interview, one is reminded of the interview some years earlier with *Melody Maker*'s Frank Owen – of two men who seem to have an affinity with each other. With strict attention to detail, Keeps described his subject as if no one had seen him before: hair, clothes, complexion, jutting jaw ('like Dudley Do-Right's'), eyes and mannerisms. Morrissey rapped at Keeps not to sit in his favourite chair, then promptly strolled across to the window to be told, 'It's no use jumping. I've got you, now!'

For several minutes without speaking, Keeps stared at Morrissey's face – enough to put anyone off – until Morrissey stuck out his tongue and burst out laughing. Assuming a Noël Coward accent, Keeps demanded, 'What *is* this thing with your tongue, sir? You stick it out rather a lot' – bringing the equally light-hearted response, 'My mouth doesn't close properly. It never did, and I suppose my tongue just falls out. It's like leaving the garden gate open!'

The ice had been broken, enabling Keeps to be bolder than he might normally have been: it had taken him a long time to get this far, and he wanted to ensure a memorable account of the proceedings, not just your standard interview. The on-stage kissing was discussed. 'More romantic than sexual,' Morrissey quipped. 'It's quite personal, and I love that. Wouldn't you?' When Keeps retorted that this would depend on the one doing the kissing, Morrissey raised one eyebrow and posed, '*Would* it?'

Partially tracing the source of this admiration to loneliness and unhappiness, which he considered the major problems faced by the youth of today, Morrissey linked this to his near-permanent depression. Admitting that he had sought professional help, but to no avail, he added, 'And when you're depressed, it is so enveloping that it actually does control your life. You cannot overcome it, and you can't take advice. People trying to cheer you up become infuriating and almost insulting.'

Upon hearing this, Keeps moved on. The pair discussed the 'evils' of the meat industry, and Morrissey's 'redefining of manhood' in the way that he and his songs had 'captured the angst of male adolescence and turned his sensitivity into strength'. And of course, with the emphasis being placed on the word *male* it did not take long for the topic of sexuality to enter the proceedings – or rather, Morrissey's fabled non-existent sex-life, allegedly restricted to the odd urge ('the first at twenty-eight') which of course no one really believed, especially when he claimed (as he had in his interview with Nick Kent) that love, for him, had always been unreciprocated and associated with pain – of how he *had* propositioned lovers, but that they had always turned him down. He concluded, 'If you're asking me if I've ever spent the night with someone in a loving way, the answer is no, I never have.'

This, of course, was *not* what Keeps was asking; neither was Morrissey confirming that he did not have sex. Admitting that he had always found it harder to say 'I love you' than 'I'm sorry' – the former pronouncement, he believed, equating to the death-knell of intimacy – he managed to maintain his composure when Keeps asked in the next breath, 'Are you still friendly with Michael Stipe?'

The conversation moved on to Morrissey's musical tastes. Did he like jazz? No: it was boring and he preferred something more spirited. Did he like gospel, then? This brought a wry smile and the response, ' "Oh Happy Day", sung by hundreds of people who are living in dire poverty in Birmingham, Alabama? No thank you!' (The British music press, of course, would have had a field-day with this one and twisted it into another example of racist stereotyping on Morrissey's part.) Did he like heavy metal, and had he been to a rave? Did he like classical music? Yes, he said of the latter. He liked Jacqueline du Pré, though he had to explain to the bemused Keeps who she was. Then, out of the blue, Keeps asked the question that he believed was on the lips of every Morrissey fan:

KEEPS: Is it true you sleep in the nude?
MORRISSEY: Yes, I do. I like freedom of movement, especially in the event of a fire.
KEEPS: (not getting this) Does that mean boxer shorts for day?
MORRISSEY: Are you asking me what kind of underwear I wear? I didn't until about a month ago.

KEEPS: Did you have some untoward incident?

MORRISSEY: No, I just suddenly decided that I wanted to. I wasn't involved in any political royal scandal. So I tried Calvin Klein. The briefs. White.

KEEPS: It's of compelling interest . . .

MORRISSEY: I couldn't doubt it for a split second.

Keeps had his answer, but at the expense of being allowed to ask any more questions. Minutes later, Morrissey gave the excuse that he had to leave for a sound-check – and allegedly to get his own back for being cut short, Keeps swapped the Morrissey cover he had planned for one of model Cindy Crawford. And in New York, stores reported a surge in the sale of white Calvin Klein briefs.

6

On Ne Badine Pas
Avec l'Amour

'Are you sure you understand the touch of his hand? Does his touch mean so much to you? . . . Love either finds you, or love either blinds you to the danger of a heartbreak ahead.'
   – Joan Regan, 'Danger Heartbreak Ahead' (Stutz/Barefoot), 1955

Back on home territory, Morrissey and his musicians barely had time to catch their breath – appearing on several television shows to promote the new single, 'Certain People I Know' – before embarking on a brief British and European tour organised by his new manager, Nigel Thomas, a stalwart individual who had handled the affairs of Joe Cocker and former Kinks frontman Ray Davies. There was also a brief but pleasing video compilation, *The Malady Lingers On* (title courtesy of Lancashire comic, Les Dawson) – and Linder Sterling's lovely book, *Morrissey Shot*. Many of the studies here were posed for, and are as arrogant as they are artistic, yet still equal anything to be found in The Kobal Collection. Many more were not, proving as with Garbo and Valentino that there was no such thing as a Morrissey bad angle – even while he is asleep. Linder captures his every mood: pensive, cynical, smiling, irate, despondent, in tears through the sheer emotion of it all. There is an inadvertent study of what the French *réalistes* call 'Le miroir, la lampe et la rose' – the mirror symbolising self-analysis, the lamp symbolising the warm glow connecting the artiste to the public, the rose symbolising love. And of course, there are the obligatory exercises in narcissism:

Morrissey hanging half-naked from iron railings; the 'oxters' shot from San Diego, which Kris Kirk only just lived to see; Morrissey in his bath or having his nails painted. And flowers everywhere.

A cold, wet Sheffield opened the eight-date British leg of Morrissey's tour on 12 December 1992. Concerts followed in Birmingham, Newcastle and Manchester – where on 15 December he played his first solo concert in his home town. At the Glasgow Barrowlands the next evening, he ducked as a bottle of water was hurled at his head, and must have been reminded of Finsbury Park. This time he accused the culprit of being an *NME* journalist. The publication had audaciously tried to secure an interview and failed; to 'compensate' for this, in the free pack of playing cards they issued shortly afterwards wherein each suit represented a musical decade, Morrissey was depicted as the Queen of Diamonds – in brackets next to his name was printed, 'The Queen Is Dead'.

The next evening, at Bristol's Colston Hall, Morrissey took another swipe at his least favourite rag by announcing just before 'The National Front Disco', 'If you think that this song is in any way racist, then I suggest that you do yourselves a very big favour. *Give up the NME!*' At London's Alexandra Palace, there were ticket concessions for those who had missed out on Glastonbury and the second day at Finsbury Park. Kirsty MacColl had changed her mind about supporting him – 'We were on home ground and it made a vast difference!' – and included in her repertoire was The Smiths' 'You Just Haven't Earned It Yet Baby'. Towards the end of her spot she was joined on stage by Shane MacGowan, and most unusually for a Morrissey warm-up they brought the house down with their massive hit, 'Fairy Tale Of New York'.

The tour closed on 20 December at the 1,600-seater London Astoria, the smallest venue on the circuit. Rumour preceded the event, on account of his persistent hounding by the music press, that this would be Morrissey's last ever concert on British soil. As such it was filmed for future audio/video release.

Two evenings later, Morrissey played the 6,000-seater Le Zénith, in the Pantin district of Paris. For him and myself, the wheel had turned full-circle. I had first become aware of his music in Paris some years before.

In January 1986, along with Catherine Deneuve, Yves Montand, Juliette Gréco and Melina Mercouri, I had been personally involved with Le Zénith's opening. The out-of-the-way venue had been especially constructed for Barbara – she and Gérard Depardieu had starred in forty performances of her musical drama *Lily Passion*, a vehicle that would have suited Morrissey down to the ground. David (named after myself) is a young serial killer who follows Lily around the tour-circuit: each time he has heard her sing, he goes off and kills someone. Eventually, Lily achieves her heartfelt ambition – like the hero of Morrissey's 'Jack The Ripper', she invites the killer into her arms, and David stabs her after a last song!

Only Barbara and Johnny Hallyday have actually sold out Le Zénith, notoriously difficult to fill, but the fact that only five hundred tickets remained unsold for Morrissey's appearance was a mighty achievement. The concert was recorded, released in May 1993 under the title *Beethoven Was Deaf*, and reached number 13 in the charts. For copyright reasons, two of the songs were replaced by ones from the London Astoria show.

The period between the close of Morrissey's tour (Düsseldorf, 23 December) and the album's release was for him fraught with sadness. On 27 February, Tim Broad died of an AIDS-related illness. The director of his finest promotional videos and one of his closest companions had been just 37. 'Tim had extraordinary patience, kindness and benevolence. The cut-throat politics of the music industry never affected him,' Morrissey reflected. A few weeks earlier, his new manager Nigel Thomas had succumbed to a heart attack and Morrissey had said at his funeral in Gloucestershire, 'Ours is not a very dignified business, but Nigel managed to make it so.' Cynics have suggested that, had Thomas not died so suddenly, like all his predecessors he would not have stood the test of time. The same might have been said for Mick Ronson, who died of liver cancer on 29 April, aged 46. Most of the obituaries were accompanied by the controversial photograph most associated with him – the infamous shot taken by Mick Rock of Bowie as Ziggy Stardust 'fellating' Ronson's guitar some years earlier during a concert at Oxford's Town Hall. *Your Arsenal*, Morrissey's definitive album, had served as

Ronson's final testament, though according to Morrissey the pair had planned an even more involved follow-up. He told American journalist Dave DiMartino in February 1994, 'Mick spoke to me a few days before he died. He was very happy, very enthusiastic about writing songs with me and getting back into the studio. He was very positive about his health. Then three days later his wife telephoned me and said, "My baby's gone." It was so incredibly painful and sad for me. I'd become so attached to him that I couldn't attend the funeral.'

One may only imagine how deeply Morrissey was affected by these tragedies, one on top of the other. Prone to bouts of deep depression, easily mistrusting, it must have seemed like the bottom had dropped out of his world. He became more reclusive than usual, later confessing that things had been so bad at one stage that he had not left the house for weeks. Then, in May 1993, came the shock announcement to *Les Inrockuptibles*' Christian Fevret that his forthcoming album, *Vauxhall And I*, would be his penultimate . . . indeed, it might even be his last:

I'm not interested in taking a break. When I stop, it will be for good. I'm starting to foresee the moment when I'll have expressed all that I want to express. An artiste's longevity isn't necessarily the proof of his worth. Are groups like The Stones of any use? I don't want to hang around just to prove that I can. There would have to be a worthwhile reason for doing so.

Throughout his entire career, Morrissey had denounced whatever had been the current musical trend: paltry Manchester pop ensembles, tuneless rap, too many rock dinosaurs, fabricated dance music, a severe lack of talent within whichever discipline one cared to mention. The time was nigh, he now declared, to search for new horizons. He had, he said, been approached with cameo roles in two major (unnamed) film productions – portraying Charlie Richardson in a gangland drama, and the part of a redoubtable playboy in an Andy Warhol biopic starring Lili Taylor. His pessimism had plunged to an all-time low:

I want to do photography, to travel, to write, but I've no desire to be recognised in the street any more. I don't really appreciate people. The ones that I care about are unreliable. I no longer believe in human nature. The human race no longer interests me. I don't care any more about the environment. People *deserve* to die out. I'll be content when all the tigers, rhinos and elephants have become extinct, then they'll no longer be persecuted. Humanity deserves nothing more than to go up in smoke.

Two days before Mick Ronson's death there had been another demise that may or may not have affected Morrissey, but which also may have caused him to breathe a sigh of relief. Kris Kirk, who had worshipped him from afar since the very beginning, succumbed to AIDS, aged 43. Almost until the week of his death, Kris had been working on a kiss-and-tell, *The Vinyl Closet*, which had threatened to send shockwaves through the pop-rock community. Keeping well within the law, Kris had been about to name names, and had more than enough proof to support his claims. Morrissey's interview with Nick Kent for *The Face* in 1990 (see page 129) was just the tip of the iceberg so far as Morrissey was concerned. Now, the unedited script lies in a vault somewhere, waiting for the day – until then we must content ourselves with *A Boy Called Mary: Kris Kirk's Greatest Hits* (1999, Millivres, edited by Richard Smith), which contains fascinating chapters written in Kris's inimitable style about Morrissey, Boy George, Dusty Springfield, Pete Burns and other gay icons.

During the summer of 1993, with the threat of retirement or abandonment hanging over his fans' heads like the Sword of Damocles, Morrissey shut himself away in a secluded studio and beavered away with fellow collaborators Alain Whyte and Boz Boorer. Of the fifteen songs completed, eleven would be selected for his alleged penultimate album, the others would be set aside for B-sides of CD and 12-inch singles. Besides these songs, there was at least one cover version of someone else's past hit, the Johnny Mercer-Henry Mancini classic 'Moon River', which had been 'crooned' in the 1961 *Breakfast At Tiffany's* by Audrey Hepburn. Danny Williams had topped the charts with it the same year: Mancini himself and Gracie Fields had had hits with it. Morrissey's rendition is passable, though the extended CD version seems to drone on endlessly. He also committed the unforgivable crime of 'massacring' a standard by changing the words – the line 'It's waiting round the bend, my Huckleberry friend' was omitted completely.

Far, far better was a cover version of a French *chanson*, Georges Delerue's haunting 'Interlude', composed in 1968 for the film of the same name. This had originally been included on the B-side of the Franco-Italian singer Dalida's 'Hurt', and had appeared in English for the first time on Timi Yuro's *Something Bad On My Mind* album in 1971:

Let's hold fast to the dream that tastes and sparkles like wine . . .
Who knows if it's real or just something we're both dreaming of?
What seems like an interlude, now,
Could be the beginning of love!

Morrissey recorded this song as a duet with Siouxsie Sioux, singer with seventies punk ensemble The Banshees. 'Move over Kate Bush and Larry Adler,' *Gay Times* enthused the following September, upon the song's long-delayed release. 'This month's Odd Couple Award goes to punk priestess, the mother of all Goths, Siouxsie Sioux, and Quiff o' the North Morrissey. It's like the Sex Pistols never happened.' In fact, the coupling worked extraordinarily well: the blending of the gentle baritone and the indigo tones of the neo-torch singer make one lament that the pair stopped here.

For these new sessions, Spencer Cobrin and Gary Day were gone – the latter, it is reputed, after some very heated set-tos in the studio – though the pair would turn up again, once the dust had settled. The replacement bassist was Johnny Bridgewood, the ex-Stingray who had played on 'Sing Your Life'. The new drummer was Woodie Taylor, formerly of The Johnson Family, who had played on two of the London dates during the *Kill Uncle* tour. Also there was another short-lived manager, Arnold Stiefel, an all-powerful American whose current stable included Rod Stewart.

The album – of which Morrissey said, 'It's the best I've ever made' – was produced by Steve Lillywhite and its title, *Vauxhall And I*, had music press cynics pointing out that the area around London's Vauxhall Bridge was the hated Johnny Rogan's 'patch' – forgetting the jacket blurb on *The Severed Alliance* stating that the author was forever changing his address. The area, of course, was most famous for the Vauxhall Tavern, the legendary gay pub in Kennington Lane – renowned for its good pint, its drag queens such as the real Dockyard Doris, and above all for its hospitality. The building was immediately added to 'Morrissey's London' and one may only wonder what the patrons of the Vauxhall Tavern have to say about the bequiffed, inquisitive and largely uninitiated individuals who wander through its portals, camera in hand, without knowing what to expect. Kanako Ishikawa, that delightful but painfully shy little Japanese lady, was still reeling from the shock two days after visiting the place when she described to me how the infamous – and regrettably no longer with us – Dockyard Doris lumbered up to her and boomed, 'Come on inside, duckie. We ain't gonna bite yer, gel!'

'Hurrah, praise him, sing hosannas, the Mozzer is back!' is how one reviewer announced the first taster single from the album, 'The More You Ignore Me, The Closer I Get', which peaked at number 8 in the charts in March 1994. This was a rare love song, the most personal to date, in which the lover – Morrissey himself – is not only completely in control of the situation, he is the one doing all the seducing, telling the deliberating object of his desire that indifference will only make the situation more appealing. 'Whether you care or do not . . . *I've* made up your mind,' he declares before warning, just in case his amour decides not to give in, 'Beware! I bear more grudges than lonely high court judges!'

The subject of the song was widely alleged to be 28-year-old Jake Walters, Morrissey's new companion: a photograph of the multi-tattooed, burly suedehead's hirsute six-pack appears on the sleeve of the single, with the word 'MOZ' mock-tattooed in large letters across his middle, the 'O' encircling his navel. Clutching a camera, he appears on the sleeve of the promotional single – this time it is Morrissey who is topless, one fist bunched as he grapples Jake in a stranglehold. Jake, who moved in with him at around this time, also features on the *Vauxhall And I* cover – or at least part of his bare shoulder and his '1 oz' medallion does, caressed by Morrissey's hand, identifiable by his signet ring.

The single was backed by two equally remarkable B-sides. Even more personal is 'I'd Love To', which makes us wonder, given the intense privacy of Morrissey's earlier years, if we should really be hearing this *chanson* that finds him ripping his heart wide open. Obviously he feels we should, as he reveals that true happiness may only be bought with tears. Before declaring that he has had a lifetime of nights he cannot bear, he confides, his voice little more than a whisper to the lover beside him, 'Gay, I lay awake and I cried because of ways I'd love to, but only with you . . . and time will never wipe you out.' [In the alternative version of the song that appears on *My Early Burglary Years*, he begins, 'Again, I lay awake . . .'] For those fans desperately trying to come to terms with their own sexuality, such lyrics coming from a man who had been seen as fighting his demons for years were an absolute godsend. The second B-side, 'Used To Be A Sweet Boy', had a lush arrangement by Alain Whyte. Here, Morrissey again opens his insular heart and grants us access to his burdening regret as he wistfully pronounces of his childhood, 'Something went wrong, and I know I can't be to blame.'

Vauxhall And I, released on 14 March, was unanimously applauded by the critics – indeed, there was not a single adverse review even from the tabloids – and in less than a week it topped the charts. It is a gentler, lyrically and spiritually more rewarding collection than any of its predecessors, an absolute work of art. 'An inordinately beautiful record, certainly the most gorgeous that Morrissey's ever done,' Andrew Harrison told me, adding in *Select*, 'If he keeps making records like this, you won't want The Smiths back.' Writing in *The Times* the previous November upon the re-release of The Smiths' entire back catalogue by WEA, the frequently catty Caitlin Moran is reputed to have infuriated Morrissey by describing him and his former partner, 'This pouting, lisping son of Oscar Wilde, almost vindictively effeminate and laying claim to the traditional "privileges" of womanhood – passivity, preening and put-down air . . . Manchester's anaemic James Dean figure, together with the vaguely ferret-like greased rocker, Johnny Marr.' Music journalists have always been notoriously two-faced, and now, with the release of *Vauxhall And I*, she attempted to redress the balance by enthusing in *Melody Maker*, 'This is magnificent, made in Gorgeous-O-Scope with supporting roles by Sarah Bernhardt and God.' Terry Deal wrote in *Gay Times*, 'The muddled miserabilist's self-pitying cries are at their most powerfully convincing, adult and human . . . not only the album of the month, but possibly Morrissey's finest hour.' The *Irish Sunday Independent* declared it, 'As homoerotic and darkly celebratory of things homosexual as anything the late Derek Jarman ever put on the screen' – which was perhaps going a little too far, for uncalculated blatancy had never been Morrissey's forte.

The eleven songs proved that, in a complex world viewed through the eyes of the all-embracing poet, Morrissey's well of inspiration showed no sign of drying up. The opener, the catchy 'Now My Heart Is Full', centres around one of his favourite films, *Brighton Rock* (1947, US title: *Young Scarface*), a heavyweight tale of gangsters and 'loafing oafs in all-night chemists' written by Graham Greene. These are referred to by name: Dallow, Spicer, Pinkie and Cubitt – to which he adds himself, the 'jammy Stressford poet' who is amorous of Bunnie. Yet amid the vibrancy of it all there is the lingering undercurrent of loneliness – the fact that, barring 'some rain-coated lovers' brothers', the narrator is still friendless as ever. And again, the fans rushed out to search for the film.

The effervescent 'Spring-Heeled Jim' has scattered among its lyrics snatches of dialogue of youngsters debating capital punishment in the seventies television drama-documentary, *We Are The Lambeth Boys*. Again, there is sexual ambiguity concerning the alleged ageing member of the Richardson gang who will 'do' but never be 'done to', yet who has had 'so many women, his head should be spinning'. And, for the man who in his heyday was afraid of no one, now that he is past his best bravado begets regret and he can only lament, 'Where did all the time go?'

Perhaps the most articulate song on the album is 'Billy Budd', the title of yet another film, based on the novel of the same name by Herman Melville, and subsequently adapted into an opera by Benjamin Britten. In the story, the First Mate has a crush on the Beautiful Sailor (portrayed by Terence Stamp in the film), only to betray him and see him hanged. Melville's biographer, Edwin Havilland Miller, was of the opinion that the tale was based on Melville's own unrequited love for novelist Nathaniel Hawthorne. Morrissey's all-too-brief song draws an ingenious parallel not just between the Beautiful Sailor's demise and his own wished-for demise by some sections of the media, but in the prejudices experienced by gay couples who, thwarted by homophobes, are unable to find work. The song ends, curiously, with a line from the 1948 film of *Oliver Twist*, in which East End actor Anthony Newley, as the Artful Dodger, begs Alec Guinness's Fagin, 'Don't leave us in the dark!'

NME's Stuart Bailie described 'Hold On To Your Friends' as 'like Noel Coward with a harpsichord'. Morrissey told *Details*' William Shaw, 'It was written about somebody I know, in relation of their treatment towards me.' In it, he decries this anonymous user, who only calls him when he needs support, while the rest of the time he is impervious to his friend's feelings. Morrissey reminds him that there are enough people to attack in the world without attacking those one cares about, and portentously concludes, 'There just might come a time when you need some friends.'

In 'Why Don't You Find Out For Yourself', on the other hand, Morrissey makes a futile attempt to warn a would-be artiste-friend of the perils encountered by trusting mentors with the money he or she might earn. It is a case of learning from the experiences of one who knows – one who really has found 'the glass hidden in the grass' – though when there is still scepticism from the other party, Morrissey more or less throws in the towel and concludes with a shrug of the shoulders that he has been stabbed so many times in the back that he has no skin left, and adds, 'but that's just the way it goes.'

In 'I Am Hated For Loving', Morrissey once more regresses into intense, crippling gloom: he feels unwanted – save by himself – alone and unloved, attacked from all sides, not specifically belonging any-where. 'I am falling,' he opines, 'and there's still no one to catch me.' Morbid irony, however, resurfaces in 'Lifeguard Sleeping, Girl Drowning', performed in a breathy falsetto. Death is played in the minor key while the elements are in the major in this *goualante* of the self-centred attention seeker who this time goes too far – a cross between Stevie Smith's 'Not Waving But Drowning' and Byron's lament for Shelley, with a dash of Jacques Brel's 'La Fanette' thrown in for good measure. 'She deserves all she gets,' declares the overworked lover who, when his girlfriend swims too far out to sea and gets into difficulties, casually lets her drown.

'The Lazy Sunbathers', the only politically controversial song on the album, epitomises *Les enfants de novembre* at its most potent. Though written in the wake of the horrors of Sarajevo, it harks back to the early days of World War II and the development of the Office of Strategic Services – the courageous American package of stars that sailed for Europe to entertain our troops at the front, while their so-called peers saw fit to lounge in the sun and continue with the good life as if nothing was happening. 'They thought the war was nothing to do with them,' Marlene Dietrich told me, 'so they just lounged around all day doing nothing, whilst innocent people were getting butchered.' In his song, Morrissey reminds us of the callousness of these cold-blooded people.

'Speedway' is the lengthy, fashionable thoroughfare that runs through Santa Monica. During the early fifties, with its wealth of uncloseted leather bars, gay clubs and bath-houses, it formed a part of the cruising area that was a mecca to the likes of James Dean, Montgomery Clift and Rock Hudson. When he wrote the song, it was one of Morrissey's favourite sojourns, a locality where he felt at peace with himself, safe from the sniping British music press. 'Speedway', the symphony-in-miniature that closes *Vauxhall And I*, begins *colla voce* and appears to be heading towards the tenderness of 'There Is A Place In Hell For Me And My Friends' – until the ear-splitting revving-up of a chainsaw directs it into a scurrilous attack on Morrissey's worst oppressors – the tabloid Shylocks hungry for their pound of flesh, who try to break his spirit and fail to do so only because he has nothing left to break. He confesses, too, that he has allowed the charade to continue in order to prevent one person in particular, maybe a clandestine lover, from being implicated in scandal. And, he concludes, he may be fighting a losing battle as he declares that these enemies will not rest until the hearse has claimed him, silencing him for ever. When later asked by Stuart Maconie whether the song was about 'gentlemen of my profession', he shot back with, 'I've never met any gentlemen of your profession.' Touché!

On 15 March 1994, the HMV store in London's Oxford Street was witness to scenes of unprecedented hero-worship when Morrissey held his very first signing session. The shop had estimated a crowd of around 500, as had happened with Cliff Richard and Tina Turner. Over 3,000 fans turned up, not just from all over Britain but from France, Belgium and the United States, many of them camping out overnight on the pavement. Morrissey breezed in on the proceedings wearing his usual denims and Doc Marten boots, and the badge on the lapel of his tweed jacket read FAMOUS WHEN DEAD. His quiff, observed the *Guardian*'s Jim White, '. . .was like the dorsal fin of a killer whale in captivity.' Casually, or so it was meant to appear, he tossed a bunch of gladioli into the crowd – and hit, not just by accident, one of the music press photographers.

The scene, with the same number of admirers, was repeated two days later at the HMV store in Manchester: he remained on home territory for over four hours, signing autographs and chatting non-stop amid scenes of frequently uncontrollable emotion. One big, very butch-looking lad had to be revived with a security man's hip-flask after kissing Morrissey on the cheek and receiving a hug and a few warm words in return. Bill McCoid reported the 'pilgrimage' in the *Manchester Evening News*:

> The fans are let through the barriers, the last steps towards their Holy Grail in total awe of their idol. This is worship, the paying of respects. Morrissey is hugged, kissed, revered. He wrings their hands. It's not unlike the Pope giving an audience. This is as near religion as you can get without the religion. Homage (and money) has been paid. Their lives are complete.

*

In the spring of 1994, several sharply contrasting Morrissey interviews and features appeared on both sides of the Atlantic. The British music tabloids were no longer interested in him – not that Morrissey lost much sleep over this – but the monthlies still held him in high esteem and found him accessible. He met Stuart Maconie, this time writing for *Q*, not in some clandestine location but in a spit-and-sawdust Battersea pub on a busy Friday evening. Effectively, Maconie was lucky to meet him at all: either Morrissey was incredibly thick-skinned, or he had not been shown the journalist's earlier review for the *Live In Dallas* video.

As had happened in Berlin, the talk was matey and Northern. Though the cover of the magazine proclaimed, MORRISSEY: 'Yes, I Am Pregnant' – MR CHUCKLE-TROUSERS UNZIPS HIS LIP, and though the accompanying photographs had been snapped atop Hollywood's Griffith Observatory (the location for the closing scenes of *Rebel Without A Cause*, though even James Dean had been terrified of straddling the balustrade, as Morrissey does here), the intro of the actual interview read, 'Goodbye, big-bloused flower-fondler; cheerio, depressed devotee of deathly doom; toodle-oo, teetotal football-fearing perma-hermit; we'll sithee, bespectacled Billy No Mates.' This, of course, was what Morrissey was all about: a cross between George Formby Sr and Norman Evans, with liberal dollops of Robb Wilton and Frank Randle. 'It never goes away,' he proudly declared of his Northernness, 'that indelible working-classness.'

Neither was the singer alone: he had brought along his new companion – who, it appears, knew his place. 'A small, bedenimed skinhead personage who answers to the name of Jake,' Maconie observed. 'Affable and barrer-boyish, Jake's role seems unclear: driver, gofer, mucker. Whatever, he busies himself with the pinball machine as Morrissey indicates a dark corner of the tap-room where, seated incongruously at a video game table, we begin.' Jake may have kept in the background for whatever reason, but this did not prevent the magazine's editor from sneaking an uncaptioned photograph of the pair into the finished feature – of the two of them getting into Morrissey's car – for readers to draw their own conclusions.

The topics of conversation were current. Of the *EastEnders* actress Gillian Taylforth's 'Did-she-didn't-she?' oral-sex episode, splashed all over the tabloids, Morrissey said, 'I think even if she did, it doesn't really matter. Do the staff of the *Sun* not do it? . . . It's very old-fashioned and very Victorian to me . . . I feel nothing but sympathy for her.' On the state of British football, now that the disastrously ineffective England manager Graham Taylor was gone, he said, 'It does seem that the current England squad is bereft of real stars. I've never been convinced by Gascoigne . . . I went to see Chelsea recently . . . I thought seeing Dennis Wise and Ian Rush and Neil Ruddock, I'd be in awe and I wasn't at all. I thought I can play better than this.' So, Maconie asked, did Morrissey actually play football? 'Yes,' came the response, 'I played football a few weeks ago . . . and I scored four goals. I should add that the game was against Brondesbury Park Ladies.'

Maconie then asked the usual chestnuts. Did Morrissey get drunk, have sex and take drugs? 'Yes,' he replied to the first part of the question, 'I have a great interest in alcohol and as time goes by I find it more comforting, although I'm not by any means an alcoholic so please don't blandish that in heavy upper case.' As to the second part of the question ('I had to ask, what with him bringing his mate along to the interview, and all,' Maconie told me afterwards) the response was a definite, 'No, I don't.' Morrissey may have been starting to come out of his shell, but some topics were still sacrosanct, even though the replies were getting less and less credible.

A little more of the Morrissey–Jake 'mystery' was unravelled with the publication, also in April 1994, of his intense, inadvertently revealing interview with William Shaw of *Details* (an edited version appeared in *Ray Gun*), which had taken place in Shaw's hotel room in Los Angeles at the beginning of the year. The first thing Shaw noticed was Morrissey's '1 oz' pendant, identical to the one Jake Walters wears on the sleeves for *Vauxhall And I* and 'The More You Ignore Me'. 'That's my secret,' he retorted when asked to elaborate, 'I do a lot of baking.' Much of the interview, a far cry from his previous one with the magazine, centred around Morrissey's depression, the fact that if there was love in his life at last, he did not give the impression that he was particularly happy.

Shaw referred to Morrissey's recent lengthy self-imposed incarceration in his London home, when for weeks he had refused to see anyone. He had tried medication and counselling, he confessed, but to no avail, and he had now learned how to live with his state of mind. 'It doesn't really matter how people try to uplift you,' he added, 'within me it's an immovable, strange, genetic medical condition that I have never escaped from.' Taking this and Morrissey's much-publicised, troubled upbringing into account, the fact that he was a survivor from a broken home, Shaw asked him if he would like to have children. Morrissey reverted to his customary pessimism – not that the conversation had been uplifting to begin with:

> Only in an ideal world [because] I'm not sure what it is about life that is supposed to make it worthwhile. I've never really enjoyed life. I've never known how. I seem to have such unbearably high standards that I set for myself that there's not really any way in which I can win. I'm not really frightened of death. It's not a particularly horrendous thing for me. I feel sad for other people, but not for me.

'Not even if it's a complete full stop?' Shaw wanted to know, bringing a wry, 'That's fine by me' in response.

Morrissey must have liked this interviewer, for when they were interrupted by Jake, come to collect him – 'He is shy and avoids my gaze,' Shaw observed, interpreting Jake's body language – Morrissey invited himself back to Shaw's hotel room the next day. He was 'delivered' by Jake, who this time hovered outside the door throughout the interview. Today the talk was of the tough new world he had begun inhabiting, probably introduced to it by his new companion. Morrissey was now a boxing enthusiast, an aficionado of the eccentric Chris Eubank. 'An astonishing machine,' he told Shaw. He also confessed to having been in a few fights himself, which he had won – whether he was speaking allegorically and referring to the British music press again is a matter for conjecture, though Jake later boasted to friends that Morrissey had actually sparred in the ring and found the whole experience rewarding, even getting hurt. Shaw's interview, however, started to take on an edgy tone when he began questioning the singer about his sexuality – a topic that today seemed especially relevant, he felt, on account of the ubiquitous Jake. The answer was a slight variation on the stock response, 'Sex is *never* in my life, therefore I have no sexuality.' Then Shaw blotted his copybook by making comparisons between Morrissey and the sex-and-self-loathing Kenneth Williams, posing the question, 'You must have had sex at some time in your life, so for that moment at least your sexuality becomes fixed.'

There must have been some sort of signal, for before Shaw could drive him further into a corner, Jake had come to the rescue. 'Simply a prearranged escape,' Shaw concluded. In the photograph he submitted for the finished feature we see the pair reclining: the younger man shirtless, the word MOZ again mock-tattooed across his bare middle – while Morrissey, feigning sleep, has an arm wound about Jake's thigh and his head resting on his crotch.

The new image was criticised in a For/Against local celebrities debate chaired and reported by Rosemary Barratt of the *Manchester Evening News*. While musician Vini Reilly praised Morrissey to the hilt and placed him in the same superstar league as Freddie Mercury and Mick Jagger, Len Brown was convinced of his sincerity, and Johnny Rogan still respected him despite the 'fatwahs', others were unimpressed. John Robb, formerly with punk outfit The Membranes, but now a member of the music press that Morrissey loathed, had been at Finsbury Park, found the whole thing amusing, and therefore had nothing flattering to say. Barratt herself concluded of this 'new' Morrissey, 'No longer portraying himself as a weak and feeble wallflower, he's flexing his pumped-up pecs and courting some rather undesirable company.'

Mark Hadfield, of the techno band Rhythm Quest, had taken great exception to Morrissey's attacks on dance music, and his self-appointed stance as spokesman for the youth of Britain. 'Dance music is made by ordinary people for ordinary people,' Hadfield said. 'Recently he's been selling records simply because of who he is and what he says, not because his music is any good. He's just not that important any more.'

Hadfield was wrong, of course, begging the question a decade on, Does anyone remember Rhythm Quest or any of the other dozens of minor celebrities who went out of their way to attack a man who today remains an active, working legend? He was and still is important, important enough for magazines and periodicals to fight to get his face on their front covers, mostly not because the editors themselves are admirers, but because he boosts circulation figures. Again, with most of these people it was purely a matter of sour grapes.

Elsewhere there was further criticism from Patrick Fitzgerald, the Manchester-raised frontman with Kitchens Of Distinction who had 'outed' himself in an interview with *NME*. 'I hate lying,' he subsequently told *Gay Times'* Richard Smith, having said that he and Morrissey had much in common, coming from the same backgrounds but above all speaking the same language, 'there's no point in doing what I do if I'm going to lie. That was Morrissey's strength on the first Smiths album and it's his weakness now. He was never out.' Richard Smith concluded,

> Morrissey's changed, too, and is now more interested in thuggery than buggery. His stylings are increasingly masculinist, both in terms of his recent records' harder guitar edges and blatant racism, and his scrapping of his fey ways in favour of professing a predilection for boxing, skinheads, the Krays, tattoos and Herman Melville. Of course, they're all as gay in their own way – though from a different tradition – as Oscar Wilde, gladioli and *A Taste Of Honey*. But one wonders if La Mozz realises how ridiculously camp his association with all these things appears? Or does he think he now comes across as one dead butch homi?

The image was toughened up further for the benefit of Morrissey's interview with Andrew Harrison of *Select*, which appeared in May 1994. The cover shot revealed him baring his teeth and wearing a knuckleduster: the subtitle proclaimed him, 'Unbeaten in ten years as World Feather Duster Champion, the man they're calling the Vauxhall Villain – Steven "Bonecrusher" Morrissey.' The photographs accompanying the feature were taken at the York Hall gymnasium in Bethnal Green – a former Krays hang-out, now one of Morrissey's preferred haunts, after he had allegedly been introduced to the place by Jake. Here, he added glamour to the somewhat spartan surroundings by posing in the ring with several prize fighters – including super middle-weight champion John 'Cornelius' Carr, whom he dwarfed. 'For me it's the sense of glamour that's attractive,' Morrissey told Harrison, 'the romance, but mainly it's the aggression that interests me. It has me instantly leaving my seat and heading for the ropes to join in.' Not long after the Morrissey feature appeared, and reputedly inspired by the photographs, the location was used for the setting of *Angels With Broken Noses*, an adult video that starred half a dozen East End twenty-somethings 'unwinding' in the locker-room after slogging it out in the ring. It would subsequently win the *Gay Times* Erotic Video Award of 1996.

To gain access to Morrissey for the actual interview itself, which had taken place at Hook End Manor on the eve of the album's release, Harrison had had to get past Jake: 'A stocky ex-boxer at the 20s-30s crossroads, with a skinhead crop, a white Fred Perry-style shirt and hard blue eyes.' According to Harrison, Jake was in a bad mood because Julie Burchill had penned an unflattering piece about 'the gaffer' in that morning's *Sunday Times*. 'He warned me,' the journalist said, 'if this piece was going to be a similar stitch-up to the Burchill story, then I'd better watch my step.' 'A very unpleasant young man,' one of Harrison's colleagues told me, 'Jake's loyalties were in the right place, but Morrissey was doing himself few favours having him trail around after him like a lap-dog. His attitude wasn't unlike that of some of the bouncers at the rougher concerts. Maybe it was a good thing for Morrissey that it didn't last.'

Morrissey risked raising his detractors' hackles by declaring during the interview how baffled he was that, despite having been the subject of several recent television debates, the National Front were yet to be given a platform to air and discuss their views. When Harrison posed the question of whether this was for the best, seeing as the National Front and the British National Party seemed intent on pursuing their political objectives through violence, Morrissey offered another logical suggestion:

If they were afforded television time or unbiased space in newspapers, it would seem less of a threat and it would ease the situation. They are gagged so much that they take revenge in the most frightening way by hurting and killing people . . . part of that is simply their anger at being ignored in what is supposed to be a democratic society.

The interview brought about the usual flurry of protest from angry readers and supplied the tabloid hacks with more ammunition for attacking him. Now he was accused of 'sticking up for the democratic rights of racists' and the issue of Finsbury Park was again regurgitated.

The rest was fairly unrevealing. '*Vauxhall And I*,' he confided, 'it's a reference to a certain person I know who was born and raised in Vauxhall.' Few doubted that this was Jake, the reason why Morrissey was self-confessedly relieved to be no longer seeking inspiration for his songs from old films and other Smiths-related sources. 'It's like being told that you've been cured of chronic tuberculosis or housewife's knee or something,' he added.

At around this time (though there is doubt as to the actual date of its submission) a script contribution by Morrissey ended up at one of the management-script meetings for *Coronation Street*. A producer's assistant told me,

> The script wasn't as ridiculous and contrived as some of the earlier efforts Morrissey had submitted. Suzie [Birchall, played by Cheryl Murray who had appeared in the 'Everyday Is Like Sunday' video] breezes into The Street looking like a younger version of Bet Lynch, but with real diamonds. She gains affection by soft-soaping everyone, and puts in an offer to buy the Rover's Return – well, we couldn't have allowed that, though had the script come later, who knows? Then, after reverting to her usual bitchiness, she suffers serious injury trying to save Betty Turpin from falling into the canal, and ends up in a wheelchair. The story was turned down, though had we known that Bet would be leaving so soon . . .

The sweat and sawdust of the provincial boxing stadium was foremost in Morrissey's thoughts during the autumn of 1994 when he entered Olympic Studios in South London to record five songs with pugilist themes. One of these was 'Sunny', released after a great deal of deliberation in December 1995, and suffering the indignity of becoming the first Morrissey record not to chart. ' "Sunny" is Moz's lament for Jake,' one of his musicians told me. 'He cared for him a lot . . . and was terribly cut up when they parted company.' It seems almost certain that Morrissey was referring to Jake in his February 1995 *Observer* interview conducted by his friend, Michael Bracewell. Under the heading, 'A Walk On The Wilde Side', Bracewell drew the time-honoured comparisons between the Stretford bard and his alter-ego:

> Both are Anglo-Irish artists, both have been feted by the English media, then savaged by them; each has been accused of the worst crime of their respective eras: homosexuality for Wilde and fascism for Morrissey. Both too have had a relationship which was as destructive as it was creative. Making a rare allusion to his private life Morrissey admits, 'I have had a relationship which opened up a crucial area in me. There is something unstoppable about the Wilde story, and my own.'

'We're really missing you,' Morrissey opines in this lovely song, 'My heart goes out to you . . . So I offered love, and it was not required. What else can I do?' The first single release from the Olympic Studio session, however, was not quite so sympathetic. 'Boxers', backed with 'Have A Go Merchant' and 'Whatever Happens, I Love You', was released in January 1995 and reached number 23 in the charts. The promotional video, by Morrissey's friend James O'Brien, was shot at York Hall in monochrome and featured new fighting buddy Cornelius Carr, then regarded as invincible by his supporters. Whether this was Morrissey's way of getting back at Jake for whatever he is supposed to have done is a matter for conjecture, given his past treatment of friends and colleagues who have erred. In this sorry vignette, Carr is seen pulverising Sunny, his opponent, a wimpish young man (which Jake was not) last seen in a television commercial for Pot Noodles – while the camera offers fleeting glimpses of Morrissey, the pugilists' hero, displayed on posters on the walls of the training room and locker room. The closing scene, where Morrissey strides into the room to console the loser – in slow-motion and unconventionally chomping gum – had even the most ardent fans cringing.

'Boxers' was feted by the *Guardian*'s Pat Kane as, 'One of the loveliest melodies and narratives Morrissey has yet penned, an acting tragedy of

working-class hardness and celebrity.' Its sleeve featured a photograph
of Billy Conn, who had fought the legendary world heavyweight
champion Joe Louis for the second time on 18 June 1946 (the date of
the photograph) and very nearly stripped him of the title he had held
since 1937: Louis had kayoed him in the eighth round. Within the CD
release, Morrissey continued his fascination with hirsute midriffs by
including one such shot of the defeated fighter.

'It's a pity he took on this phoney tough image,' Kirsty MacColl said.
'Not that I'm saying Morrissey was a wimp, because he wasn't. I'm pretty
sure he would know how to handle himself in a fight. But in pretending
to be something he was not, rather than sticking to the *Arsenal* and
Vauxhall trusted formula, he was preparing himself for an almost certain
slump in his career.'

7

Sweet and Tender Hooligan

'Violence isn't a hobby of mine. I would like it to disappear entirely from life. But when people treat me as if I'm abnormal, as if I'm not like they are, isn't that already the beginning of violence?'

– Morrissey

The Boxers tour would be the most uncommercial so far: few official posters, programmes and T-shirts on account of a dispute with the merchandising company, hardly any backstage passes because of increased problems with nuisance fans. It opened on 3 February 1995, a wet and miserable Friday, at Glasgow's Barrowlands. Supporting were Joe Moss protégés Marion, a five-piece outfit from Mansfield – from their opening number onwards, the fans yelled for Morrissey. Their frontman, Jamie Harding, later complained about this and was offered an option: put up with being regarded as second-best like any other Morrissey support, or leave the tour. They stayed.

For this tour, the ear-shattering squealings of Klaus Nomi had given way to the equally tuneless rendition of William Blake's 'Jerusalem', as delivered by the borstal boys in *The Loneliness Of The Long-Distance Runner*. The backdrop was a thuggish shot of Cornelius Carr – whose face also adorned the sleeve of the just-released midprice compilation album *World Of Morrissey*. Gone too were the diaphanous/samite/satin tops, replaced by the more serviceable but less flattering 1960s collectors' items Ben Sherman checks, which mostly stayed on during this tour. 'Compared to the pectoral majesty of his album cover on *Your Arsenal*, the singer kept his dark bumfreezer jacket on till the end,' observed the *Guardian*'s Pat Kane. 'It was eventually shrugged off in the surly manner of a reformed Chippendale.' The denims too were 'antiques' – dating from 1944 and costing a cool £2,000 a pair.

There was also another Morrissey first: complementing his new image, he was seen on and off the stage sporting an impressive collection of fighting 'injuries' – provided by his make-up lady, and which looked so realistic that many people meeting him thought that he really had been beaten up. 'Looking like a man who's thrown himself down the stairs of his Primrose Hill residence – a music-hall vision of a Victorian boxer,' was how *Vox* described the wealth of black eyes, split lips, bruises and scars. Morrissey however was the first to realise that by making himself appear overtly ridiculous, he had played straight into the hands of his detractors – telling Christian Fevret of *Les Inrockuptibles* when it was all over, 'At the time I considered those photographs very beautiful. Now, I don't know *what* to think.'

In Glasgow, Morrissey opened the show with 'Billy Budd', worked his way through most of the new album – a collection of mainly laddish B-sides, with nothing pre-1991 – and closed with The Smiths' 'Shoplifters Of The World Unite'. The next evening, in Motherwell, this 'blast from the past' was aborted halfway through due to an aggressive stage invasion, bringing the concert to an abrupt conclusion. 'Proactive and relentless, the stage-invading became a kind of theatre in its own right,' observed David Cavanagh of *Q*. Asked by Cavanagh why he had chosen a Smiths song to end with, Morrissey grandly responded, 'It's just as much mine as anyone else's. I wrote those words. It doesn't belong to some fictitious brickie from Rochdale. It actually belongs to *me*!' David Sinclair of *The Times* caught up with him on the road, and during their brief chat reminded him of what I had written in the preface to *Morrissey: Landscapes Of The Mind*: 'He is an authority on the human condition, quite probably the most influential entertainer of his generation.' 'If such a role is thrust upon me, I'll take it and stick it on the mantelpiece,' he replied, 'but I'm not really trying to be the Lord Mayor of Pop or anything like that.'

Craig McLean, who covered the trio of Scottish concerts (the third was in Edinburgh) for *Spectrum*, observed,

> Like any god, Morrissey has his disciples. Like any disciples, Morrissey's feel compelled to record their own gospel and spread the word. The fanzine culture that has sprung up around the arch-Hulmerist is an international industry. Their mutual love of one man is why they're all standing in a car park in Scotland in the middle of winter.

A major cause for concern amongst these fanzine editors was Jake's departure. Those who had a tough job managing their own lives believed that Morrissey was as weak as themselves, and therefore on the verge of breakdown. Others handled the situation in such a way that some readers actually believed Jake had died. The French *Lonely Planet Boy* printed the lyrics to 'I'd Love To', and a photograph of Morrissey sobbing at the edge of the stage. *Wilde About Morrissey* (USA) and *Drive Me Home* (Spain) included the lyrics to 'Sunny' – the latter alongside the head-on-lap shot from *Details*. Others printed black-edged pictures. *The Mighty Quiff* (Belgium) underscored the lines, 'With your jean-belt wrapped around your arm/And with a needle pressed onto tight skin.' Though photographs of Morrissey, taken by Jake, would appear on promotional material for a while longer, allegedly the singer now had a new companion – wisely, perhaps, kept out of public view for the duration of the tour.

Meanwhile, on 7 February, fans entering Sheffield's City Hall were handed leaflets – written by a former fanzine editor on behalf of the anti-fascist magazine *Searchlight*. Headed, 'Morrissey's Dirty Laundry', these detailed his non-existent political views and urged fans to boycott the concert; they ended up where they belonged, scattered across the theatre steps. The concert, introduced by an overweight Dockyard Doris lookalike drag queen, was filmed by James O'Brien – as was the one the next evening in Blackpool – and later released on a video, *Introducing Morrissey*. Not dissimilar to the earlier *Hulmerist*, the concert footage was interspersed with clips of the more 'interesting' Morrissey fans: Matt, a young skinhead who (in view of Jake's absence) was paid £150 to walk into Blackpool's Empress Ballroom with a copy of *World Of Morrissey* tucked under his arm. Then there was Libby, a pink-quiffed admirer filmed backstage at Birmingham's Aston Villa Centre on 11 February, holding aloft a card inscribed I BLAME YOU, while Morrissey posed on the couch behind her. I met Libby soon afterwards: the singer had autographed her arm, and she had had this tattooed over. 'It's a lasting reminder of the most important day of my life,' she said.

Morrissey went on to play Cambridge, Birmingham, Ilford, Portsmouth, Hull, Bradford, Ipswich (where he rattled a tambourine inscribed SHAG), Cardiff, Croydon and Brixton. At each venue, in addition to 'Jerusalem', he was introduced on stage by Gorecki's Third Symphony, a work composed as a eulogy to those who had died during the Warsaw Ghetto Uprising, which had effectively ended the Nazi occupation of Poland during World War II. This stunning piece, which had topped the British album charts in 1993, also closed the show. In Bradford, despite suffering from the flu and sweating profusely throughout his set, the performance was faultless. 'I'm afraid that I picked up something nasty in Hull,' he announced. When someone yelled, 'Who was it – Jake?' he sniggered and replied, 'Thank you, from the heart of my bottom!'

In Newcastle, on 17 February, there were problems with security, which Morrissey solved by yelling at the bouncers – bringing about a huge wave of fans who rushed the stage and knocked him off his feet. The tour ended in spectacular fashion at London's Theatre Royal Drury Lane on 26 February, where the concert was recorded and the guests included then Morrissey favourites Echobelly, Adam Ant, Blur, P J Harvey, The Pet Shop Boys, Gianfranco (the aforementioned gay porn star), my wife and myself. In terms of location, timing and sheer vocal brilliance, this undoubtedly was the finest moment in Morrissey's career: his Piaf at the Paris Olympia, his Judy at Carnegie Hall. He was in sparkling form.

Touts were selling tickets for £300 a pair – this was how much I was offered for my own in the royal box, organised by his manager. The support was McAlmont – to my way of thinking just a horrendous noise, which was why Jeanne and I headed back to the bar (missing Morrissey, who came up looking for us!) where we spent half an hour chatting to a 'displaced' musician who confessed that though he was looking forward to the show, he had no intention of meeting the man afterwards. 'The last time we met,' he added, 'Moz got so bloody mad, I thought he was going to deck me. But I still think there's nobody like him. Moz is like a drug. The more you take, the more you want, even though you know it's fucking you up!'

Tonight, Morrissey was more loquacious than ever. 'You can either be as playful as you like, or you can be your own boring self,' he announced before attacking a wild and nifty 'Spring-Heeled Jim', and he would not be disappointed. Taking advantage of the unusually relaxed security, and encouraged by a tuxedoed young man named Darren – pretending to be a security man – the stage was assailed by admirers. A leggy, leonine blonde hitched her flouncy red dress up to her thighs, wrapped these around Morrissey's middle and 'grabbed a handful'. A handshake with another female in the front row went purposely wrong and saw him all but dragged headfirst into the crowd. Emerging from this melée, minus his shirt and proudly flaunting an enviable, glistening physique, he slyly remonstrated, '*That* was *very* enjoyable!'

After 'The More You Ignore Me, The Closer I Get' there was more wit and a huge roar of approval when Morrissey pronounced, weighing each word cautiously as if wondering whether he would get away with a few deserved expletives, 'You may have noticed that I didn't get a BTI Award last week – and I was so *relieved*!' He was actually referring to the BRIT Award for Best British Male Singer, which had gone to Paul Weller. The previous year, Morrissey had received a *Q* Award for Best Songwriter and had commented during his acceptance speech, 'I would like to thank the people who have stood by me and bought the records over the years. It can't have been easy!' He did not, of course, need such over-hyped accolades – which outlived the recipient's popularity in the world of five-minute wonders – to prove his worth.

Although a not-unprecedented flurry of over-excitement from a group of fans (clambering on to the stage and almost flattening him) caused Morrissey to abandon ship seconds into his 'Shoplifters' finale, the climax to the evening had occurred earlier when, after 'The National Front Disco', Morrissey had performed 'Moon River' and stood stock-still throughout an astonishing seven minutes of multi-strobed, mind-blowing feedback – 'In silhouette, like a noble savage', Max Bell had enthused in the *Evening Standard*. Bathing majestically in the silvery spotlight, as he had all those years ago at the Eldorado, he reminded me of the tragic French actor Gérard Philipe in Alfred de Musset's *On Ne Badine Pas Avec L'Amour* – no mere 'savage' arrogantly savouring the love but, 36 years on, Perdican reborn.

In Newcastle, Morrissey had been interviewed by *Les Inrockuptibles'* Emmanuel Tellier – but only after the journalist had convinced security that he was there on official business. He told me:

That's the trouble with some of today's entertainers. They themselves are usually charming, but first of all one has to get past some of the horrid people who look after them. These people are often too big for their boots and end up giving the stars a bad name. Eventually, after some deliberation between this thug and Morrissey's hairdresser, I was escorted into his dressing room where the stench of vapour-rub was overpowering, almost unbearable. Morrissey looked white as a sheet. He could hardly stand. This was the face of a man close to death, yet the moment he stepped on to that stage, he seemed to shrug off his illness like an old shirt. The transformation was amazing!

The conversation centred around the forthcoming album, *Southpaw Grammar*, Morrissey's first for RCA now that his contract with EMI was almost expired. Work on this had already begun, in the South of France at the Miraval Studios. Pointing to the mock scar across the back of his hand, he declared, 'These new songs are tougher, more aggressive, frightening and disturbing than anything I've ever done before.' French footballer Eric Cantona had recently hit the headlines with his kung-fu attack on an abusive fan at Selhurst Park, resulting in a six-month ban from the game. Speaking of him as though he was a friend, which he was not, Morrissey said, 'There's no place for me in the pop world. I'm lonelier, lonelier than ever. The only person I feel close to is Cantona. I've so much compassion for him. He responded to aggression and if such a thing had happened in the street, no one would have been shocked. I understand Eric only too well. I'm the Cantona of rock!' Then, as if to make a point, Tellier recalled how he had shouted for his tambourine and scrawled CANTONA across the vellum in large letters. A few evenings later, the tambourine would be inscribed ERIC . . .

The non-obligatory British interview was granted to Stuart Maconie and appeared in the September issue of Q. Clearly by this time regarding himself as some sort of neo-Ronnie Kray figure – minus the actual violence, but besotted with thuggery, things tough, gangland duffers and 'bovver' boys – the heading to the piece this time was an atypically aggressive Morrissey quote: DO YOU FUCKIN' WANT SOME? The accompanying photographs, by Andy Earl, were in keeping with the new image: immaculately groomed as usual but sweaty with 'bruised' cheeks, fake slash marks across his forearm and the mock tattoo SOUTHPAW GRAMMAR, the words ENGLAND SWINGS 'carved' into his chest – alternatively posing in a collector's item Ben Sherman shirt, and an Eric Cantona T-shirt. The sub-heading was also his own: ON LIFE, DEATH & ANTHEA TURNER.

When asked the touchy question of why he had moved to RCA, Morrissey quipped, 'I was in the [EMI] building so often that I was surprised they didn't give me a janitor's bucket!' (Replying to the same question a few weeks later, posed by Christian Fevret of Les Inrockuptibles, he would less flippantly reply, 'Because I wanted to work under my own steam, without being told what to do all the time.') Of actor Hugh Grant's infamous oral sex episode on Sunset Boulevard, he professed of Grant's actress girlfriend – whose own career had taken off like a rocket as a result of the publicity – 'If I was Elizabeth Hurley and he hadn't done anything, I wouldn't stand by him. He's so overrated. All he seems to have is an English accent.' Liam Gallagher, the laddish lead singer with Oasis, regarded by some as 'yet another bunch of Smiths challengers', was dismissed with a gruff, 'Very runt of the litter. You can tell that he'd run off with the fillings from his grandmother's teeth, but that doesn't mean he doesn't love her.' Later, he would revise his opinion after meeting Liam and brother Noel in Australia: the newspapers, he declared, made people out to be monsters when in reality most of them were 'terribly sweet'.

Of the other show business names currently making the news, Morrissey was able to sympathise with Kurt Cobain over his suicide, but expressed only loathing towards the ever-smiling television presenter Anthea Turner, currently fronting *The National Lottery Live*. If *she* handed him a cheque for £20 million, he said, he would hand it back. 'That fixed smile, that fraudulent jollity,' he added. 'If she were telling you that a planeload of children had died in the worst Air India crash ever, she would *still* keep on smiling. Her happiness actually makes me depressed.' Next up were the stock attacks on 'elderly' rock stars, politicians, and a professed indifference towards wealth: 'You may be a billionaire, but if you contract cancer you may as well live in a bedsit in Birmingham – the poor remain poor. *Someone* has to work in Woolworths.' And of course, in keeping with this new Morrissey there was overt praise for Eric Cantona and the boxing ring.

Morrissey's interest in thuggery, of course, had always been there and evenly spread across the board – whether this had been his championing of murderers and gangland heroes, or lesser rapscallions such as rough trade, skinheads and big-headed sportsmen. 'My songs are but a reflection of life,' he had confessed to *Les Inrockuptibles*. This passion for the tougher, seamier side of life reached its zenith in August 1995 with the release of *Southpaw Grammar*, generally regarded as one of Morrissey's poorer albums, though any successor would have been hard put to supersede *Your Arsenal* and *Vauxhall And I*. Paul du Noyer commented in *Mojo*, 'If only Morrissey's tunes were as good as his titles, he would be the Burt Bacharach of his generation.' Housed in a sleeve featuring a long-forgotten boxer named Kenny Lane, the album reached number 4 in the charts, but dropped out of the best-sellers list after just three weeks. Many fans and most of the critics accused Morrissey of short-changing them by including just eight songs – two of these running in excess of ten minutes. This problem might have been avoided had he, say, waited a little longer and added some of the songs that were subsequently relegated to B-sides – though one, 'Whatever Happened To Love?', appears to have disappeared altogether.

A superb song recorded at around this time was 'Swallow On My Neck', one of the B-sides (the other was the lacklustre 'Black-Eyed Susan') of the 'Sunny' single. One of the best *chansons-propres* Morrissey ever wrote sets out to be a hymn to self-outing: 'I have been smashed again with the man from the Old Valhalla Road crematorium,' adding, 'He drew a swallow on my neck . . . and soon everyone knew.' This had the more impressionable fans, the ones who had sacrificed their quiffs for 'Jake' haircuts, rushing to the nearest tattoo parlour, not always aware of the motif's gay implications: Marc Almond had a tattooed swallow on his neck, and Morrissey sports a mock one on the *Vauxhall And I* sleeve. The fact that this little masterpiece was actually left off the album almost constitutes a crime. Paul Goddard of *Grooves*, for whom Morrissey could do no wrong, gave the new album a very definite thumbs-down:

> Once upon a time This Charming Man had us all Reeling Around The Fountain with admiration. We thought his talent was a Light That Never Goes Out and we were wrong. These days, The World Won't Listen – and of the evidence of this, who can blame us? To borrow a baseball term, Bigmouth Strikes Again!

'*Southpaw Grammar* is the school of hard knocks,' Morrissey had told Stuart Maconie, 'it's coming up the hard way and taking your bruises with you.' The cynics, of course, were quick in pointing out that 'southpaw' meant fighting with the left hand – and in gay parlance, 'batting for the other side'. The opening track, 'The Teachers Are Afraid Of The Pupils', has as its central theme Shostakovich's Fifth Symphony, therefore brevity would be deemed inappropriate. Morrissey had certainly done his homework. The great Russian composer, himself castigated for his views (accused by the Communist Party of having anti-democratic tendencies) and a chronic depressive on account of this, had composed the piece in 1937, giving it the subtitle, 'In Answer To Just Criticism'. It had re-established his reputation in the Soviet Union, and like the later Gorecki piece was a firm favourite amongst pacifists. Morrissey's lyric was effectively a complete volte-face from 'The Headmaster Ritual' in that, whereas teachers had once been allowed to discipline their charges and had frequently gone too far, nowadays they were virtually prohibited from disciplining them at all, resulting in classroom anarchy. In Morrissey's schooldays, as in my own, the maxim had been, 'Don't tell your father you got a clout from the teacher, otherwise *he'll* clout you harder!' Now, no matter what the child has done, the riposte from the parents is, 'Say the wrong thing to our children, and we'll have you!' And the teacher, hinting at retirement or perhaps even driven to the point of suicide by all of this, can only opine, 'To be finished would be a relief!' The phrase, however, was double-edged, as Morrissey explained to *Les Inrockuptibles*: 'On a more intimate level, it's about my life and career. Going away would effectively be a relief – no longer feeling the pressure, being allowed to breathe a little more freely.'

The criticism continues in 'Reader Meet Author', a bouncy attack against biographers, and more specifically Johnny Rogan and some members of the music press who, according to the narrator, fail to scratch beneath the surface of their subjects – a point that all reputable biographers would fervently disagree with! It also contains a rare silly line from Morrissey, 'You don't know a thing about their lives/Books don't save them, books aren't Stanley knives.'

The next, much better track on the album – 'The Boy Racer' – is reminiscent of Edith Piaf's 'L'Homme A La Moto', the inspiration behind Twinkle's 'Terry'. It returns the singer to the more familiar territory of gay fetishism. 'Morrissey as the man in the mac', is how *Select* described it. 'He thinks he's got the whole world in his hands, stood at the urinal,' Morrissey declares, confessing his jealousy of the beautiful, Brandoesque youth who has too much money, too many girlfriends. Then he vehemently concludes, indicating that if he cannot have the young man then no one will, 'I'm gonna kill him, he's just too good looking.' Earlier, Stuart Maconie had asked Morrissey, leaving the most personal question until last – as others had done so as not to jeopardise the interview – 'Do *you* ever stand in front of the urinal and think you've got the whole world in your hands?' The gentle reprimand had been, 'I don't need to walk to the urinal. I already know. And *you* should know better than to ask.'

One of Morrissey's musicians told me, 'Two of the new songs were Mozza's way of getting Jake out of his system, once and for all.' In 'Best

Friend On The Payroll', Morrissey gives no indication as to who pampered whom – 'More breakfast in bed, and I'll bring the paper in later' – but he is very firm when declaring, 'No, it's not gonna work out.' In 'The Operation' he laments, 'You fight with your right hand and caress with your left hand . . . sad to say how once I was in love with you.' Before we hear this, however, we are party to the most thrilling chunk of percussion work in any Morrissey recording since Andrew Paresi's contribution to *Kill Uncle* – two and a half minutes described by *Mojo* as, 'Like waking up with a hangover, stumbling out of bed for some Paracetamol and discovering the Boys Brigade are marching through your kitchen, while the Orange Lodge are coming in from the lounge.' 'Jake started off as a very nice guy,' the aforementioned musician told me, 'but he took his position far too seriously. It went to his head. He became bossy. I guess that's why he had to go.'

The most engaging song on the album is 'Dagenham Dave', a brief tale of envy brought about by suppressed homosexuality, the saga of the loveable Essex rogue (thought to be a rare Morrissey-friendly music journalist) who walks through the streets, 'Head in the clouds, with a mouth full of pie' – and who has transfers of his girlfriends' names on his windscreen, possibly to fool his friends. This, however, is a Morrissey song and as such the veil is soon torn aside to reveal how, 'He'd love to touch, but he's afraid he might self-combust.' By comparison, the album's closing tracks, 'Do Your Best And Don't Worry' and 'Southpaw' were, according to the majority of critics and fans, lyrically dull for an artiste of Morrissey's standing.

The launch party for *Southpaw Grammar* took place at England football coach Terry Venables' Kensington nightclub, Scribes West – the sleeve of 'Dagenham Dave' has an unflattering shot of Venables with his tongue sticking out, taken in 1964 when he was a twenty-year-old striker. As for the guest of honour, Morrissey was conspicuous by his absence – he claimed because he had wished to avoid the 'undesirables' from the music press who had been invited against his wishes.

As had happened with his previous album, there were near-hysterical in-store signings: the Virgin Megastores in Dublin and Belfast, and the huge FNAC under the shadow of Paris' Montparnasse Tower, which saw

Morrissey travelling through the very Chunnel he had so often vowed would cave in. Here, thousands of fans were in attendance for what *France-Soir* called, 'A papal visit without the purple robes.' Some had jetted in from Japan, Australia and the United States – dossing down in shop doorways, sleeping in parks, going without sustenance for a twenty-hour wait in a seemingly endless queue, a rushed embrace, and thirty seconds of their idol's time. One couple from Canada told of how they had remortgaged their house to raise the funds for this particular trip! The tattoo parlours around the rue de Rennes also reported good business, working over the various slogans and scribblings on arms, shoulders and hearts. There was also a new breed of fanatic, an adherent of the faction that had attempted to trash Morrissey's name a few years earlier in Chicago. Nicknamed 'The Girl Racer' for obvious reasons – the theory being that if *she* could not have Morrissey, then no one else would – this young American woman had begun by bombarding Morrissey with expensive gifts, including jewellery and a Cartier wristwatch. 'The gifts became so costly,' bassist Johnny Bridgewood said, 'Moz thought it wouldn't be right to accept any more.' This was the same fan who had been searched at Drury Lane after she had boasted to another fan that she had been carrying a knife. One of the FNAC employees told me,

> We were told of an incident outside Morrissey's dressing room, when this woman had become hysterical and threatening after he had refused to see her. It wasn't his fault she'd used up her savings to fly out for a handshake. His management were terrified that she might turn out to be some female Mark Chapman, so as soon as she was pointed out to us, we collared her and escorted her out of the store. She was extremely abusive and lucky not to have been handed over to the police.

Christian Fevret and Emmanuel Tellier of *Les Inrockuptibles* were party to what may now be regarded as Morrissey's most portentous interview. Under the heading, 'My Bitch Of A Life', he appeared on the cover of the magazine's 6 September issue – photographed by Eric

Mulet 'en pleine crannerie' ['in full swagger'], squatting between two huge, slobbering Rottweilers. Time and time again these journalists had proved that they could be trusted to quote his comments verbatim. He explained why he had dispensed with the services of his high-flying American manager, Arnold Stiefel: 'He organised a series of concerts in New York which sold out like lightning. Unfortunately, he forgot to check if I was free to do them. That's one of the great regrets of my life, that I've never had anyone intelligent enough to represent me. Such a person doesn't exist.' What he did not add was that these concerts had been at the city's most prestigious venue, Carnegie Hall, and that – whether or not it was true that Stiefel hadn't checked with Morrissey first – cancelling such engagements for any reason other than sudden death invariably led to the doors of other major American establishments being unceremoniously slammed in faces.

On a personal level, such gaffes aside, Morrissey was this time truly seen to be wearing his heart on his sleeve. No British journalist would have got away with asking him if he held his parents responsible for his permanent state of sadness! His mother, he confessed, had been forced to contend with his 'unsatisfied state' for years. 'She would love to see me happy and in full bloom,' he added. 'Therefore she can't be blamed for the way I am.' The mere mention of his father's name, however, brought an adverse reaction. Emmanuel Tellier told me, 'He turned very pale and grimaced. Then he signalled for me to switch off the microphone. The silence was crippling. I could have pursued the subject, but we both respected his feelings too much to even try.'

In this interview, Morrissey spoke of his desire to form another relationship. He had written 'Now My Heart Is Full' when there had been love in his life, and now he was alone again, though strangely at peace within himself. One of the problems associated with finding someone, he said, was that would-be suitors were always too much in awe of him to let themselves go. Another fault lay with himself: he spent too much of his time arguing with people, he could be just as cruel towards women as he could towards men, he was ever on the alert. Also, he added, he was surrounded by people who thought solely of their own agenda and never tried to understand *him*. He concluded, seemingly finding it no longer necessary to conceal his light under the proverbial bushel:

> It's become, as it were, impossible to meet someone profoundly generous, someone capable of offering his feelings, his emotions. Most of the people I meet always say the same things. And what's the point of seeing people if you know *exactly* what they're going to say, if every move's premeditated and regulated by rules?

This, of course, was a classic malady of the superstar loner: because they are so big, because they rarely settle for anything less than having all their own way, they render themselves feared and unattainable – they needlessly put themselves through the mill and actually enjoy the process, they spend much of their lives alone, and inevitably die likewise. Emotionally and psychologically, Morrissey fitted into the same bracket as Garland, Piaf and any number of post-war torch singers whose lives were lived in the full glare of the media and the public. He might easily have shared a theme song with Judy: 'The Man That Got Away'. When asked about long-term relationships – the enemy of the torch singer in that, if lasting love is found and all the soul-searching stops, the performances themselves have no meaning – he responded, 'If such a relationship was a reality for me, it would no longer be fascinating. I'm drawn towards what I can't have. Accessible things are of no interest to me. If I find calm and serenity, doubtless you would never see me again. That would be the end of my career.'

Morrissey was also by now utterly obsessed with violence. 'It's a macabre fascination,' he told *Les Inrockuptibles*. 'It's *not* a hobby of mine, and I wish it would go away. But for me, violence is a daily part of my routine. People treat me like I'm abnormal, and *that's* also the beginning of violence.' But, his interviewers wanted to know, had Morrissey ever met the woman of his dreams? His response was suitably acerbic, but honest:

> More often than not I've met the woman of my *nightmares*. *Most* women are nightmares, physically and mentally. There again, I was

never very interested. Even as a child I found it easier to fall in love with photographs. I find the whole idea of attraction embarrassing, whether it's attraction towards a man or a woman. So if I bump into someone I find attractive, I flee in the other direction. What's the point in telling him you think he's attractive when you know it's never going to work out? I get those kind of letters from some fans, but if they ever found out what I was *really* like, they'd soon refrain from desiring me.

Emmanuel Tellier put to Morrissey that, as a handsome, healthy 36-year-old male he must get sexual urges. How, therefore, did he control these?

I don't have that many. Honestly! I have no sex life, therefore I don't *get* urges . . . and whenever the hormones start to manifest, I have a shave! I've never known sexual satisfaction, but right now I *want* to have a sex life, to find out what it's *like* to feel satisfied. I'm working at it! It's my greatest wish!

Like William Shaw of *Details*, Emmanuel Tellier had observed the Morrissey–Jake body language. He told me, 'When they were together, Morrissey looked happy, like a child on Christmas morning. But there was something about Jake. He was a very polite young man, but his mannerisms were too affected for my liking. Somehow I was given the impression that he was more attracted to the celebrity and all that went with it than he was to the man himself.' For the benefit of his readers who might not have known, Tellier therefore asked, 'When was the last time you were in love?' Jake is said to have been upset by the response, 'Very recently, but it wasn't the real thing – more like a kind of dream. He was solid and real enough, but our love affair was impossible.'

A few weeks after this interview, Morrissey announced that he would be augmenting David Bowie's Outsiders tour at the end of the year – not on equal billing, but as Bowie's support. Dates were scheduled for London, Birmingham, Belfast, Dublin, Exeter, Cardiff, Aberdeen, Glasgow, Sheffield, Manchester and Newcastle – an 'unlucky' thirteen shows, most of these not in the smaller, more intimate venues Morrissey preferred, but in the impersonal arenas he had always sworn he would never set foot in. The term VERY SPECIAL GUEST was used in the publicity material, but only Bowie's photograph appeared on playbills, therefore it is not difficult to imagine the response from fans of both camps, who predicted a mighty clashing of egos and a fight to the death for artistic supremacy between these undisputed icons of differing generations.

The music press – no real surprise here – labelled Morrissey 'Bowie's underdog' from Day One. So why, then, did he agree to do the tour in the first place when he was well aware that he would be positioning himself for the music press's most vitriolic attack since Finsbury Park? 'He wanted to give his enemies a good kick in the balls,' one of his closest friends informed me. 'It's like the John Major thing. You know, when the PM decided to resign so that he'd be re-elected, more powerful than ever? That's how Moz sees himself.'

Morrissey's victory over the 'adversary' he had elected to take on, to prove a point, would prove almost tragically pyrrhic.

On the eve of the tour he was interviewed for the *Observer* by Will Self, a gravel-voiced, towering six-foot-six presence, and photographed in intense close-up by one of Britain's most eminent photographers, Jane Bown: the result was a candid, beautiful image of an attractive, pensive young man whose penetrating gaze bespeaks a mélange of wisdom and mocking wit, the faint lines of stress just starting to show, along with the odd grey hair, which gave him a look of Byronesque distinction. 'Life finds Morrissey in mature mode,' Self observed. 'Has the boy outsider become an adult and joined the rest of the human race?'

Aware of Self's reputation, like Julie Burchill, of being a law unto himself in the journalistic world, Morrissey got in the first punch by telling him, 'You've actually got the face of a criminal I've met.' Self had his own way of interpreting this. Describing his subject as 'very attractive in the flesh' he asked his readers, 'Is this a man tortured by his own sexuality and that of others? His body language is far from craven. Setting aside the context of this remark, it struck me that this was not the sort of thing that someone intent on denying corporality would be likely to say.' However, when Self broached the subject of Morrissey's so-called 'vexed sexuality' he was very quickly put in his place: 'It doesn't vex *me*. I don't exactly think it vexes other people. I don't think people *assume* anything any more about me. I'm sort of classified in a non-sexual, asexual way, which is an air of dismissiveness which I quite like.' Self summarised this by quoting Oscar Wilde: 'Celibacy is the only known sexual perversion.'

From sexuality, the natural progression for Self seemed to be – via linking the singer with campology and Kenneth Williams – whether or not Morrissey wanted children. This was no doubt a sly way of asking him (from a man who reprimanded a *Gay Times* reporter, ten years later, with the comment, 'I'm not *that* straight!') if he liked sleeping with women, and anticipating some remarkable confession. The response was a variation on the one he had given to *Details* a few years earlier, 'What happens when your child turns around and says, "Look, I don't like this world. Why did you bring me into it?" ' – enabling Self to draw his own conclusion:

> I get the feeling that these kinds of sallies are a form of bluff for Morrissey, and that he throws them out in much the way that aircraft in World War II dropped strips of metal to fool radar. If his interlocutors rise to such chaff, then they're not really worthy of consideration. But he's also adept at side-stepping the conventional psychoanalyst thrusts of the interviewer . . . He is responsible – among other things – for encapsulating two hundred years of philosophical speculation in a single line: 'Does the body rule the mind or does the mind rule the body? I don't know.' He told me he could 'do anything'. I certainly hope he does. England needs him.

The tour opened on 14 November with the first of four concerts at the Wembley Arena. Ticket sales had been poor on account of the prices: two top-notch stars did not come cheap, and fans found themselves paying twice as much to get in as they had earlier in the year. Even so, with the same musicians and Cornelius Carr backdrop, Morrissey easily proved that despite the 'stiff competition' he was still a force to be reckoned with. The *Independent*'s Ryan Gibney described this opener as, 'His most startling performance in years, launching himself at the songs like an Exocet missile.' Will Self, invited to the show, went a step further, writing in the *Observer*, 'The band crashes into the opening chords of "Reader Meet Author", and Morrissey begins to flail at the air with the cord of his microphone, pirouetting, hip-swivelling for all the world like some camp version of Roy Rogers.'

Yet behind the bravado of verve, vigour and general bonhomie there lurked much apprehension, particularly when he drawled after this first song, 'Good evening, we are your support group.' He also looked tense towards the end of his set, the first time since The Smiths' early days that he had been officially listed second fiddle on any bill, when in an attempt to silence the Bowie hecklers he announced, 'Don't worry, we won't stay *too* long!' – before flinging himself into 'Dagenham Dave'. Manuel Rios of the Spanish *Drive Me Home* fanzine witnessed the spectacle from the front of the half-full auditorium. He told me,

> Morrissey *looked* great, in a designer suit and plain shirt. Along with his medallion, his bracelet, his whiskers, his ring and such a cool band behind him, he looked like somebody in a Tarantino film – that is, a sort of gangster. His singing was brilliant, but he seemed *bored* at times and the atmosphere was far from being what it usually is. And you know just how essential that is for his performances.

The non-gutter press were generally sympathetic, but almost certainly contributed to Morrissey's burdening neurasthenia and, looking back on the period, his encroaching breakdown. David Bowie's performances were not up to his standard, either, and saw large sections of the audience walking out on him along with the Morrissey fans. 'Next to Bowie, Morrissey is a parochial pleasure, but at least he has a coherent sense of himself,' observed Roy Wilkinson of *Select*, 'and the rousing "Now My Heart Is Full" that comes at the end of the Moz set is a more affecting evocation of *The Long Day Closing* than all of Bowie's *fin de siècle* poltroonery.'

Tristan, of *The Mighty Quiff* fanzine, was more direct, saying, 'Most of us who stayed to watch Bowie fell asleep.' David Sinclair reported in *The Times* how Bowie had emerged from behind the drumkit:

> Singing and walking as if in his sleep . . . the show seemed mired in a joyless aesthetic. Poor Morrissey. He sang well enough, but performing too early, on a borrowed stage to someone else's cold audience, the man with the rapidly thinning quiff fell flat as a pancake. It is hard to imagine Morrissey putting up with this level of indifference for the whole of a lengthy tour.

The Outsiders fiasco chugged around the circuit, and at each venue the response from the media and fans was the same. Then on 29 November, only minutes before he was due to go on stage at the Aberdeen Exhibition Centre, Morrissey was taken ill in his dressing room and the audience were told, in lieu of his performance, that Bowie's would be brought forward. The next day, some of the tabloids ran stories of a supposed backstage bust-up between the two singers, while Morrissey 'insiders' fed the music press with a variety of fabricated stories. The truth was, Morrissey had been driven to the city's privately run St John's Hospital, where a few days later his condition was explained to me – as much as was permitted, anyway – by an off-the-record spokesman:

> Yes, it's potentially serious. That's why we're expecting to keep him under very close observation over the next few weeks. But as you know, Mr Morrissey is a strong, hefty laddie, and we have every confidence that he'll make a splendid recovery.

It was rumoured that he had a complete mental breakdown and friends felt it was too much for him. Kirsty MacColl told me, 'He should never have done that tour, Morrissey is far too great a star to be supporting one of the rock dinosaurs he's persistently slagging off.'

Whatever the cause of his condition, within the week, apparently ignoring the advice of doctors and friends but promising to take care of himself, Morrissey discharged himself from hospital. Everyone expected him to recuperate at home for several weeks, then rejoin the Outsiders tour's European leg, scheduled to begin in Lyons on 11 February 1996. He had absolutely no intention of further humiliating himself, however, and is thought to have personally made up for any losses and refunds. For some time now, despite the horrors with security the first time around, he had been wanting to return to Japan. Accompanied by the companion who had got him through the worst of his illness, he flew to Tokyo for a 'stationary' tour – four concerts in different Tokyo halls (Shinjuku, Kawasaki, Ebisu, Tokyo Bay) on 13, 14, 16 and 17 December. Each was a sell-out, there were no problems with security, and the sojourn appears to have done him more good than any psychiatrist's probing, enabling him a swift return to normality. He even managed a few words of Japanese between songs! Then he flew home, hopeful of placing the anguish of the last two months behind him. And to what seemed like semi-retirement . . .

8

I Will Live My Life As I Will Undoubtedly Die . . .

'I do feel I'd be disappointed if I got to fifty. It would show a lack of resolve, or something.'

– Morrissey

Andy Rourke, Mike Joyce and Craig Gannon, despite the hysterical ambience of Morrissey's 'rebirth' at Wolverhampton in 1988, had for years claimed that he and Johnny Marr owed them money. In March 1989 – with *Viva Hate* selling like hot cakes around the world – Stephen Street took out an injunction on Morrissey's single 'Interesting Drug', preventing its release until his particular financial beef with the singer had been settled. Prior to this, Rourke and Joyce had been told by Morrissey and Marr that they were not entitled to the quarter-share of Smithdom they had demanded (extant of songwriting royalties) because the group, contractually, had not extended beyond Morrissey and Marr. The two of them had been told they were each legally entitled to 40 per cent of mechanical royalties (revenues largely from record sales), which left the remaining 20 per cent to be shared by Rourke and Joyce – and by Gannon when he had tagged along. Hoping to resolve the situation, Morrissey and Marr had proposed an 'ideal solution' – 10 per cent of the group's general royalties. This had been rejected and the pair threatened with legal action. The royalties war would rage for years, seriously threatening Morrissey's reputation, though in the dew-kissed eyes of the fans he could have committed mass murder and still been put forward for beatification.

'The Fifth Smith', Craig Gannon, had been the first to take the plunge, challenging the might of Morrissey during 1986's autumn of discontent. Gannon had been fired from the group not just because he had accused Morrissey and Marr of under-paying him during The Smiths' last American tour, but because, he claimed, they had short-changed him by not paying him co-writing royalties for 'Ask'. A few years later – hypocritically perhaps, because he had worked with Morrissey in the interim period – Gannon took the matter to court and won. Denouncing the case as 'heartbreaking, deeply sad and an outrage of public justice', a somewhat smug Morrissey told *Vox*'s Len Brown in November 1993, 'Everybody involved knew he didn't have a leg to stand on yet, through some perversion of justice, he walked away with £42,000 . . . but my opinion is that Craig Gannon didn't really win because he's still Craig Gannon. Ha ha!'

On 3 December 1996 the *Daily Mail* – whom Morrissey had once suggested might publish a photograph of Prince Charles wearing his mother's wedding veil – ran the headline, 'Smith Versus Smith'. After almost a decade, Mike Joyce was taking his former 'employers' to the cleaners. The accusation: Morrissey and Marr had, he claimed, 'swindled' him out of thousands of pounds.

His was a lone stance. In 1989, Andy Rourke had accepted an out-of-court settlement of £83,000, plus 10 per cent of The Smiths' future mechanical royalties. Even so, he was summoned to give evidence. Joyce's lawyers estimated that, in view of the recent abundance of Smiths re-releases, his client was entitled to at least £1 million – along with a full 25 per cent of future mechanical royalties.

There were many who thought Joyce might have been on to a hiding over nothing. The press were reminded of Morrissey's interview with *NME*'s Danny Kelly in June 1985, when Kelly had asked, with regard to Morrissey and Johnny Marr's perception of the other group members, 'You must be aware that the drone Smiths seem like session men?'

Morrissey had replied, apparently without the slightest hint of malice, 'Yes, but I positively know that they're not as upset about it as people think they should be . . . they have their position and they know what it is. We all have our roles. We all know our limitations.'

In Berlin, during the spring of 1991, *NME*'s Stuart Maconie had asked Morrissey, quite likely with Joyce in mind, 'Do you love your enemies?' – bringing the Machiavellian response, 'I *sympathise* – and then I arrange to have their heads kicked in. I *do* have friends in high places. Tower Hamlets, for instance.'

More recently, there had been Morrissey's self-righteous outburst to the *Observer*'s Robert Chalmers: 'I believe that if Andy Rourke and Mike Joyce had had another singer, they would have gotten no further than Salford Shopping Centre.' 'He almost *spat* that out,' Chalmers told me. Joyce had since bumped into Morrissey, demanded an explanation, and in lieu of 'chinning' him had accepted an invitation to go for a drink. Subsequently, Morrissey had come up with the excuse that he had been 'misquoted' – not possible with Chalmers who, as I know from personal experience, tapes everything to ensure there is no comeback.

The London High Court hearing lasted seven days, and did Morrissey few favours, for here he was subjected to criticism not from educationally challenged music press journalists, but from a wily, no-nonsense QC, Nigel Davis, and Mr Justice Weeks, who was not in the least interested in trying to 'decipher' some of his Wildean phrases. Indeed, both are alleged to have never heard of Morrissey or The Smiths until preparing for the case.

The proceedings opened with QC Davis explaining to the court how Morrissey and Marr had persistently denied that Mike Joyce had been a partner in their company, Smithdom Ltd – until November 1995, when they had offered him £273,000, which he had refused, preferring to sort out the matter legally. While The Smiths had been in existence, no formal contract had ever been drawn up about the sharing of profits; neither had there been any verbal agreement to do this. It was avowed that Joyce had been sent a copy of the company's accounts in July 1986, but that with no knowledge of figures, and trusting Morrissey and Marr, he had shoved this into a drawer without even looking at it.

QC Davis added that Joyce had subsequently showed this to a friend who had a knowledge of accountancy, and that after taking advice from this friend, he had decided to take the matter further. Neither Morrissey nor Marr attended the first day of the hearing, but QC Davis explained to the court how Morrissey had described Joyce and Rourke as 'mere session musicians as readily replaceable as the parts in a lawnmower'. He summarised,

> Mr Joyce says he is entitled to 25 per cent of income, deriving from the group's activities, except for activities of songwriting. Mr Morrissey and Mr Marr say he is only entitled to 10 per cent. Mr Joyce never agreed to 10 per cent. On the contrary, he thought he was getting 25 per cent. Morrissey and Marr place the greatest possible emphasis on how much more important they were to the group. They had the highest profile so far as the public were concerned, but it would seem that they would go further and claim they are much more talented. They seek to downplay the importance of Joyce and Rourke. It was Mr Joyce's perception throughout that all the real decisions were made by Morrissey and Marr. In particular, the financial decisions were made by Morrissey. Mr Joyce was happy to do so because he trusted them. Morrissey now seeks to disparage Mr Joyce and Mr Rourke by saying they were mere session musicians.

Morrissey and Marr's effective undoing, so far as QC Davis was concerned, was that in offering Mike Joyce a large sum of money the previous year, they were admitting that there had been at least a verbal partnership agreement. At once, public sympathy was on the side of the apparent underdog. In the 8 December issue of the *Sunday Times*, John Dugdale denounced Morrissey as 'an insecure miserablist' and called Joyce, 'An innocent who has apparently idolised the songwriting duo,' adding, 'He had the great attraction of doormat-like docility. Until last week, that is.'

Not all the subsequent sessions were open to the press, allegedly because 'personal accusations and comments were in danger of being levelled by one side or the other'. So far as is known, Morrissey made just the one appearance in court, looking every inch the star – immaculately dressed and groomed like a Hollywood matinee idol of yesteryear, smiling shyly. What was said is on file, accessible, but under embargo and not always pleasant. One of the few snippets released to the press was Morrissey's admission that he had 'kept back' almost £500,000 in royalties because, he said, the other group members 'weren't interested in business'. He and Johnny Marr sat close to each other for the first time in over nine years. When the question arose that Mike Joyce should have studied the Smithdom accounts sheet before assigning it to a drawer, QC Davis declared that even if he had, it would have been too complicated for him to comprehend. When Mr Justice Weeks reached his verdict on 11 December, Morrissey, surprisingly, was not in court, though he was closely informed of the outcome by his solicitor. Joyce won his case. In his summing up, Mr Justice Weeks delivered his assessment of the four group members, working his way downwards:

> Morrissey, the oldest and more assertive member of the group, held the purse-strings. He and Marr signed the accounts on behalf of The Smiths. Morrissey was more complicated and did not find giving evidence easy or a happy experience. He was devious, truculent and unreliable when his own interests were at stake. Marr was a more engaging, reasonable character, probably the most intelligent of the four, but seemed to be willing to embroider his evidence to the point where he became less credible. Joyce and Rourke impressed me as straightforward and honest, unintellectual and certainly not financially sophisticated or aware.

The cost to Morrissey and Marr would be phenomenal: as Mike Joyce's lawyer had predicted, £1 million plus interest dating back to the spring of 1983 to come out of their own pockets, along with costs in excess of £250,000. Johnny Marr, snapped leaving the court ashen-faced, declined to comment. Morrissey's solicitor issued a statement on his behalf, 'I am disappointed and surprised at the Judge's decision, particularly given the weight of evidence against Mike Joyce. I will be considering the terms of the judgement with my solicitors to assess possible grounds for an appeal.' Joyce told a hastily assembled press-conference outside the court, 'This was never about money. It will not change my lifestyle, but it will secure the future for my wife and children. I still have the highest regard for Morrissey and Johnny, but I always knew ten years ago when I started this action that I would win. And I always believed that I was an equal partner with The Smiths.'

The newspaper headlines the next day unanimously contained the words 'devious' and 'truculent' (Morrissey claimed the latter word had been spray-painted across his mother's front door), along with some variations of The Smiths' song title, 'Heaven Knows I'm Miserable Now'. Almost all of the accompanying photographs were of Morrissey: of the national dailies, only the *Guardian* published one of Johnny Marr.

For a man who could probably win any battle with words, revenge should have been sweet. In the wake of the Joyce affair, Morrissey penned a song that makes one shudder and sympathise with the badly-done-to drummer – not for winning the case, but for being apparently so loathed as to have become the central subject of 'Sorrow Will Come In The End', a tremendous piece of theatricality so barbed in its attack that, next to it, 'Margaret On The Guillotine' and '*The Queen Is Dead*' seem like nursery rhymes. A spokesman for Island Records told me, 'Mozza was informed, "Sing *that*, and you'll end up doing time!" So he tried to get round the problem by *speaking* it!' Even so, the song was banned from appearing on the *Maladjusted* album and is unlikely to ever be released in Britain. In brief, the song's narrator – who has recently lost a court case – wishes a hex on his oppressor, concluding the piece with the foreboding lines, 'I'm gonna get you . . . You think you've won. Oh, no!' Beastly, but brilliant.

Against a force more powerful than himself – justice – Morrissey was a poor loser, though being relieved of a half-share of £1.25 million arguably would have sent anyone over the top. Johnny Marr settled his debt promptly, but Morrissey lodged an appeal, and in April 2003 – using the newly founded *Word* as his sounding-board – he launched a blistering attack on Mike Joyce, listing a catalogue of the drummer's supposed calumnies. According to Morrissey, not sure how to actually get the damages he had been awarded, Joyce had taken to turning up at the stage-door after Morrissey's concerts to ask for money. On top of this, claiming that Joyce had put a charge on his only British assets – his mother's and sister's houses – he scathed, 'He is a purely evil person and he has persecuted my mother, my sister and my nephews, but he presents the public face of a person who's hard done-by and has been thrown to the wayside.'

Morrissey then went off on a tangent, proclaiming how benevolent he and Johnny Marr had been to their former protégé: Marr was alleged to have designed Joyce's drum patterns for him; Joyce had never had to attend business meetings, or even fill in his own tax returns. The supreme accusation, however, was that the court had only sided with Mike Joyce in the first place because Mr Justice Weeks had been 'primed' on Morrissey's character through his former press attacks on the Queen and Margaret Thatcher! 'It's likely that Thatcher had appointed the judge,' he concluded, 'so I was not a very sympathetic character, whereas Joyce was playing the part of the wounded soldier.'

Mike Joyce was either not asked, or denied any attempt to defend these accusations, doubtless because the appeal was close at hand and prudence of the essence. The hearing took place on 22 July 1998. Morrissey lost and immediately lodged a re-appeal.

To date, Mike Joyce is apparently still waiting for Morrissey's portion of the settlement, and in June 2004, ironically speaking to *Word*'s Andrew Harrison, seemed distressed that he might not receive a penny in the wake of Morrissey's having transferred most of his business affairs to the United States. And finally he was offered a platform for his grievances, enabling him to deny Morrissey's claims of the previous year. 'I've got a fair claim on Morrissey's own property and he owes me a lot of money,' he declared, 'but I don't want to throw anyone out of their house.'

It seems unlikely that Morrissey will refrain from denouncing his former drummer at every opportunity – besides 'Sorrow Will Come In The End', at least two Morrissey songs have been 'dedicated' to Mike Joyce. As Kirsty MacColl had said to me some years earlier, 'As a friend, Morrissey is one hell of a guy. But as an enemy – well, you wouldn't want to know.'

*

In July 1998, at the time of Morrissey's appeal against the £1.25 million judgement awarded to Mike Joyce, many of his so-called peers (who had and always would pale in the shadow of his sun) regarded Morrissey as a redundant enigma. He had no record contract. For whatever reason he had hardly ever been capable of holding on to a manager. His 'downfall', it was said, was the result of almost paranoid perfectionism, a mercurial temperament – and greed, the fact that he reputedly would not consider any recording contract under $2 million.

Even so large a sum should have been chickenfeed for any major company to have one of Britain's biggest ever stars on their books – one of almost twenty years' standing who, unlike the Justin Timberlakes and Britney Spears of the fickle pop world, was no here-today-gone-tomorrow sensation. However, because he had always been against the 'down-your-throat' publicity such acts attracted – the tabloids' and weekend supplements' tittle-tattle about their sex-lives, which in any case would have caused him and his clandestine coterie of companions untold grief – most record companies did not know quite how to market him. Such a problem, of course, could have easily been resolved, with decent media advertising and his fair share of airplay. Subsequently, his last album had been largely left to chance: the fans had bought it out of loyalty and force of habit, but there had been few fresh recruits to the Morrissey fan base as had happened with its predecessors.

Then there was the rumour that struck a chill in the hearts of his admirers: Morrissey did not want to go on singing and end up a 'rock relic'. In the spring of 1988, when Shaun Phillips of *Sounds* had spoken to him after a Shirley Bassey concert and posed the question, 'You'll be taking the Shirley Bassey route to stardom, then?' he had exclaimed, 'Good heavens, that means that I'll have to stay alive for another twenty-two years. Could you imagine that? It's a ghastly thought – all those Christmas Morecambe and Wise shows?' On a much more serious note was the rumour from one source very close to Morrissey that he planned to die at 46, like his idol Oscar Wilde.

Had there *really* been a suicide attempt in November 1995, as one of Morrissey's friends had reported to Kirsty MacColl? Indeed, would a true friend have imparted such information before excommunication from the

Morrissey camp? He certainly had not balked at the suggestion of a violent exit from the world when speaking of Kurt Cobain's death: 'I felt sad and I felt envious. I admire people who self-destruct,' he had told Stuart Maconie in the autumn of 1994. 'They're refusing to continue with unhappiness, which shows tremendous self-will. It must be very frightening to sit down and look at your watch and think, in thirty minutes I will not be here.'

Vauxhall And I had been effectively an ode to newfound love and had shimmered with optimism; the fans had shared Morrissey's happiness, and this had been reflected in sales. Much of *Southpaw Grammar* had been a lament for lost love, and this had also been reflected in sales, effecting a curious reversal of attitude by some fans. 'I feel so happy having the flu now that he's got it,' a young Frenchman had told me after Morrissey's Bradford concert – while an inordinately good-looking American fanzine editor who could have had the pick of the crop confessed at Drury Lane, 'I tried sex with a girl and didn't like it much, so I tried sex with a guy and I still didn't like it. Then when I saw the picture of Moz with his head on Jake's lap I tried it again with a girl and a guy and it was like, WOW! Then when I found out that they were no longer together, all of a sudden sex was such a turn off!'

The autumn of 1997 was marked by several show business anniversaries: twenty years since the deaths of Elvis Presley, Maria Callas, Joan Crawford, Marc Bolan and Bing Crosby – and ten years since The Smiths' demise. Morrissey was expected to mark this in some way, but for him there was no going back and he brought out his ninth solo album – *Maladjusted*, better perhaps than its predecessor, but still several rungs down the ladder from *Your Arsenal* and *Vauxhall And I*. Alan Jackson of *The Times*, while enthusing that Morrissey was in 'better voice than ever', still wanted to know,

> Where are the searing melodies, the chiming guitars, the deftness and grace with which a complementary band leavened the bequiffed one's famous tendency towards mordancy and introspection? Such virtues are in short supply here, as is another old-fashioned commodity, the tune that can be whistled.

Richard Smith of *Gay Times* was similarly unimpressed:

> The songs are more sprightly than those on *Southpaw Grammar*, but they're just as slight, and just as before I've no idea what most of them are about. *Maladjusted* largely is the sound of a man who has no interest whatsoever in modern life. And to paraphrase some old queen or other, to make one boring album may be regarded as misfortune, to make two in a row looks like he couldn't care less. Maybe Morrissey shouldn't be surprised if these days people care less and less about him.

The *Guardian*'s Caroline Sullivan disagreed. Recalling Mr Justice Weeks' 'devious, truculent, unreliable' accusation, she declared, 'One must take exception with that "unreliable". In the past few years, Morrissey has been the soul of reliability, turning out one lachrymose record after another. This is his ninth, which makes for a pretty formidable canon.' Suzie Mackenzie, writing for the publication's weekend supplement, was more enthusiastic: 'The whole album – elegant, elegiac, with nods to the past to The Smiths – is in fact a hymn to himself. Morrissey burbling dolefully on like a sad but resilient saint inventing his own religion.'

The focal point of the album should have been 'Sorrow Will Get You In The End', the brilliant, unforgivable attack on Mike Joyce, not surprisingly removed for legal reasons. Even so, aside from the weak but catchy 'Alma Matters', the confusing 'Ammunition' and the rather silly 'Roy's Keen', there are a few gems. The album opens with the title track, an explosion of guitars and with Morrissey's lyrics more in keeping with those of Michael Stipe or even William Burroughs. He takes on the persona of the 'working girl' (in gay parlance, this could refer to either sex) who runs away from home 'with a soul full of loathing for stinging bureaucracy' and ends up in a rough district of London. The song, however, is too long and there is too much repetition of the musical stanza that is redolent of the Frank Sinatra standard, 'It Was A Very Good Year'.

'Ambitious Outsiders', the most moving song on the album, is also profoundly disturbing, a brave subject even for Morrissey to tackle for it deals with the threatened kidnapping of children. What makes it more chilling is that it is delivered in the same minor register as the missing 'Sorrow Will Get You In The End', drenched with shimmering strings. The narrator takes pleasure in being an acquaintance of his victims, who are blithely unaware that he is the one terrorising them. He warns that though they may take whatever precautions they see fit to protect their offspring, he knows 'when the schoolbus comes and goes'. And he arrogantly concludes, 'It's your fault for reproducing – we're just keeping the population down.'

The stimulation provided by difficulties emerges in the very lovely 'Trouble Loves Me', the fact that the narrator feels more comfortable with his problems because these have always proved more reliable than any lover may hope to be. For this reason, love is always best when paid off – among the rough trade of Soho. Lyrically, 'Papa Jack' is reminiscent of the earlier 'Spring-Heeled Jim': the unloveable rogue who never wanted his children when they needed him ('Papa Jack just pushed them away') and now he grieves alone, desperate to turn back the clock. The ambiguously titled, self-deprecating 'Wide To Receive' returns us to more familiar Morrissey territory, and opens with him plagiarising his own work – a musical stanza from 'The National Front Disco'. The narrator is logged on to an Internet chatroom, yet even unseen he fails to score and can only opine, 'I don't get on with myself, and I'm not too keen on anyone else.'

'He Cries' has Morrissey rising phoenix-like from the ashes of attempted destruction – 'Stoned to death, but still living' – while the final, and finest song on the album, 'Satan Rejected My Soul', sees him defiantly proclaiming that such has been his life, the Devil himself wants nothing to do with him ('As low as he goes, he never goes *this* low!') and, as heaven is similarly out of bounds, there is nowhere else to go. Superb!

The album's release coincided with the first Gay & Lesbian Morrissey Convention taking place at the ICA, in London. The event was organised and hosted by Amy Lamé, the owner of Duckie, a gay pub in South London, and covered by the *Independent*'s Bunty Clynch. Four hundred revellers participated. 'Gladioli were shipped in,' Clynch reported, 'as were NHS black-rimmed specs (without lenses), hearing aids, and two hairdressers equipped with enough hairspray to coif a few hundred quiffs.' Inevitably there were straight gatecrashers, some of which nevertheless headed straight for the venue's central feature – a large bed 'where fans were encouraged to writhe around and dream of Morrissey'. Asked to sum up the evening in a few words, one of these repeated the Morrissey gospel, 'People who wade through happiness all their lives don't know what pain is.'

The interviews this time around were more selective, the concerts rather thin on the ground. 'I'm in exile, I'm box-office poison as far as I can gather,' the singer told *Big Issue*. Under duress, it would appear, he 'granted an audience' with the *Guardian*'s Suzie Mackenzie. 'God forgive that I should be normal,' he told her, before asking her if she had any pets – and if she had, would she consider *eating* them? Then he threw a confusing spanner into the works by 'confiding' that he and Johnny Marr had first met not in 1982, but three years earlier at a Patti Smith concert, when Marr would have been sixteen. Otherwise, he spoke mostly of nothing in particular, perhaps because in this instance – interviewed away from the pub, gymnasium or similar laddish environment, and face to face with a woman who might easily to his way of thinking turn out to be another Antonella Black or Julie Burchill – he felt out of place and did not know what to talk about. He no longer wanted to discuss celibacy: 'Can't think why I ever did. It's incredibly boring.' He offered a rare vote of disapproval for the Church, explaining how as a child he had been forced to go to Confession and, to please the priest, invent sins he had not committed:

God forbid that [priests] feel redundant. It is probably the worst thing you can do to a child, to make it feel guilty, and guilt is astonishingly embedded in Catholic children without knowing why. It is a ferocious burden to carry. How evil can children be?

What impressed Mackenzie about her subject was that he was no longer the wilting wallflower of yesteryear, but now perceived as the 'supreme survivor'. 'Don't ask me how,' he admonished, 'but if a plane crashed at 38,000 feet, I'd be walking on the ground. And if there were eight survivors and one had to be eaten, it wouldn't be me.'

The quills were sharpened for this undisputed survivor when, on 10 December 1997 (as part of a two-event deal with a venue in Chester), Morrissey gave a concert at the unlikeliest of locations: Battersea Power Station. The last two albums had been savaged by some critics, often for the sheer want of something or someone for them to attack. Therefore, would this performance suffer the same fate? The answer was No, because by and large the event was ignored by the tabloids and music press. Stephen Eastwood of Channel 4's text service was enthusiastic: 'Appearing in front of a *Carry On*-style "homoerotic" backdrop, saucy old Moz greeted all the "sexy Londoners" who had trudged through the mud surrounding the Power Station to view their idol. All in all, the show proved there's life in the old Moz yet.' The unsigned reviewer from London's *Eye On Friday* was surprised how the singer had filled out since he had last seen him: 'The rampaging sweaty buffalo of a man careering around the stage was not the Morrissey we know . . . The physique suggested that he now does his moping around in the gymnasium rather than the library. What's more, he was positively jubilant.'

Morrissey was in tremendous form, though many among the audience might have been happier had he ditched some of the *Southpaw Grammar* songs and stuck to the standards. The wit was also razor sharp. 'Hello, you sexy Londoners,' he boomed, as the flowers rained down on him, 'I love being petalled!' This last observation brought guffaws from some of the scene-queens next to the stage, who knew exactly what the term meant. Then, before 'Paint A Vulgar Picture', here given its first airing since The Smiths' split, he announced, 'As some of you may know, I used to be the drummer with The Smiths!'

The *Guardian*, having enjoyed a brief Morrissey-friendly period, incurred his wrath in July 1998 when it published Dave Simpson's very disturbing feature, 'Heaven Knows He's Miserable Now'. Simpson barely drew the line that prevented Morrissey's lawyers from breathing down his neck – what he did not say, he left his readers to work out for themselves, throwing in plenty of double-edged clues along the way. This was the Morrissey the fans did not want to know about: the Howard

Hughes-like unemployed and unemployable manic depressive, deserted by The Gang, a fallen idol who spent much of his time dabbling with prescription drugs, who smashed up apartments, who consorted with 'hard-looking characters beating a pathway to his door'. One 'East Side informant' had reputedly told Simpson, 'Morrissey? He's evil in a way damaged people are.'

Simpson appears to have coaxed friends and colleagues to speak unusually openly. They were only too willing to hammer nails into his coffin before the seemingly inevitable suicide. Former Smiths soundman Grant Showbiz was more dramatic than most, declaring, 'I suspect it'll be the lonely garage with the poison.' Gary Day explained how Morrissey had fired him, how he had loathed the male companions, particularly Peter Hogg. Jo Slee, blaming his depression on 'repressed feelings, repressed pain and emotions', added, 'He's childlike, very extreme in his emotional reactions to people . . . not in touch with the consequences of his actions.' Slee also confirmed his breakdown during the Outsiders tour: 'He was very ill, coming apart at the seams.' Jake dismissed him as, 'The hardest character I've ever met.' Vini Reilly mentioned 'physically wrestling' with Morrissey and also referred to their 'sharing of anxieties'. Such was the severity and finality of Simpson's feature that one imagines the obituary writers already scribbling away. Only Michael Bracewell, now Linder Sterling's partner, seemed to have anything worthwhile to say. Counteracting the suicide predictions, he told Simpson, 'I think he'll be like the heroine in *Far From The Madding Crowd* – where she says, "I shall awake before dawn and astonish you all!"' But it was left to former manager Gail Colson to 'sum' Morrissey up:

It's so sad. He's his own worst enemy. He's cut everybody out and is back where he was before fame, only stuck in a hotel room, not a bedroom, with his mother running everything. Everybody yearns to love him but he is incapable of receiving affection.

Such adverse criticism, of course, was nothing new to a man who over the years had, or so he liked everyone to believe, forcibly developed the hide of an ox. No matter how tough he was, or appeared to be, some of these comments must have hurt, and now he had had enough. In September 1994, Stuart Maconie had asked him, 'If you were forced to leave England at gunpoint, where would you go?' 'Jersey, Guernsey – anywhere with a decent postal service,' he had replied. 'Not Los Angeles?' Maconie had posed, bringing the response, 'No. I need grit and struggle, and Los Angeles is terribly nice, but people once they get there cease to be real.'

'That was Moz playing Johnny Opposite again,' one of his musicians told me. 'He's done it all the time I've known him. Saying he's ugly when even a blind man can see he's anything but. Saying that he's unloved when everyone worships the ground he walks on. And don't believe all that rubbish about his genitals being a joke, either. He's more than regular in that department!'

Morrissey *was* living with his mother when Simpson wrote his feature, but only because he was in the process of relocation. For a reputed $1.25 million he had bought arguably the gayest property from Hollywood's Golden Age, the former Lincoln Heights home of screwball comedy actress Carole Lombard. The self-proclaimed 'Queen Of Fag-Hags', Lombard had purchased the neo-Hispanic house in 1934 and employed disgraced actor turned interior designer William Haines to completely refurbish the place. Lombard and Haines went back a long way: the biggest silent movie star after Valentino, his career had ended abruptly after he had been arrested by the vice-squad, caught out with a marine in the notorious gay cruising area around Pershing Square. The original plans for refurbishment included the instruction, 'Must be light, feminine and slightly screwball like myself.' Haines had not charged for the work, knowing that if a huge star like Lombard 'put the word out', he would have a solid business foundation, which is exactly what happened. At the time of his death in 1973, Haines had been worth millions.

During the refurbishment period, the promiscuous Haines had brought many of his lovers to the house, including Clark Gable, whom Lombard subsequently married. She was killed in a plane crash during a war-bonds tour, and for a while the grieving Gable had held on to the house as a shrine to her memory. Subsequent owners or leasers have included P G Wodehouse, Joan Crawford, film director John Schlesinger, F Scott Fitzgerald – and Tallulah Bankhead who once observed, 'Willy Haines laid more men in Lombard's house during the six months he was doing the place up than he laid carpets in the next thirty years!' Such were Haines' powers of 'persuasion' that he is even alleged to have seduced Boris Karloff, who lived next door. When Morrissey moved into the house, it only vaguely resembled Carole Lombard's mini fun-palace: stripped of most of William Haines' furnishings, it looked more like the interior of a Roman villa, its walls bare but for the huge portraits he hung of Steve McQueen, footballer Billy Wright, and The New York Dolls. Even the massive stone fireplace in the living room – allegedly purloined by a previous owner from San Simeon, the Randolph Hearst mansion – looks out of place. 'Morrissey has turned the place into a mausoleum,' Kirsty MacColl said.

Amongst the first visitors were Michael Bracewell and Linder Sterling, commissioned to provide text and photographs for a feature about the relocation. By now these British press interviews were starting to become boring, even when conducted by friends, constantly regurgitating the same tired topics: The Smiths' split, Mike Joyce, Finsbury Park. The novelty here was the revelation of Morrissey's interest in things Mexican. 'I spend hours just driving around the small rundown Mexican areas of Los Angeles,' he said, 'that is, the areas where the small, rundown Mexicans live.' The area was notorious for its poverty-inspired relaxed morals. Sixty years earlier, Errol Flynn and David Niven had patrolled its streets in search of what Niven called in his memoirs 'San Quentin Quail' – underage partners of both sexes. 'I really like Mexican people,' Morrissey later declared in a television documentary, 'I find them so terribly nice. They have fantastic hair and fantastic skin and usually really good teeth. Great combination!' He used the neighbourhood as an inspiration for his work – resulting in 'Mexico', though no new songs would be brought back to Britain for his brief tour at the end of 1999.

Morrissey had received rave reviews for his latest batch of American concerts, yet the instant he stepped on to British soil, the hacks were out in force, reopening the familiar wounds. 'He arrives on stage to "Who

Wants To Be A Millionaire?" and leaves, impeccably, to "My Way". Against all odds, his way sounds irresistible all over again.' This was the *Guardian*'s Dave Simpson, the man who had effected the biggest character assassination since the *NME*'s Finsbury Park attack – too late to make amends, and reminding us yet again of the events leading up to Morrissey's press-enforced exile. And why on earth these people assumed him incapable of performing without a manager or record label was ludicrous. It is no small wonder that he ever chose to visit Britain again, though of course his absence would only have punished the fans who had stuck by him through thick and thin. Some of the broadsheets, too, had now sunk to tabloid level, notably the *Independent*'s Stephen Dalton, who saw Morrissey at Nottingham's Rock City and accused him of having 'an unhealthy fixation with a homoerotic fantasy underworld of racist thuggery'. Indeed, Max Bell of the *Evening Standard* might almost have been putting the singer's thoughts into words when he concluded, 'As far as Morrissey is concerned all of Britain can die from BSE and stuff the gladioli where the sun don't shine.'

Morrissey, like many of us, is said to have been traumatised by the death of Kirsty MacColl at the end of 2000. Like him, she had recently discovered a new source of inspiration – South America and Cuba – the latter the subject of an eight-part series for BBC Radio Two, which she had just completed. A few years earlier she had called and asked me for a copy of *The Piaf Legend*. 'Morrissey has a copy,' she said, 'and Piaf and I have a little in common. The same tragic make-up. A few more hours and I would have been born on the anniversary of her death.' How ironic then, that on 18 December – the day before what would have been Piaf's birthday – Kirsty and her teenage sons were swimming off Chamcaanab Reef, just off the Mexican coast, when she was struck by a speedboat that should not have been in the swimming-and-diving-only area. Its deck hand, Juan Jose Cem Yam, would subsequently be fined a paltry $100 for negligence. Her death was harder for Morrissey to deal with because he had been the one, he told *Word*'s Andrew Harrison, who had got her interested in Mexico in the first place. 'She is irreplaceable to me,' he said.

*

1498 North Sweetzer Drive – the Lombard house, as it will eternally be known no matter who lives there – has become Morrissey's refuge, a safe haven from which he emerges from time to time to remind us that the wit and sparkle of his interviews and performances have not diminished. As the new millennium dawned, however, there was evidence that lethargy and lack of willpower not just from the record companies but from Morrissey himself were winning the battle that might have ensured that his glory days were behind him – which would have been tragic, for though he was now the same age as some of those rock dinosaurs he begged to 'get off the stage', he had so much more to offer.

When he arrived in Britain in October 2002 for a rare visit – two sell-out concerts at the Royal Albert Hall, and a handful of others including Bradford, Blackpool, Dublin and Glasgow – he was interviewed for Radio Two by Janice Long, and lost no time in cynically denouncing the industry that had turned its back on him, as it had many other major stars in favour of the 'fast-buck' *Pop Idol* boom. He had, he said, a certain amount of sympathy for the kids themselves, fabricated and pushed towards uncertain stardom mindless of the stress wrought upon them by money-mad executives who always stayed in the background when such enterprises failed, leaving the inexperienced singers themselves to suffer the humiliation of having it all blow up in their faces. These artistes were the subjects of the first of three new songs he performed live in the studio: 'The World Is Full Of Crashing Bores'. There is no doubting that the line 'Lock-jawed upstarts [later amended to 'pop stars' for the album version], thicker than pig-shit' referred to *Pop Idol* contestants – yet Morrissey is even more irreverent towards taxmen, and to policewomen, whom he addresses as 'uniformed whores' and 'educated criminals', and in the next breath adds himself to this undistinguished list because he is unloved.

In March 2004 Morrissey would still be denouncing the all-too-obvious lack of originality within *Pop Idol* contestants, telling New York's KROQ Radio, 'They should be put in a cage and sent out to Thailand. They think all they have to do is sing an old Diana Ross song, and suddenly they're a pop idol.' The following month, a little hotter under the collar, he would tell *NME*'s Alex Needham, 'They're worse than terrorists . . . they're idiots. It's just the hideous process of wheeling them on, stripping them down and throwing them off. It's just so degrading and sad. You actually do feel pity for them, and you can only shudder at the working mind of the young people who enter the competition.' To which Needham's colleague, Mark Beaumont, added the comment, 'I think that's a No to the duet, Gareth!'

In the meantime, when asked by Janice Long to name one crashing bore in particular, Morrissey jauntily replied, 'Elton John, because he's pushing his face in all the time and telling us about his private life. Nobody's interested. He's incredibly rich and I think he should just go away.'

'. . . Crashing Bores' was a collaboration with Alain Whyte. Despite recent press reports, and despite some of the barbed comments they had made, Whyte, Boz Boorer and Gary Day were still working with Morrissey, though Spencer Cobrin had been replaced by Dean Butterworth. The second song he performed, complementing a new speech affectation (pronouncing the word 'any' as 'annie', Irish-style) was the sublime 'Irish Blood, English Heart' – 'The components that make up my tubby little body,' he told Long. In this the narrator is Morrissey himself, the rebel who fearlessly declares, 'Irish blood, English heart, this I'm made of/There is no one on earth I'm afraid of' – and who yearns for the day when standing beside the Union Jack will no longer be deemed shameful or racist, and for the time when Englishmen will 'spit upon the name Oliver Cromwell/And denounce this royal line.' 'And', he concludes, 'I will die with both of my hands untied.' When later asked by *Sonic*'s Sebastian Suarez-Golborne if the number was a comment on Anglo-Irish relations and the failure of the British parliamentary system, he would say, 'It's a comment on the whole British monarchy. Oliver Cromwell was no more than a general, but he behaved like some of them by slaughtering thousands of Irishmen just to get them out of the way. As for British politics, the only choice you have is between the Tories and Labour, neither of which are spokesmen for the people. It's an age-old, ridiculous circus.'

Janice Long asked Morrissey if the rumour was true that he had begun writing his autobiography. He affirmed that he had, but that the book might never reach the shelves on account of the large number of injunctions it would attract. She asked if there would ever be a Smiths reunion, and received the humorous reprimand, 'Janice, I'm going to head-butt you in five minutes. The Smiths may reform, but not with me.' Finally, she wanted to know what was happening in his love life, if there was anyone special to give him a cuddle when he wanted one. As usual, he was keeping schtumm, though he did confess that he was no longer celibate. And, hinting that there may have been someone special, he finished with 'I Like You', the ode to the lover who gets away with so much because he likes him, albeit that this object of his affection is not always nice to know: 'You're not right in the head/And nor am I'!

Two other new songs introduced to British audiences at the Royal Albert Hall (where there was a reported one-night-only reunion between Morrissey's parents) were 'Mexico', an anti-racist ode to the difficulties frequently experienced in that country by poor, non-white migrant workers – and 'First Of The Gang To Die'. Here, Morrissey transfers his attention from East End skinheads and riff-raff to the Latino hoodlums of East Los Angeles and the luckless Hector, the 'silly boy' with the gun in his hand whose ultimate reward for thuggery is 'a bullet in his gullet'. There was also an excellent cover version of the 1970 Gilbert O'Sullivan hit 'Nothing Rhymed', one of David Bowie's 'Drive-In Saturday', and new arrangements of 'There Is A Light That Never Goes Out' and 'Hand In Glove'.

Morrissey was riding the crest of a potentially enterprising wave on Good Friday, 18 April 2003, when Andrew Harrison interviewed him at his Los Angeles home for the recently founded *Word* magazine. Harrison told me,

He was in such good spirits. Talkative, the perfect host, ever vain about his appearance. We drove around in his flashy Jag, and he insisted upon taking a change of clothes for the photographs. 'I don't want the people back in England thinking I've only one shirt to my name,' he said. He changed in the back of the car – so yes, I got very close to the fabulous Morrissey torso!

The general air of bonhomie centred around Morrissey's delight over being 'three dotted i's' away from signing a reputedly very lucrative contract with Sanctuary Records – actually his fourth in recent months, though he claimed he had rejected the others because the companies had wanted him to ditch his musicians. Sanctuary were reported as having assigned him the former reggae label, Attack, for his personal use – and to permit him to acquire its extensive back catalogue of music he had mostly denounced in the past. Launched in 1969, the label's luminaries had included Family Circle and Gregory Isaacs. Morrissey's first album for Attack, according to a shaky press report, had been scheduled to go into production that summer.

He proved as eccentric as ever – eschewing the latest rock sounds to play Andrew Harrison of *Word* magazine a John Betjeman interview full-blast on his car stereo, discussing the problems encountered in this most modern of cities buying decent vegetarian cheese. There was the obligatory dig at the latest over-hyped music sensations. Of Radiohead and Coldplay he observed, 'If you fail with that amount of promotion you must be pretty atrocious. The music mystifies me because I don't understand why I have the monopoly on the word miserable. Both of these bands sound very unhappy, with not a sign of a witty lyric.' Morrissey was similarly unimpressed by Robbie Williams, whom he felt had been 'foisted' upon the Americans. 'Personally,' he added sarcastically, 'I think that almost everything about Robbie Williams is fantastic – apart from the voice and the songs.'

Morrissey had been wholly accommodating of Andrew Harrison: the interview had been set up with little fuss; unlike most of its predecessors, the time and location had been adhered to. A few weeks later he was interviewed by Manchester's *City Life* magazine, who wanted to know if living in Los Angeles had given this most English of Englishmen a different perspective as a songwriter. One gets the impression that he still felt he did not belong here:

Slightly. It's a very nervous and frightened city. If you brush against someone accidentally on the street, they jump five feet into the air because they think you're going to kill them. If you wave over to ask someone directions they run off in the opposite direction without answering you – whereas in, say, Dublin or Copenhagen you can literally sit on a complete stranger's knee in the park and they don't especially mind.

Not surprisingly, Morrissey would have nothing to do with *NME* when, in June 2003, it published *The Smiths Special 20th Anniversary Souvenir*, a glossy commemorative magazine which, though generally laudatory, could not resist ruffling a few feathers. Within was an extraneous feature that depicted the 'archetypal' Morrissey fan: an Asian youth, transformed from a beer-guzzling, hamburger-munching yob into an aesthetic Oscar Wilde apostle of ambiguous sexuality. There were over-the-top eulogies from minor pop stars, the 'stigmata' photograph of Morrissey, a selection of his 'wit and wisdom' quotes and letters to the editor, and naturally a reference to the Finsbury Park incident – which, of course, had not involved The Smiths.

Far better was the sixteen-page tribute in *Record Collector*, penned by Simon Goddard, detailing twenty essential Smiths songs that had come about as a result of Morrissey's and Johnny Marr's 'borrowing' from artists who had influenced them – described by Goddard as, 'A near flawless body of work from one of the greatest British guitar bands of all time.' Thus we learned, among other snippets, how 'Hand In Glove' owed much to Leonard Cohen, that 'Reel Around The Fountain' had been inspired by James Taylor's 'Handy Man' (the mind boggles), and less gallantly, perhaps, how 'Panic' had been modelled on T Rex's 'Metal Guru'.

Morrissey had also just completed his first television documentary since The Smiths' *South Bank Show* – effectively, his first major celluloid interview in sixteen years. *The Importance Of Being Morrissey* opens with the claim, 'At last, the record is going to be set straight' – but ultimately tells us little that we do not already know. The other Smiths and two former lovers were asked to appear, but not surprisingly declined, and one gets the impression that the celebrities who do appear and have little or nothing to do with Morrissey are here simply to make up the numbers: a giggly J K Rowling, belying the fact that she possesses any intelligence at all, Michael Bracewell, Ron and Russ Mael, Alan Bennett declaring that Morrissey has 'an interesting face', Chrissie Hynde, Morrissey's nephews, a somewhat nervous Alain Whyte and a copiously vulgar Kathy Burke, who describes him as, 'A good-looking bloke who don't fuck – very cool!' Fortunately his musical contemporaries offer a sensible insight into his genius. Bono, quoting 'Girlfriend In A Coma' as an example, gently denounces the detractors who accused Morrissey of being miserable: 'They're just miserable people that don't get the humour!' Noel Gallagher says, 'Whatever you put down in a lyric to define your love or hate for anyone he'll do one better because he's the best lyricist I've ever heard.' Gallagher further denounces the racist slurs about Morrissey in his own no-nonsense manner: 'If he was, the fucking *News Of The World* would have uncovered it first. Forget the fucking *NME*!'

Soul-mates Linder Sterling and James O'Brien speak of Morrissey's depression. O'Brien, who lived nearby in Los Angeles, observes that when Morrissey comes knocking on the door in the early hours and is wearing spectacles (as opposed to contact lenses), the conversation is guaranteed to turn heavy. Whether Morrissey approved of such comments from those closest to him is not known. He had not been shown the rushes for the film, and with no post-production input from himself was certainly unhappy with much of the finished result, as he explained to *City Life*:

> I did some lengthy interviews with them that were great, but they only focused on all those tired old subjects such as celibacy and racism. I was embarrassed because it looked as if this was all I could talk about. Also they kept filming me from the chin, which made me look as if I've got no teeth – and they positioned the lights every time to give me a greenish-white deathly pale look. In the Australian clips, for example, I actually had a great tan, but the Channel 4 camera technique made me look as if I'm just coming round after emergency surgery. I think it was a deliberate ploy to make me look grey and miserable. But, that's tabloid telly.

Morrissey is seen on stage: the lithe, androgynous creature of yesterday being kissed and hugged at Wolverhampton – the Morrissey of today, stiff-shouldered and burlier but no less charismatic, still sending the mostly male fans wild with emotion and desire as they join in with the chorus of 'There Is A Light That Never Goes Out'. As Gianfranco, the gay porn star, told me, 'The expressions on their faces leave little doubt that they really would lay down their lives for him.' He is seen attacking the archetypal British Bulldog in his London hotel: 'How many people did he send to their deaths, just to make up the numbers?' he asks, punching a bust of Winston Churchill in the suite that bears his name – a precursor to what he would say later in the film about other politicians and the royals.

On the tour circuit, Morrissey meets an Australian fan who has been waiting years for this moment after winning a competition to meet her idol. She tells him, 'You've made me and so many people so happy' – and he responds, humbly and without so much as a hint of sarcasm, 'I didn't mean to!'

The 'exclusives' here are the briefish conversations with Morrissey himself in and around the Lombard house or at his Mayfair barber's shop, filmed over a six-month period. He alternates between looking suave in neat-fitting shirt, and not so icon-like in denim jacket and cheap spectacles. He speaks lovingly of The Smiths ('Like launching your own diary to music') but is contemptuous of their drummer: 'I wish the very, very worst for Joyce for the rest of his life.' He likens meat-eating to child-abuse and admits that he felt smug about mad cow disease – the animals getting their revenge at last. Linking this to one of his least favourite people he pronounces, 'Bring me the head of Elton John, which would be one instance where meat would not be murder!' He says of the hierarchy he has left behind, 'It seems I'd have had a better chance of being struck by lightning than I had of being accepted by the British music industry.'

Elsewhere in the film, Morrissey 'receives' Nancy Sinatra, play-acting for the camera's benefit, and now looking and acting very much like the poor man's Mae West. Yet almost in the next breath he is denouncing David Bowie as a has-been, recalling of their ill-fated tour, 'You have to worship at the Temple of David when you become involved. He was a fascinating artist – 1970, '71, '72 – but not now.' As for those fans who had been horrified to see Morrissey posing in Speedos, they are said to have been mortified to see him visiting a heterosexual strip-joint and seemingly enjoying the experience, while gay fans delighted in watching the filmed footage of Linder Sterling photographing the 'oxters' shots that had featured in her book. Of course, this all leads to the usual, in this instance off-camera questions regarding Morrissey's sexuality – followed by the snappiest put-down ever, 'I'm not telling you. I can't see that it's anybody's business. People can think what they like!'

Coinciding with the documentary, Morrissey had consented to a 'Questions & Answers' interview with *i-D* magazine for its July 2003 Beat Issue – one of his most entertaining and provocative for some time, and yet another missed by many fans because of its inclusion on the back page. The entire magazine was given a similarly 'unadvertised' Smiths/Morrissey theme: computerised advertising mock-ups featuring Alain Whyte, mock-ups of Morrissey at Cadogan Gardens, and re-created Smiths record covers (Dallesandro, Davalos, Morrissey, Fury, Marais) turned into an attractive fashion spread, handsome androgynous models masquerading as Dilly Boys, and various related chapter headings such as 'This Night Has Opened My Eyes', 'I Know It's Gonna Happen Someday', 'The Boy With The Thorn In His Side', etc.

The questions were set by Ben Reardon, who asked, 'What would be your perfect Friday night?' – hardly anticipating the response, 'I'd like to give sex another go.' Then on, this being a fashion magazine, the conversation moved on to clothes. Morrissey had gone a long way since ill-fitting denims and Evans Outsize Shop blouses, and now preferred Helmut Lang and Gucci. 'I have a few pleather [mock leather] jackets,' he added, 'but people keep pinning notes on the car saying "How the fuck can you wear leather, you hypocrite?" . . . So I don't feel quite right in pleather because some very caring and gentle folk think it's the real thing.' Reardon wanted to know how friends addressed him – Morrissey, Steven, Mozzer or Moz? He replied the former, adding, 'I've asked people to stop calling me Moz. It's like something you'd squirt on the kitchen floor.' The wittiest anecdote, however, came when Reardon

demanded, 'What is the freakiest thing one of your fans has ever done?'
Recalling an earlier incident when a 25-year-old American fan had been
arrested for plastering Morrissey's car with photographs, then
masturbating over it, he told Reardon, 'He took all his clothes off and
danced in the road outside the house. I think he was trying to tell me
something. Somebody called the police . . . I believe they charged him
with being too happy and enjoying his body too much.' Then it was back
to titillation when the journalist brought up the two names that had
hogged the British tabloids' headlines for as far back as most cared to
remember: 'Posh or Becks?' – i.e. which might Morrissey have preferred
sexually? 'I'll take them both and leave them howling,' he replied, 'I
often form the third part of a very messy triangle.'

Morrissey's new album (at that point untitled) was recorded off and
on at the Sarm Studios in Berkshire, and at Los Angeles' Conway Studio.
The producer was Jerry Finn, who had worked with big-selling pop-punk
outfits Green Day, AFI, Bad Religion and Blink-182. Again he was backed
by Alain Whyte, Gary Day, Boz Boorer and Dean Butterworth – and
completing the line-up was Roger Manning, the keyboard player from
Jellyfish who had also worked with Blink-182 and Beck.

There was a supposed embargo on interviews, but two reporters from
American magazine *Index* slipped through the net: James Murphy and
Tim Goldsworthy of the New York record label, DFA. These proved
fawning, their queries amounting to little more than blasé chit-chat, and
from Morrissey naturally there were the inevitable put-downs. Of
Christina Aguilera and her ilk, much favoured by the American pair,
Morrissey denounced, 'The most successful singers in pop music can't
sing! They make a meal of every note, they chew it to pieces, but that's
not singing.' Then he introduced one of his own favourites into the
conversation, a performer who, technically and vocally, many might
have argued was little better, albeit that he had been a pioneer of sorts:
Jobriath, for whom Morrissey had been asked to compile a *Greatest Hits*
album (though Jobriath had had no hits!) for the Rhino Homemade
label. Morrissey's own forthcoming album was scarcely touched upon,
other than that he was apprehensive over how it would be received by
some sections of the media. He concluded, with a shrug of the

shoulders, 'But I never made music in order to please. I know I don't fit in. Nothing has changed for me in that regard. I don't fit in, and don't want to.'

Early in 2004, Morrissey announced the title for his new album. Tauntingly, he told *i-D*'s Ashley Heath, an impressionable young man who had first flipped his lid over the Smiths at fourteen, '*You Are The Quarry* is actually a title aimed at one person who – no – I won't name. It's not the obvious person, though it is aimed at my audience in general, saying they are a target for me to win their affection now.'

Sanctuary Records issued a somewhat grandiose press release that opened with Morrissey's declaration, sure to have the detractors sharpening their quills in advance, 'This is the best album I've ever done.' Producer Jerry Finn left himself wide open to future comment by describing the album as 'creamy' and 'just purely organic' – and gave every impression that he was criticising the singer's proven working methods by concluding, 'I think *Quarry* is Morrissey's best work because of how it was recorded.' He was referring to the fact that, for the first time ever, Morrissey had eschewed his usual way of supplying the vocals for his musicians to work around and had this time joined everyone else in the studio – suggesting, many thought, that his previous albums would be inferior to this one. Neither did the anonymous writer of the press release do himself any favours by proclaiming, 'As lead singer for The Smiths, arguably the best alternative act of the 80s, Morrissey blazed a trail for dozens of modern day alternative rock acts including The Strokes, The Raptures and The Skins amongst others' – outfits who had yet to make their names outside the parochial pages of the music papers. Worse still, in mentioning the snippet that Nancy Sinatra had recorded Morrissey's 'Let Me Kiss You', he 'upped' her status by calling her 'a legendary chanteuse' – which she was not. Morrissey issued an additional statement that he had assigned Sinatra to the Attack label, along with old pal James Maker.

Recording the album appears to have been a happier experience for Morrissey than usual, on account of the way he was treated by Sanctuary. He told *Les Inrockuptibles*' Jean-Daniel Beauvallet how, on the day he signed the contract, the head of the record company had presented him with the white Vox Teardrop guitar formerly owned by Johnny Thunders, along with a huge basket of fruit. 'It's the first time ever that a record company thought about making me feel welcome,' he added.

In the meantime, with little publicity, two new books appeared. Privately denounced by the singer, Mark Simpson's *Saint Morrissey* had taken several years and at least one change of publisher to reach the shelves. Floridly written and hailed by its author as a 'psycho-bio', its pages revealed nothing new and it was attacked by *Uncut* magazine's Simon Goddard as, 'Fawning hagiography posing as highbrow criticism . . . a strangely boring read (considering its endlessly fascinating subject) which reveals nothing about Morrissey that hasn't been suggested more eloquently before.' Goddard's own book, *The Smiths: Songs That Saved Your Life*, is on the other hand a work of art, luxuriously unsparing in its attention to detail and one no Smiths or Morrissey enthusiast can afford to be without.

On 4 March, having decided not to be interviewed at home again, Morrissey met *Esquire*'s James Medd at Los Angeles' Viceroy Hotel. He was photographed in a Venice Beach car park – feeding the birds and sitting cross-legged in front of a Salvation bus – by Mischa Richter, who enthused, 'He is genuinely lovely. He is totally into animals and made us stop the car to let some pigeons cross the road.'

With his flair for surprising utterances – to put interviewers at ease, or merely to confuse them – Morrissey greeted Medd by asking him if Sanctuary's marketing people had brought him the bread he had ordered – 'Warburtons, the one with the yellow wrapping.' Humour persisted throughout the interview. 'Did you think you'd still be doing this at forty-four?' Medd asked, bringing the response, 'I didn't think I'd still be doing it at twenty-four. I thought I'd be floating face-down in the nearest canal.' Speaking of his disappointments, and the people who had harmed him over the years, he added, 'I think the human race is extremely overrated, and the older I get, the more I feel that way.' Medd wanted to know how he was faring with his autobiography. 'It's bubbling,' he replied, 'but I don't think it will ever see print because when the proofs are distributed I'll probably be immediately assassinated.'

Many believe, of course, that the closest one will ever get to Morrissey will be by listening to his songs, that certainly there will never be such a book during his lifetime because this would only defeat the objective of his very existence: Morrissey, stripped and laid bare for all to see, would no longer be of interest because it is his mystery that attracts the most.

And, Medd asked, would he ever consider returning to live in Britain? 'Only if I'm given a prison sentence,' Morrissey quipped. Then it was to the obligatory 'dig of the day', aimed at one of America's current top box-office draws. When asked if he had seen any good films of late he shot back, 'I'm sorry, I only have to catch a distant glimpse of Jim Carrey's teeth and I'm in agony. I never go to the cinema.'

Also in March, Morrissey announced that he would be celebrating his 45th birthday (on 22 May) by giving a concert on 'home ground' – for 18,000 fans at Manchester's G-Mex. His contract contained a clause stipulating that no meat products be sold at the venue while he was rehearsing, performing or merely visiting. The tickets all sold within forty minutes. Then a press statement announced that he had been appointed curator of the South Bank's prestigious Meltdown Festival, to be held in June. Morrissey declared a list of pencilled-in hopefuls – an eclectic, frequently bizarre mixture that included the three surviving New York Dolls, Gene, Maya Angelou, Jane Birkin, ageing French crooner Sacha Distel (subsequently dismissed by Morrissey as 'an Egyptian cabaret singer'), Nancy Sinatra, Françoise Hardy and Brigitte Bardot – along with 'contemporary sensations' The Libertines, and friends Linder Sterling and Alan Bennett. Much of this may have been wishful thinking, and one may only imagine Morrissey's fans' reaction to Angelou, or Birkin's sublime interpretations of late husband Serge Gainsbourg – indeed, if they had ever heard of them. The final line-up announced in *Time Out* was only slightly less surprising. Morrissey would be topping the bill, naturally, with three concerts at the Festival Hall; Birkin would be plugging her new album and singing Gainsbourg – supported by James Maker, who would also be working with The New York Dolls. Loudon Wainright III, Sparks, Italian impressionist-mine Ennio Marchetto and Alan Bennett would have shows of their own. Linder would be supporting Nancy Sinatra, gay playwright Neil Bartlett would be directing

An Evening With Oscar Wilde, and there would be 'special appearances' by The Cockney Rejects, The Ordinary Boys, Lypsinka and The Libertines.

Morrissey was also booked for the Leeds Carling, Reading and Glastonbury festivals and immediately expressed his dislike of one of the supports, The Darkness, regarded by many detractors as the poor man's Queen. He told New York's KROQ Radio, 'I've never been interested in heavy, soft or medium metal. It's not my bag!'

Over the long weekend of 19/21 March, Morrissey 'held court' in his plush suite at London's Dorchester to around a dozen journalists, admitted single-file, and most of them led to believe that they would be getting that all-important exclusive. His 'official' reason for being back in England, he told one of these, was to help his mother move from one Manchester home to another. His first visitor was the *Sunday Times'* Robert Sandall, who told me that the singer was so jet-lagged, the interview was virtually a waste of time (indeed, much of his piece was packed out with anecdotes from myself). When Sandall hinted that Morrissey might have been on the comeback trail, he was met with a waspish, 'I'm not coming back to anything, but a lot of people might be coming back to me.' Tackling the subject of why he had left England to live in America in the first place – according to the journalist, to make it harder for Mike Joyce to pursue the court settlement – Sandall added, allegedly incurring Morrissey's wrath, 'One aspect of LA living that might appeal to him, you might imagine, is its gay scene. Morrissey is widely presumed to be gay though he has never said so directly . . . He has been seen around with a number of male companions, notably a photographer, Jake Walters. But nobody has ever kissed and told.'

Dorian Lynskey of the *Guardian*, said to be Morrissey's favourite British broadsheet, fared only slightly better – resulting in his subsequent feature being padded out with the oft-repeated lesson in Smiths and Morrissey history. Lynskey described his subject as 'a verbal fencer, thrusting and parrying', 'thin-skinned but hard-headed', and interpreted his body language as 'a choreography of discomfort'. 'He fidgets around the sofa, crossing his arms, chewing his lip and wearing a curious smirk that could either mean he's having a high old time or that he's never hated an interview more,' he concluded. Alternating between the maudlin and the sarcastically enthusiastic, Morrissey bypassed his seven 'lost' years since *Maladjusted* – 'I went through great gulps of doubt wondering whether there was actually any point to it' – before stepping on to his podium, arrogantly declaring of his immense popularity, 'I think if I was shot in the middle of the street tomorrow, a lot of people would be quite unhappy. I think I'd be a prime candidate for canonisation.' Yet in the next breath, he was on the attack again: 'I'm not really that hot on the human race, to be honest. Very few people have anything to offer . . . the world . . . [or] themselves.' And, was he still lonely? Morrissey hedged on this one. Loneliness, he opined, was a privilege that permitted him to develop. 'You don't when you're with someone else,' he added, 'you put your own feelings on hold and you end up doing things like driving to supermarkets and waiting outside shops – ludicrous things like that.' And of course, the interview could not end without bringing up the topic of Morrissey's sexuality. Having been assured that his subject had 'skirted' love on a few occasions and even 'plunged in', Lynskey asked, 'Were all these people women?' The response was an ambiguous, 'They seemed to be, as far as I knew. They would all be women if they had a choice!'

Next in line was *i-D*'s Ashley Heath, writing for the magazine's Drama Queen Issue, though Morrissey's alleged wish to grace the cover was denied – it was primarily a fashion publication, and he had to make do with his name appearing in small print beneath a photograph of a gurning teenage Japanese model. As such, the impressive ten-page spread was overlooked by many fans.

This particular journalist was more interested in discussing the homoerotic aspects of the Morrissey persona than the new album, and the piece was the brief conclusion of an interview that had ended abruptly the previous week at Los Angeles' exclusive Alexandria Hotel. Here, according to one unsubstantiated Internet press report, Morrissey had actually asked to be photographed in the Rudolph Valentino Suite. The piece declared that this was his way of asserting that I, as Valentino's biographer, was aiming to claim Morrissey as a gay cultural icon the way I had the Italian actor. Utter tosh, of course. The fans had done this long before I appeared on the Morrissey scene. He did, during the course of the interview, refer to my new biography – announced that week – which met with a torrent of abuse from the same 'bedroom Google whackers' who had done their best to bring Morrissey down in the wake of his aborted 1992 American tour. 'It's unsettling to read supposedly factual accounts of you and your life from people who have never come within twenty feet of you,' he observed. Needless to say, he was forgetting how he had once written supposedly factual accounts of his idols (James Dean, The New York Dolls) without knowing or meeting them – and he should have been well aware that reputable biographers do check their facts, if for no other reason than not to be sued!

Since seeing The Smiths in Brighton during their *Meat Is Murder* tour, Ashley Heath had carried a torch for their former frontman and felt he could ask him anything, before being asked to leave by Morrissey's manager. Even so, he got him to open up more than any predecessor since Nick Kent before being ejected. Of his interest in James Dean, Morrissey confessed, 'It was purely physical obsession, certainly nothing to do with his films or the art he may have striven for.' There was another icon from his youth, never mentioned until now: an exceedingly handsome model/gay pin-up named Michael Schoeffing, whose chiselled features and hunky physique had frequently adorned the cover of the American *GQ* magazine during the late seventies, when the publication had only been available in this country on import. 'He was an absolute hero to me, and I used to write to this magazine claiming I would be the next Michael Schoeffing,' Morrissey told Heath, adding cockily that he had also forwarded unsolicited glamour shots of himself to the editor.

Suffice to say, this confessed fascination for beautiful men (Morrissey also observed how, years before it had wound up on the sleeve of 'William, It Was Really Nothing', the *GQ* photograph of the male figure sitting on the bed had held pride of place on his bedroom wall) led Heath to pose the question that caused Morrissey's new manager to see red: 'Were you in love with Johnny Marr?' The response now came over tea at the Dorchester with a muted, 'Why doesn't anyone ever assume Johnny Marr was in love with me? That perhaps Johnny Marr was in fact madly in love with me, but didn't feel he could act on that – or that he didn't have the courage to ever take it any further?'

The following month, *Mojo* would publish a rarely seen photograph of The Smiths, part of a Stephen Wright collection of prints about to be sold on the Internet, and which may have added credence to Morrissey's claim. Snapped at the University of Leicester in February 1984 and captioned, 'Used to be sweet boys', it shows a smiling Johnny Marr taking obvious pleasure in clasping a similarly gleeful Morrissey in a bear-hug from behind. In all probability it is all very innocuous, gung-ho clowning around, but it led to Johnny Marr being asked some rather awkward questions by the press.

The surprise interview – and an act of extreme hypocrisy on both sides, considering how the magazine had tried to end Morrissey's career, and how he had never stopped publicly slagging them off in the twelve years since Finsbury Park – was granted to *NME*. Morrissey was interviewed by Alex Needham, who began his two-part feature with such cloying sycophancy, one is hard-put to determine whether the journalist is being genuinely laudatory, or taking his subject for a ride. 'Rock 'n' roll has seen many heroes,' Needham observed, 'but one stands quiff and shoulders above them all.' And as if this and the opening paragraph were insufficiently syrupy, the magazine cover boasted the subtitle, 'New Mozza Express'.

The interview was no great shakes, other than that it enabled both adversaries to profit handsomely: the magazine's circulation soared, as per usual, through having Morrissey on its cover – and he received invaluable publicity for his 'comeback'. Why he had submitted to an audience with *NME* in the first place was of course high on Alex Needham's agenda. Claiming that the people working for the magazine were 'a different breed' than back in 1992 – as he believed they were generally within today's music press now that 'the nasty old guard' had disappeared – Morrissey concluded, 'It isn't the smelly *NME* any more.' This topic, and the essential regurgitation of Finsbury Park, were quickly brushed aside: Morrissey had moved on, if the publication had only pretended to have done. He spoke of his current favourites, The Libertines, though in the age of five-minute wonders not without reservation for their future: 'I think if they can possibly keep themselves together, which is a long shot really, I think they'll take a firm place in history.' Well, maybe. Two months later, the group's frontman, Peter Doherty, would enter the Priory rehabilitation centre for treatment for drug addiction – two weeks after this, he announced his departure from the group.

Yet again comparing Tony Blair with camp comic Larry Grayson (and with *NME* supplying side-by-side photographs to 'prove' this point), Morrissey declared his hatred of the British prime minister: 'I think people liked Blair initially, but in the end – those teeth. I think Blair is just a bumbling fool as well as a liar. I mean, surely he's doomed? Surely people are not going to vote for him again? How can anyone gaze at that face and be optimistic?' Earlier at the Dorchester, he had accused Tony Blair's ally, George W Bush – in the wake of the recent terrorist attack in Madrid – of making the world a more dangerous place to live in, adding ominously, 'I am sure there will be bloodshed in Britain now. It's bound to happen. There will be explosions at a shopping centre – very soon, very likely.'

Well aware that he would only get an honest answer – perhaps the response he might have received from every other man or woman in the street, yet one which would spark controversy – Needham posed, 'What do you think of the current furore about asylum seekers?' The response was a logical, 'Well, it's a question of how many people you'll continue to allow to flood into the country, regardless of where they're from or why they're arriving. It's a question of how it affects the people who still live here. It's a question of space.' Morrissey was not in any way making a racist comment, and he did conclude, 'It's very difficult when people are being persecuted.' Even so, he had opened the floodgates for the obligatory attendant detractors, and *NME* reputedly received scores of letters of protest. Unusually perhaps, the magazine's Asian letters editor, Imran Ahmed, half-defended him (though only after assuring his readers, 'Speaking personally, I was also uncomfortable with Morrissey's comments') by observing, 'I think it's important to see Morrissey's comments in such a context . . . Like most of us, I think Morrissey is guilty of ignorance over the issue of asylum, rather than any deep-rooted prejudice.'

In his interview with Alex Needham, Morrissey enlarged on an incident, the previous year, when a passport mix-up had led to him being apprehended by the Los Angeles airport police and incarcerated in a cell for three hours – hence the attack on the establishment in 'The World Is Full Of Crashing Bores'. 'I was put through the whole process of tagging and searching,' he confessed. 'It was harrowing . . . they thought I was a threat to national security.' The interview ended on a frivolous note – more probing into Morrissey's love life, when Needham asked him if people were queuing up to have him as a boyfriend or partner. Of affection, he quipped, 'It comes in and out, but it's not something I ever speak about because it isn't lasting.' Then he turned the tables on his interviewer, discovered that Needham was still unattached at 29, and doubtless cheered him up no end by advising, 'Buy yourself a nice budgie. That's my advice to you. You've been roaming the planet for twenty-nine years, and if it hasn't struck you on the head by now, I think you'd just better get used to that television set and get yourself a nice comfortable armchair.'

Even more sycophantic was Swedish journalist Sebastian Suarez-Golborne, interviewing Morrissey for *Sonic* in advance of that summer's Hultsfred and (Danish) Roskilde festivals. Declaring that Morrissey fans were the closest one could get to *übermensch* ('supermen', as defined by Nietzsche in *Thus Spake Zarathustra*), and vulgarly attacking anyone who dared criticise their demi-god (this author included) he asserted, 'If someone is a Moz fan on a credible foundation, you can assume this person is intelligent and beautiful with a good sense of humour – that all these features are most probably imbued by a profound hatred against Mankind and an everlasting self-hatred.' Oh, dear! And as for the actual interview, this was such a non-event that its content is scarcely worthy of mention.

Similarly inane, certainly by the time it had been edited for the finished feature, was Morrissey's interview for Flemish-language magazine, *Humo*: more attacks on Mike Joyce, regurgitated stories about Morrissey's likes and dislikes and the disbanding of The Smiths – tedious subjects by now. Journalist Serge Simonart also revealed that the singer had a new companion: 'During our conversation, the woman from the Gucci shop called to ask if they could deliver . . . Jed's new outfits. Morrissey fled into the adjacent room for a while, looking rather embarrassed. Then he returned, and our interview continued.'

Next in line was *Les Inrockuptibles*' Jean-Daniel Beauvallet, who got to spend more time with Morrissey than anyone else – primarily because he was trusted more than the others not to read too much between the lines and jump to his own conclusions. Some years earlier, Morrissey had told the French magazine that he had found it necessary to set aside a few hours each day to practise being Morrissey. Now, he said, the fresh air of California and being allowed to jump into his car and drive for hours on end had liberated the prisoner within the Morrissey persona: 'Even if I ended up in Bangkok, I would still be Morrissey. I'm no longer play-acting. I never considered myself the prisoner of some caricature. I feel free.'

Having earlier confessed that he had had lovers, he now denied that there was anyone special in his life: 'I'm my best friend. I sleep with myself, I wake up next to myself, we'll never get divorced, and we have our moments. I'm a lucky man!' He further denied ever having set foot in a gay bar, and when Beauvallet quipped that no Morrissey song had ever evoked homosexuality quite so much as 'All The Lazy Dykes', he cajoled, 'Doubtless because that's because I myself am a lesbian!'

Having discussed his harsh upbringing, choking back the tears when his father's name had entered the conversation, he now declared, 'No one in my family ever had a drink problem, and there was never the slightest hint of aggression back home – only outside, in the streets of Manchester.' And finally, he was similarly contradictory on the subject of his alleged autobiography, claiming that as an acknowledged storyteller, he had already discussed his personal life in the hundreds of songs he had written – 'It's necessary that a whole slice of my life should run to no more than three minutes fifty seconds,' he concluded, 'I've never got stuck working to that format.'

Morrissey's final visitor to the Dorchester was Keith Cameron, of *Mojo*. Having confessed that he was submitting to this seemingly endless stream of interviews on account of pressure from his record company – 'I'd rather say nothing. I'd rather absolutely let the music speak for itself and do what it can do' – Morrissey cut the session short, but promised to meet Cameron again in Los Angeles three weeks later.

Cameron had duly turned up, only to be informed that the singer had just been discharged from hospital: according to their spokesman, a viral infection had developed into meningitis. 'Uncharitable it may be, but one's instinct is to feel sceptical,' Cameron wrote in his feature. 'For him, the importance of being Morrissey is ensuring no one knows who Morrissey really is, or what he does (and with whom). Which is, of course, one of the reasons for his enduring fascination.' One week later, speaking to the journalist on the telephone, Morrissey confessed that he had been stricken with meningitis, that additionally he had suffered a five-day migraine, and that he had undergone two brain scans. Yet with typical irony, he added that his greatest ordeal had occurred when the doctors had left him alone in his room, strapped to his bed and connected to a drip – while loud hip-hop music had been playing in the background!

It is hard to determine which parts of Keith Cameron's interview were conducted where, and how. Though much of the eleven-page spread is padded out with historical anecdotes and Kevin Westenberg's stunning photographs of a pensive Morrissey, there were some treasured quips. Of his last two largely critically unacclaimed albums, Morrissey was disapproving only of the artwork, declaring, 'I made such a holy mess of *Southpaw Grammar* that I left *Maladjusted* to be pieced together by the record company – and it was even worse than *Southpaw Grammar*. I've got Tony Blair's hairline and I look as if I'm sat on the lavatory crying my eyes out.' And if this was a comeback, he said, then it should be compared to Frank Sinatra's triumphant return from the wilderness (in 1953, when Montgomery Clift had persuaded the producer of *From Here To Eternity* to cast him in a major role). Then he went on to criticise *Q* (and implicitly *Mojo*, for it was the work of both magazines) for their soon-to-be-published The Smiths & Morrissey special edition. 'Rounding up all those little left-over people who met me on the stairs in 1986 for an hour,' he expostulated. 'So boring!' And of The Smiths, he confessed to having had a friendly chat with Johnny Marr the previous summer, only to add, portentously, 'The whole story is so black and twisted, I'm convinced the story will only end with . . . a murder. And you're talking to the potential corpse!'

'Irish Blood, English Heart' was released on two separate CDs (along with a vinyl EP) on 10 May. It shot to number 3 in the charts, his highest entry ever: it was his best single in years, and the B-sides were exemplary. 'It's Hard To Walk Tall When You're Small' sees a Mexican gang member boasting that, because of his diminutive size, he must fight dirty. In 'The Never Played Symphonies', the dying narrator reflects upon his life but can only recall the negative points: the people who cared but whom he can no longer visualise because they cared, the lover who flitted in and out of his life but whose memory still haunts him. He therefore concludes that death will be a merciful release. As for 'Munich Air Disaster 1958', this is doubtless Morrissey's most moving song since 'I've Changed My Plea To Guilty' and was similarly wasted on a B-side. Dedicated to Manchester United's 'Busby Babes', who died in arguably the worst disaster in British sporting history, and backed by the droning of a plane's engine, it brings to mind the newsreel footage of the time and a tearful team-mate's admission, 'I wish I could've died with them.' When Morrissey sings, 'I wish I could have gone down – gone down with them to where Mother Nature makes their bed,' slanting his notes like a torch singer, it breaks your heart.

It was a grave mistake for Morrissey to appear on *Friday Night With Jonathan* Ross (pre-recorded before a studio audience and broadcast on BBC1 on 14 May), though he should have been well aware of the chirpy host's offbeat, frequently smutty interview approach. Matters were made worse by the inclusion of arch-camp television personality Dale Winton, first on the bill – introduced by Ross's houseband, Four Poofs And A Piano, all wearing Morrissey T-shirts and belting out 'Boy Racer'.

Almost at once, the conversation turned to gay sex, and Morrissey was seen cringing in his Green Room corner seat when Winton blurted out that he was 'crazy' about Morrissey's straight drummer, Dean Butterworth. 'He's warming you up, Dino. Watch out!' Ross pronounced as the camera zoomed in on the embarrassed young man. Then, after telling Winton to return to the Green Room and 'work his magic', Ross added, 'All I ask is, if anything happens, come back on the show as a couple and tell us all about it.' His next guest was newly crowned snooker champion Ronnie O'Sullivan (a few weeks earlier, The Smiths'

'This Charming Man' had played over the television credits for the championship as he had received his trophy), who now came on to 'The Last Of The Famous International Playboys' – and was asked by Ross if he shaved his pubic hair. All of this was hugely unsettling for Morrissey, about to give his first television interview in seventeen years, and no doubt terrified of what humiliating questions Ross might have been about to fling in his direction.

Morrissey looked striking in his vermilion jacket, but was tremulous during the first few bars of 'Irish Blood, English Heart' despite the rip-roaring welcome from the audience. He quickly got back into his stride, though, and gave a dazzling performance. Unfortunately, from this point it was downhill most of the way. Half-expecting Ross to interview him on the stage and no doubt keen to get it over with, he stalled before being invited to the sofa, where he fidgeted constantly, tugged at his hair, often seemed short of breath on account of his frayed nerves, and persistently glanced off-camera as if in search of the nearest escape route. He managed to get in an early dig at President Bush, and received a mighty cheer from the audience of mostly non-fans when, after Ross asked him if they might be friends after the show, he responded, 'I don't think so.' When the host mockingly addressed him as Steven and, failing to raise a smile from the singer, demanded if there was such a thing as Morrissey turning on the charm, he replied just as drily as before, 'There is no Mozza charm.' Then he criticised Ross for calling him a performer – 'What I do is real. Only seals perform.'

By now looking every bit as uncomfortable as his guest, and having been rebuked for not taking Morrissey's vegetarianism seriously – 'Would you eat your cat?' – Ross asked him if he was a fan of Britain's cult Saturday night television show Stars In Their Eyes. 'Why would I be watching Stars In Their Eyes?' he asked, before cringing again – covering his ears – at the footage of comedian Harry Hill murdering 'This Charming Man'. Then the real, absolutely inimitable Morrissey showed everyone how it should be done, closing with a stupendous 'special' version of 'Everyday Is Like Sunday', complete with new introduction. 'I can't understand why my life has been cursed, poisoned and condemned/When I've been trying every night to hold you near me,' he sang, drawing a welcome curtain over quite possibly the longest 25 minutes of his career.

You Are The Quarry was released on 17 May 2004 in an unprecedented blaze of mostly positive publicity. Even the cover was innovative: Morrissey, looking like a spivvish Chicago gangster of yesteryear, levelling a machine-gun as if about to mow down any detractor who might dare challenge the unwritten proclamation, 'I'm back, and this time I'm back to stay, so you'd better beware!' 'For a nation that seemed sick of Morrissey back in the late 90s, there's a remarkable amount of folk dying to get their hands on his mammary glands once again,' enthused *Gay Times'* Jo Heaney, nominating it the magazine's Album of the Month and issuing a proclamation of his own: 'Morrissey releases new album! It's almost too much excitement to deal with. A hundred thousand gay men across the country dive into their local record shop and shell out £16.99 to find out what their great leader is up to!'

Referring to the singer's so-called 'lost years', and linking Morrissey with the reclusive has-been star from Billy Wilder's cult film *Sunset Blvd.* (though portrayed by Gloria Swanson, not Greta Garbo as the journalist seemed to think), *NME*'s Mark Beaumont wrote, 'He was big – it was the music that got small.' And referring to the latest musclebound pop comeback sensation (courtesy of an appearance on television's *I'm A Celebrity, Get Me Out Of Here!*) he added, 'Eat Keats, Peter Andre: the true Comeback King has arrived and this proud chest can't be inflated by footpump . . . This is no cap-in-hand shuffle back into the limelight; as if taking bloody revenge on a world that allowed him to fall, Moz deals out the poetic spite-fire like a Uzi-toting renegade holed up in a reference library.'

Victoria Segal made an even more potent comparison in *Mojo*, declaring, 'Morrissey's very own '68 Comeback Special proves that despite the demons, rumours of his death have been much exaggerated' – a point she supported with a brilliant mock-up portrait of the singer (by Paul Slater) recreating the infamous Elvis pose while these demons peer through the letters MOZ spelled out in huge red neon lights. And after using every superlative in the book she ended her review, 'The knives might have been out, but for Morrissey the Ides of March are long since gone. The king is not dead. Long live the king.' Segal's colleague, Keith

Cameron, would observe in the same magazine's next issue, 'What makes his seventh album such a treat is it has the musical flair to match his lyrical blunderbuss . . . not a bullet is wasted . . . There's wit and passion and pathos in every meticulously measured line.'

Morrissey's one-time friend David Peschek erred by writing a double review feature in *Uncut*, covering *You Are The Quarry* and the latest offering by Prince – the two had absolutely nothing in common. 'Morrissey sings better with every passing year,' he observed, though he was generally dismissive of much of the album. And did we really need to know, 'They were born 11 months and 3,876 miles apart'? The wittiest observation, one which one imagines Morrissey would have appreciated, came from *Times Online*'s Ian Watson who wrote, with reference to the Morrissey/Marr/Joyce court hearing:

> If the Morrissey of The Smiths was a Tom Courtenay character, misunderstood and aching for love, then the Morrissey of the 21st century is a Bette Davis monster – spiteful, egotistical, outrageous and utterly compelling. Seven years of being shunned has sharpened the ogre's teeth and he's back on fearsome form . . . being devious, truculent and unreliable has never sounded so good.

From my own point of view, there was absolutely no doubting the fact that it was Morrissey's best album by far since leaving the Smiths, proof of the fact – as in the case of Barbara, Brel and Sinatra – that absence, and the recharging of one's artistic and inspirational batteries, do make a significant difference.

Of the twelve songs, several have already been mentioned. 'Well, America, you know where you can shove your hamburger,' Morrissey expostulates in the album's opening track, 'America Is Not The World'. 'Not since "Margaret On The Guillotine" has Morrissey been so deserving of an FBI or MI5 file,' quipped Mark Beaumont in *NME*. Indeed, the biting lyric is hardly the kind of thing one should be singing when, technically, one is a guest of Uncle Sam. Morrissey does of course have a point in denouncing this so-called land of opportunity, whose president has 'Steely-blue eyes with no love in them' and 'a humourless smile', where bigotry ensures, 'the President is never black, female or gay'. And only Morrissey could repeat the line 'You fat pig' time and time again and make it sound so harmonious. Yet after making the attack he did offer an apology of sorts, telling *i-D*'s Ashley Heath, 'I can't live with the notion that America is George W. But simply because I can't live with that doesn't mean that I despise the place, because I don't.'

Despite Morrissey's claim, in the album's press release, that 'There are no links to the past', 'I Have Forgiven Jesus' furnishes the listener with the first of several. In this disdainful prayer of sorts, made delicious by the wonderful key changes as the drama of the song rises, he harks back to his unloved-and-unwanted phase, recalling how as a dutiful Catholic boy he withstood humiliation and condescension to attend church, 'Through hail and snow I'd go/Just to moon at you.' Religion, he declares, instilled within him so much love to give – while, on the other hand, there has never been anyone there to love him. Even so, he concludes, 'I have forgiven Jesus'.

The theme of loneliness persists with 'Come Back To Camden', lyrically reminiscent of 'Everyday Is Like Sunday', where 'taxi drivers never stop talking/Under slate-grey Victorian sky' in the dreary setting where Morrissey pines for his lost love. From Roger Manning's simple piano opener to the song's gorgeous, heart-wrenching falsetto finale, the song has one wondering just how much sadness one man can withstand. Indeed, 'Come Back To Camden' is superior to the earlier piece – quite probably Morrissey's best song ever, a classy excursion in which John Betjeman meets Judy Garland for a suburban reworking of 'The Man That Got Away'. Recalling the initial intimate moment between two lovers – 'Your leg came to rest against mine/Then you lounged with knees up and apart,' Morrissey issues a plea that may have come from either party, 'Come back/To Camden and I'll be good.'

Many drew the conclusion, rightly or wrongly, that the song was a *cri de coeur* to Jake, particularly when Morrissey told *i-D*'s Ashley Heath, 'The song is about a particular person. I have a history, yes. And that whole time in my life is a very emotive period for me.' If it was about Jake, then one cannot begin to imagine how special this young man must have been to have left such a void in the singer's life, albeit one that inspired a veritable masterpiece.

Sexual ambiguity and confusion form the central theme of 'I'm Not Sorry'. Plangent once more, but brazenly unrepentant over the break up of his relationship, Morrissey pronounces over Dean Butterworth's feisty drumbeats, 'I'm not looking for/Just anyone', then almost throws in the towel by asking, 'When will this tired heart stop beating? . . . Existence is only a game.' Harking back to an earlier French interview when he had skittishly confessed that most of the females he had encountered had been nightmares, he affirms, 'The woman of my dreams/Well there never was one'. Then he blames his attitude on a wild man in his head before the song ends, unusually but pleasantly, with a fade-out flute coda, not dissimilar to the one that closed Marianne Faithfull's 1965 B-side (of 'This Little Bird'), 'Morning Sun'. It was the *Guardian*'s Dorian Lynskey who asked Morrissey if this song was his 'Je Ne Regrette Rien' – prompting at least one Internet 'authority' whose musical sphere progressed no further than Morrissey to pose, 'What's a je ne regrette rien?' As for Morrissey, he merely added to such people's confusion by responding, 'No, it's my Chirpy Chirpy Cheep Cheep!'

Alain Whyte's feisty guitar playing – described by *NME*'s Mark Beaumont as, 'like a flame-thrower burning the stalkers out of the Chez Moz bushes' – dominates 'How Can Anybody Possibly Know How I Feel?' This is Morrissey at his most self-deprecating. 'I've had my face dragged in/Fifteen miles of shit . . . and I do not like it,' he growls, only to contradict himself by declaring it incredible that anyone should like him at all. The woman who said she loved him must be insane; the man who wanted to befriend him cannot possibly know him; and absolutely everyone who observes his pain just walks away. He therefore takes his frustration out on the authoritarian figure to whom he is telling his tale, concluding, 'as for you in your uniform . . . you think you can be rude to me . . . but even I as sick as I am/I would never be you'. Brilliant!

Morrissey is only slightly less critical of himself in 'Let Me Kiss You' – according to Mark Beaumont, 'The first evidence that Morrissey has working genitals and the will to use them.' Opting for the maxim

'Everyone has a someone, somewhere,' he tells the person he believes to be his heart's desire, 'Close your eyes/And think of someone/You physically admire' – only to remind them that, when they open them again, they will be seeing someone they physically despise!

In the so-called age of 'renewed queer culture', which has seen the gay and lesbian communities embracing formerly homophobic terms such as 'faggot' and 'dyke' to neutralise their insult level, 'All The Lazy Dykes' backfires on Morrissey because he has hinted and teased, but neither willingly confessed nor denied being a part of this community. The song purports to be about a female friend, trapped in a conventional marriage, who is personally urged by Morrissey himself to 'come out' by visiting a lesbian club – The Palms, in Santa Monica, a favourite haunt of Hollywood's so-called 'Girl Titans'. Questioned by NME's Alex Needham about how he knew so much about the establishment if he had merely driven past it, he replied, 'The clientele were all spilling out on to the pavement and they looked absolutely fascinating . . . very, very strong women who know who they are, what they want, where they're coming from and where they're going.' Even so, it remains the most offensive song in the Morrissey catalogue, an unnecessary tirade from an acknowledged communicator who should know better – a song that, despite its attractive, plaintive melody, leaves an aftertaste of bitterness and one that may bring him grief in years to come.

The album closes with 'You Know I Couldn't Last', Morrissey's criticism of the detractors who have plagued him over the years. Rumour, he says, may hurt but it is the irrevocable printed word that causes the most damage. Hence he seeks revenge. 'Don't let . . . the blue eyes fool you,' he warns, 'They're just gelignite/Loaded and aiming right between your eyes'. He speaks of himself as a meal-ticket for many – 'There's a cash-register ringing and/It weighs so heavy on my back'. Then, having avowed that adverse publicity unwittingly only brings success, he laments the pitfalls of this and attacks those who steal his hard-earned cash: the 'evil legal eagles', 'accountants rampant' and 'the Northern leeches [who] go on/Removing' – a comment that seems very like a thinly disguised dig at Mike Joyce and the court case.

Morrissey performed 'Irish Blood, English Heart' on *Top Of The Pops* on 21 May – he and the band sported matching black Jobriath T-shirts; for some reason he also wore a sprig of eryngium on his jacket lapel. Two days on, and the single had dropped from three to eighteen in the charts: nothing had changed in the respect that once the hordes of die-hard fans had rushed out and bought the latest record on the day of its release, few others were interested.

The next evening, Morrissey headed a particularly dire line-up on BBC2's *Later With Jools Holland* – the most painful of all, to this writer's ears, being future supports The Ordinary Boys. He took up 25 minutes of the hour-long show, and was in sensational vocal form, performing the single and two songs ('First Of The Gang To Die' and 'Let Me Kiss You') with another newly acquired affectation – a habit of rolling his r's like Piaf. He proved no less nervous in an interview with Holland, however, than he had with Jonathan Ross. He twitched, fidgeted and refused to respond to Holland's attempt to raise a laugh with a 'knock-knock' joke, telling him, 'I'm not in. I refuse to open the door.'

Sitting next to Morrissey at the piano, and apparently wondering how to tackle an edgy subject who obviously did not want to be sitting there, Jools Holland seemed exasperated and at one stage, after Morrissey had made a quip about life flying past, was heard to mutter, 'This is flying past!' Morrissey eased up only slightly during the course of the interview. Asked if he liked Los Angeles he replied, 'It's a very pleasant place as long as you don't meet people.' And when asked what he missed about Manchester he retorted, 'I miss the kind of things that nobody could understand why they could be missed. I miss the grey slate of the sky. But you're Southern – you wouldn't understand. When you're Northern, you're Northern for ever and you're instilled with a certain feel for life that you can't get rid of.'

Morrissey, of course, was not being completely honest here. One of his earlier predecessors, Gracie Fields, had said almost the same thing many times when asked what she missed about Rochdale, after spending most of her life living in luxury on Capri – whereas everyone close to her knew only too well, as with Morrissey no doubt, that she would never want to return. The situation was saved by Holland leading the audience into a rousing 'Happy Birthday' (just after midnight on

22 May, though the show had been taped three days previously), and with Morrissey declaring that the ideal birthday gift would be for George W Bush and Tony Blair to exit the political arena – to make way for himself! Then, doubtless pleased that it was over, he closed with a cracking rendition of 'There Is A Light That Never Goes Out', disappearing during the applause as he did at the end of his concerts.

During the early summer of 2004, Morrissey, who had castigated the powers behind *Pop Idol* for placing personal appearance before artistic merit, went out of his way to fanfare latest-flavour-of-the-moment Franz Ferdinand, who would be supporting him in the near future. He had told *i-D*'s Ashley Heath,

> They have that 'It'. Physically, they're all the same height so their eyes are always meeting each other, and they seem to be the same weight so they look fantastic stood together. I think all groups should be like that. The 'It' factor is everything in life, isn't it?

Named after the Austrian archduke whose assassination had sparked off World War I, the four-piece outfit hailed from Glasgow, and their half-Greek frontman, Alex Kapranos, certainly belonged to the Morrissey school of self-promotion when it came to making extroverted statements. 'We are a proper band who are totally apart from the pop industry and have done everything on our own,' he would tell the *Sun*'s Jacqui Swift in May 2004, adding, 'We have no stylist, hairdresser or make-up artists.' Unfortunately, this showed during their earlier television appearances. Hobnobbing with these new-kids-on-the-block was without question infinitely good for the Morrissey image, proving that despite his seven-year absence he had kept in touch with the latest trends. Therefore what better way of adding a younger element to his fanbase of mostly ex-Smiths aficionados than to be seen with Franz Ferdinand, sharing the cover of *NME*?

Previously, some time in March 2004, *NME*'s Alex Needham, allegedly in an attempt to woo Morrissey back to the magazine he despised, had arranged a meeting 'between pop heroes as sharp of mind as they are of trouser' in a Paddington hotel – ostensibly a gathering of egos for a feature which, though unrevealing, was a brilliant publicity exercise. 'The Mozfather was meeting his heirs,' Needham observed. And on 22 May 2004, Morrissey's 45th birthday, this 'fusing of talents' was put to the test when Franz Ferdinand opened for him at the *Manchester Evening News* Arena – 'An event which came very close to ruining the evening,' claimed 'Mozza superfan' Mark Nicholson. 'He's opened with some pretty bad supports in the past, but these took the biscuit. They were completely lacking in the three requisites that make a decent band – they couldn't play, they couldn't sing, and they totally lacked charisma.'

The local media made a meal of this latest 'Morrissey Mania', this 'private party for 18,000 plus one,' with the *Manchester Evening News* devoting its front page to the city's biggest ever star under the banner headline, BIRTHDAY BOY MOZZA IS BACK WITH A SMILE. The other three Smiths had reputedly been invited to the party, sparking rumours that they might join Morrissey on the stage – as if! Only Andy Rourke took advantage of the publicity, showing up at the Salford Lads Club to stage an impromptu performance, including a clutch of Smiths songs (with singer-songwriter Vinny Peculiar) for the benefit of around a thousand fans. Asked why he had elected not to attend Morrissey's concert, Rourke told the press, 'I would have loved to have gone, but it would have been chaotic and too distracting for all parties concerned.'

Journalists had fought and back-scratched to be given the oppor-tunity to interview Morrissey, mindless of the fact that the Jonathan Ross fiasco was still at the back of everyone's mind. The 'winner' was DJ/columnist Pete Mitchell, who got to spend a few minutes with Morrissey, though the latter appears to have been edgy and as non-loquacious as he had been with some of those summoned to the Dorchester. The questions and answers were routine. It was only when Mitchell asked him if returning to Manchester was like coming home that Morrissey seemingly warmed to his interviewer, responding, 'It does indelibly feel like home. I was born and raised there, and for better or worse, it made me. You can rally against the negative things that you don't particularly like about yourself, and you can easily blame Manchester for that. The only thing I blame Manchester for is my terrible education, not because of anything else.' Cynics may remark that in stating, 'I was born there' and not 'here', giving the impression that he was not speaking in the city of his birth, Morrissey did not come across as altogether sincere.

Sincerity, however, was the essence of the evening of 22 May. The Manchester concert, even more so than Morrissey's first official comeback at the Dublin Point, was all that it had been hyped up to be – and more. Replicating Elvis Presley's 1968 comeback special and the Judy Garland recitals of the previous decade, his name was spelled out in twelve-foot-high red neon letters. There was a 'Je Ne Regrette Rien' fanfare of sorts, followed by a voiceover pronouncing modern maladies: Tiananmen Square, cancer, scandalmongering and the Liverpool comedian Jimmy Tarbuck. Wearing a dark blue jacket, and with a strand of ivy dangling over the front of his trousers, Morrissey walked on drawling a couplet from 'My Way' – 'Regrets, I've had a few, but then again too few to mention' – perhaps less a link with Sinatra than with Dorothy Squires, whose theme song this had become in Britain after the litigious years preceding her 1970 London Palladium comeback.

The audience, some of whom had paid as much as £300 for tickets on the black market, went wild. 'His elevation to national treasure status has made it easy to forget just how nuts Morrissey's diehard fans are,' quipped the *Guardian*'s Alexis Petridis, 'but tonight provides a handy reminder.' The *Manchester Evening News*' Eric Jackson enthused, 'He was among family. Thousands of mostly fellow Mancunians for whom this was more a spiritual rally than a mere pop concert.' Morrissey was, of course – and despite his own categorising himself thus – much more than a pop singer because he had progressed way beyond the Robbie/Elton/Rod megastars stable to join the ranks of the *monstres sacrés*: Leonard Cohen, Bob Dylan, Jacques Brel and a very small band of brothers.

Beginning with 'First Of The Gang To Die', Morrissey performed nineteen songs – working his way through most of the new album, and throwing in a few Smiths classics for good measure: 'The Headmaster Ritual', 'A Rush And A Push And The Land Is Ours' (the perfect companion-piece for 'Irish Blood, English Heart'), 'Rubber Ring' and 'Shoplifters Of The World Unite'. He sang an obscure number by the group Raymonde (James Maker's 'No One Can Hold A Candle To You', from their 1987 *Babelogue* album), and 'Don't Make Fun Of Daddy's Voice', recorded for *You Are The Quarry* but left off. Blasts from the past included 'Jack The Ripper', 'Hairdresser On Fire', 'I Know It's Gonna Happen Someday' (crooned wonderfully to the mirrorball) and the obligatory 'Everyday Is Like Sunday'.

The waspish wit and inevitable put-downs were in plentiful supply. Britney Spears was referred to as 'Satan' before Morrissey ploughed into 'The World Is Full Of Crashing Bores'. The pair of sparring ex-lovers and five-minute wonders who had swapped top spots in the charts (with the expletive-peppered 'Fuck You, I Don't Want You Back' and 'Fuck You Back' – a level to which Morrissey would never have sunk) and thereby relegated Morrissey's single to number 3 were denounced with a sarcastic, 'How very nice and right it feels to be in the British Top Ten again – alongside such major talents as Eamon and Frankee.' When the crowd chanted 'Happy Birthday' he shot back, 'Manchester, you've made a happy man very old. I can't believe I'm twenty-nine. Where did the years go?'

The proceedings were rounded off, after three shirt changes and a flash or two of still finely honed torso, with an even more emotional than usual 'There Is A Light That Never Goes Out', and half of the auditorium were in tears after Morrissey's pronouncement, 'Whatever happens, just don't forget me.' 'It was as if he was saying goodbye, absolutely and finally, despite all the gigs he had been booked for that summer,' Mark Nicholson said.

Other fans believed the same – worse still, that after his recent brush with meningitis, Morrissey might have been ill. Whether there was a reason for the utterance, or whether Morrissey was merely play-acting or carried away by the excitement of the whole thing, would remain to be seen. For the time being, the *Independent*'s Fiona Sturges concluded,

Just at the point when pop music seems lost to bimbettes, the erstwhile frontman of The Smiths has chosen to come out of exile and show them how it's done. It's clear that this most eccentric star won't be content with anything other than world domination.

*

In 1986, Morrissey had posed for two photographs that recalled James Dean's comment, 'Die young and make a beautiful corpse.' In the first, clutching one of George Formby's ukuleles, he reclines on top of a grave the headstone of which bears the inscription, MORRISSEY 1959–1986. In the other he is half-naked, prostrate on a mortuary slab and looking almost ethereal. Asked what he would like his epitaph to be, he had discounted the former picture and told Martin Aston, apparently very seriously, 'I think I'd have a jam jar instead of a headstone – saying, "He lived, he died." That says enough, really.'

Two decades later, in *The Importance Of Being Morrissey*, Noel Gallagher pronounced – as only he could – 'He's fucking revered, man! His records'll be listened to until George Bush blows up the planet!' It was Morrissey himself, however, who provided the best eulogy, just before the recently deceased Nina Simone sang 'Please Don't Let Me Be Misunderstood' over the documentary's closing credits:

> I've left my fingerprints somewhere. That's good enough.
> I'm my own person and that's good enough.
> I stand my ground. That's good enough.

Discography

The following represents Morrissey's complete recorded output as a solo performer from 1988 to the present day. Bootlegs are included and are of variable quality, some having been issued more than once on different labels. Flexis and trade promos are not included.

1988

'Suedehead'; 'I Know Very Well How I Got My Name' (HMV POP 1618 7-inch)

'Suedehead'; 'I Know Very Well How I Got My Name'; 'Hairdresser On Fire' (HMV 12 POP 1618 12-inch); the CD POP 1618 also contains 'Oh Well, I'll Never Learn'

'Everyday Is Like Sunday'; 'Sister I'm A Poet' (HMV POP 1619 7-inch)

'Everyday Is Like Sunday'; 'Sister I'm A Poet'; 'Disappointed' (HMV POP 1619 12-inch); the CD POP 1619 also contains 'Will Never Marry'

Viva Hate: 'Alsatian Cousin'; 'Little Man, What Now?'; 'Everyday Is Like Sunday'; 'Bengali In Platforms'; 'Angel, Angel, Down We Go Together'; 'Late Night, Maudlin Street'; 'Suedehead'; 'Break Up The Family'; 'The Ordinary Boys'; 'I Don't Mind If You Forget Me'; 'Dial-A-Cliché'; 'Margaret On The Guillotine'. (HMV [CD] CSD 3787)

1989

'The Last Of The Famous International Playboys'; 'Lucky Lisp' (HMV POP 1620 7-inch)

'The Last Of The Famous International Playboys'; 'Lucky Lisp'; 'Michael's Bones' (HMV 12 POP 1620/CD POP 1620)

'Interesting Drug'; 'Such A Little Thing Makes Such A Big Difference' (HMV POP 1621 7-inch)

'Interesting Drug'; 'Such A Little Thing Makes Such A Big Difference';

'Sweet And Tender Hooligan' (live) (HMV POP 1621/CD POP 1621)

'Interesting Drug'; 'The Last Of The Famous International Playboys';
  'Such A Little Thing Makes Such A Big Difference'; 'Lucky Lisp';
  'Michael's Bones' (EMI-Toshiba Japan, CD CP15-5889)

'Ouija Board, Ouija Board'; 'Yes, I Am Blind' (HMV POP 1622 7-inch)

'Ouija Board, Ouija Board'; 'Yes, I Am Blind'; 'East West' (HMV 12 POP
  1622/CD POP 1622)

1990

'November Spawned A Monster'; 'He Knows I'd Love To See Him' (HMV
  POP 1623 7-inch)

'November Spawned A Monster'; 'He Knows I'd Love To See Him'; 'Girl
  Least Likely To' (HMV 12 POP 1623/CD POP 1623)

'Piccadilly Palare'; 'Get Off The Stage' (HMV POP 1624 7-inch)

'Piccadilly Palare'; 'Get Off The Stage'; 'At Amber' (HMV 12 POP
  1624/CD POP 1624)

Bona Drag: 'Piccadilly Palare'; 'Interesting Drug'; 'November Spawned A
  Monster'; 'Will Never Marry'; 'Such A Little Thing Makes Such A Big
  Difference'; 'The Last Of The Famous International Playboys'; 'Ouija
  Board, Ouija Board'; 'Hairdresser on Fire'; 'Everyday Is Like Sunday';
  'He Knows I'd Love To See Him'; 'Yes, I Am Blind'; 'Lucky Lisp';
  'Suedehead'; 'Disappointed'. (HMV [CD] CSD 3788)

1991

'Our Frank'; 'Journalists Who Lie' (HMV POP 1625 7-inch)

'Our Frank'; 'Journalists Who Lie'; 'Tony The Pony' (HMV 12 POP
  1625/CD POP 1625)

'Sing Your Life'; 'That's Entertainment' (HMV POP 1626 7-inch)

'Sing Your Life'; 'That's Entertainment'; 'The Loop' (HMV 12 POP
  1626/CD POP 1626)

'Pregnant For The Last Time'; 'Skin Storm' (HMV POP 1627 7-inch)

'Pregnant For The Last Time'; 'Skin Storm'; 'Cosmic Dancer'*;
  'Disappointed'* (HMV 12 POP 1627/CD POP 1627) *Live in Utrecht.

'My Love Life'; 'I've Changed My Plea To Guilty' (HMV POP 1628 7-inch)

'My Love Life'; 'I've Changed My Plea To Guilty'; 'There's A Place In Hell
  For Me And My Friends' (HMV 12 POP 1628/CD POP 1628)
'My Love Life'; 'I've Changed My Plea To Guilty'; 'Skin Storm' (SIRE USA,
  941276-2)
'My Love Life'; 'The Loop'; 'Skin Storm'; 'That's Entertainment';
  'Pregnant For The Last Time'; 'I've Changed My Plea To Guilty' (EMI-
  Toshiba Japan, CD TOCP-6909)
Morrissey At KROQ: 'There's A Place In Hell For Me And My Friends'; 'My
  Love Life'; 'Sing Your Life' (SIRE USA, CD 940184-2)

Kill Uncle: 'Our Frank'; 'Asian Rut'; 'Sing Your Life'; 'Mute Witness';
  'King Leer'; 'Found, Found, Found'; 'Driving Your Girlfriend Home';
  'The Harsh Truth Of The Camera Eye'; 'The End Of The Family Line';
  'There's A Place In Hell For Me And My Friends'. (HMV [CD] CSD
  3789)

1992

'We Hate It When Our Friends Become Successful'; 'Suedehead'* (HMV
  POP 1629 7-inch) *Live at the Hammersmith Odeon.
'We Hate It When Our Friends Become Successful'; 'Suedehead'*; 'I've
  Changed My Plea To Guilty'*; 'Alsatian Cousin'* (HMV 12 POP/CD
  POP 1629) *Live at the Hammersmith Odeon.
'We Hate It When Our Friends Become Successful'; 'Suedehead'; I've
  Changed My Plea To Guilty'; 'Pregnant For The Last Time'; 'Alsatian
  Cousin' (SIRE USA, 12-inch, CD, Cassette 940560-2)
'You're The One For Me, Fatty'; 'Pashernate Love'; 'There Speaks A True
  Friend' (HMV 12 POP/CD POP 1630)
'Tomorrow'; 'Let The Right One Slip In'; 'There Speaks A True Friend';
  'Pashernate Love' (SIRE USA, 940580-2)
'Certain People I Know'; 'Suedehead'; 'Our Frank'; 'November Spawned
  A Monster' (USA, CD 8803652)
'Certain People I Know'; 'You've Had Her' (HMV POP 1631 7-inch)
'Certain People I Know'; 'You've Had Her'; 'Jack The Ripper' (HMV 12
  POP/CD POP 1631)

Your Arsenal: 'You're Gonna Need Someone On Your Side'; 'Glamorous
   Glue'; 'We'll Let You Know'; 'The National Front Disco'; 'Certain
   People I Know'; 'We Hate It When Our Friends Become Successful';
   'You're The One For Me, Fatty'; 'Seasick, Yet Still Docked'; 'I Know It's
   Gonna Happen Someday'; 'Tomorrow'. (HMV [CD] CSD 3790)

1993

Beethoven Was Deaf: 'You're The One For Me, Fatty'; 'Certain People I
   Know'; 'The National Front Disco'; 'November Spawned A Monster';
   'Seasick, Yet Still Docked'; 'The Loop'; 'Sister I'm A Poet'; 'Jack The
   Ripper'; 'Such A Little Thing Makes Such A Big Difference'; 'I Know
   It's Gonna Happen Someday'; 'We'll Let You Know'; 'Suedehead';
   'He Knows I'd Love To See Him'; 'You're Gonna Need Someone On
   Your Side'; 'Glamorous Glue'; 'We Hate It When Our Friends Become
   Successful'. Live at Le Zénith, Porte de Pantin, Paris. (HMV [CD] CSD
   3791)

1994

'The More You Ignore Me, The Closer I Get'; 'Used To Be A Sweet Boy';
   'I'd Love To' (1) (PARLOPHONE CD, CDR 6372)
'The More You Ignore Me, The Closer I Get'; 'Used To Be A Sweet Boy';
   'I'd Love To' (2) (SIRE USA, 941276-2)
'Hold On To Your Friends'; 'Moonriver' (extended) (PARLOPHONE CD
   CDR 6383)
'Interlude'*;   'Interlude'   (extended)*;   'Interlude'   (Instrumental)
   (PARLOPHONE CD CDR 6365) *Duet with Siouxsie Sioux.

1995

World Of Morrissey: 'Whatever Happens, I Love You'; 'Billy Budd'; 'Jack
   The Ripper'; 'Have-A-Go Merchant'; 'The Loop'; 'Sister I'm A Poet';
   'You're The One For Me, Fatty'; 'Boxers'; 'Moonriver'; 'My Love Life';
   'Certain People I Know'; 'The Last Of The Famous International
   Playboys'; 'We'll Let You Know'; 'Spring-Heeled Jim'. (PARLOPHONE
   CD 7243-8-32448-2-9)

'Boxers'; 'Have-A-Go Merchant'; 'Whatever Happens, I Love You' (PARLOPHONE CD 7243-8-81888-2-1)

'Dagenham Dave'; 'Nobody Loves Us'; 'You Must Please Remember' (RCA CD 7432-1299-802)

'The Boy Racer' (1); 'London'*; 'Billy Budd'* (RCA CD 7432-1332-942) *Live in London.

'The Boy Racer' (2); 'Spring-Heeled Jim'*; 'Why Don't You Find Out For Yourself?'* (RCA CD 7432-1332-952) *Live in London, courtesy of EMI/PARLOPHONE (both).

'Sunny'; 'Black-Eyed Susan'; 'A Swallow On My Neck' (PARLOPHONE CD CDR 6243)

'Now My Heart Is Full'; 'Moonriver'; 'Jack The Ripper' (SIRE USA, 94100-2)

Southpaw Grammar: 'The Teachers Are Afraid Of The Pupils'; 'Reader Meet Author'; 'The Boy Racer'; 'The Operation'; 'Dagenham Dave'; 'Do Your Best And Don't Worry'; 'Best Friend On The Payroll'; 'Southpaw'. (RCA CD 743-212-99632)

1997

Maladjusted: 'Maladjusted'; 'Alma Matters'; 'Ambitious Outsiders'; 'Trouble Loves Me'; 'Papa Jack'; 'Ammunition'; 'Wide To Receive'; 'Roy's Keen'; 'He Cried'; 'Satan Rejected My Soul'. (ISLAND CD CID 8059)

'Alma Matters'; 'Heir Apparent'; 'I Can Have Both' (ISLAND CD CID 667)

'Roy's Keen'; 'Lost'; 'The Edges Are No Longer Parallel' (ISLAND CD CID 671)

'Satan Rejected My Soul'; 'Now I Am A Was'; 'This Is Not Your Country' (ISLAND CD CID 686)

'Suedehead' – *The Best of Morrissey*: 'Suedehead'; 'Sunny'; 'Boxers'; 'Tomorrow'; 'Interlude'; 'Everyday Is Like Sunday'; 'That's Entertainment'; 'Hold On To Your Friends'; 'My Love Life'; 'Interesting Drug'; 'Our Frank'; 'Piccadilly Palare'; 'Ouija Board, Ouija Board'; 'You're The One For Me, Fatty'; 'We Hate It When Our Friends

Become Successful'; 'The Last Of The Famous International Playboys'; 'Pregnant For The Last Time'; 'November Spawned A Monster'; 'The More You Ignore Me, The Closer I Get'. (EMI CD 7243-8-59665-2-1)

Viva Hate: 'Alsatian Cousin'; 'Little Man, What Now?'; 'Everyday Is Like Sunday'; 'Bengali In Platforms'; 'Angel, Angel, Down We Go Together'; 'Late Night, Maudlin Street'; 'Suedehead'; 'Break Up The Family'; 'The Ordinary Boys'; 'I Don't Mind If You Forget Me'; 'Dial-A-Cliché'; 'Margaret On The Guillotine'; 'Let The Right One Slip In'; 'Pashernate Love'; 'At Amber'; 'Disappointed'*; 'Girl Least Likely To'; 'I'd Love To' (1); 'Michael's Bones'; 'I've Changed My Plea To Guilty'. (PARLOPHONE CD 7243-8-56325-2-5) *Live in Holland.

1998

My Early Burglary Years: 'Sunny'; 'At Amber'; 'Cosmic Dancer'; 'Nobody Loves Us'; 'A Swallow On My Neck'; 'Sister I'm A Poet'; 'Black-Eyed Susan'; 'Michael's Bones'; 'I'd Love To' (2); 'Reader Meet Author'; 'Pashernate Love'; 'Girl Least Likely To'; 'Jack The Ripper'; 'I've Changed My Plea To Guilty'; 'The Boy Racer'; 'Boxers'. (REPRISE USA, CD 9-46874-2)

2004

'Irish Blood, English Heart' (1); 'It's Hard To Walk Tall When You're Small' (ATTACK CD ATKXS002)

'Irish Blood, English Heart' (2); 'Munich Air Disaster 1958'; 'The Never Played Symphonies' (ATTACK CD ATKXD002) Also issued on vinyl EP.

You Are The Quarry: 'America Is Not The World'; 'Irish Blood, English Heart'; 'I Have Forgiven Jesus'; 'Come Back To Camden'; 'I'm Not Sorry'; 'The World Is Full Of Crashing Bores'; 'How Can Anybody Possibly Know How I Feel?'; 'First Of The Gang To Die'; 'Let Me Kiss You'; 'All The Lazy Dykes'; 'I Like You'; 'You Know I Couldn't Last' (ATTACK CD001)

'First Of The Gang To Die' (1); 'My Life Is A Succession Of People Saying
   Goodbye' (ATTACK CD ATKXS003)
'First Of The Gang To Die' (2)*; 'First Of The Gang To Die'; 'Teenage Dad
   On His Estate'; 'Mexico' (ATTACK DVD ATKDX003); this release
   contains a photo gallery which plays during the audio tracks. *DVD
   version.

Bootlegs (Author's Choices)

Morrissey (untitled): 'Stop Me If You've Heard This One Before';
   'Disappointed'; 'Interesting Drug'; 'Suedehead'; 'The Last Of The
   Famous International Playboys': 'Sister I'm A Poet'; 'Death At One's
   Elbow'; 'Sweet And Tender Hooligan'. Morrissey's first solo concert,
   recorded at Wolverhampton, 22/12/88.

Posing In Paris: 'Interesting Drug'; 'Mute Witness'; 'The Last Of The
   Famous International Playboys'; 'November Spawned A Monster';
   'Will Never Marry'; 'Pregnant For The Last Time'; 'That's
   Entertainment'; 'I've Changed My Plea To Guilty'; 'Everyday Is Like
   Sunday'; 'Piccadilly Palare'; 'Suedehead'; 'Trash'; 'Cosmic Dancer';
   'Disappointed'. Recorded at the Elyseé-Montmartre, Paris, 29/4/91 by
   Bernard Lemoin and featured on José Artur's France-Inter *Pop-Club*.

Higher Education: 'Mute Witness'; 'Will Never Marry'; 'Pregnant For
   The Last Time'; 'Everyday Is Like Sunday'; 'Cosmic Dancer';
   'Disappointed'; 'Our Frank'; 'That's Entertainment'; 'I've Changed My
   Plea To Guilty'; 'Piccadilly Palare'; 'Sing Your Life'; 'Asian Rut'; 'King
   Leer'; 'The Last Of The Famous International Playboys'; 'November
   Spawned A Monster'. Recorded in Utrecht, Holland 1/5/91.

Morrissey: London 1991: 'Interesting Drug'; 'The Last Of The Famous
   International Playboys'; 'Piccadilly Palare'; 'Trash'; 'Sing Your Life';
   'King Leer'; 'Asian Rut'; 'Pregnant For The Last Time'; 'Mute Witness';
   'Everyday Is Like Sunday'; 'November Spawned A Monster'; 'Will
   Never Marry'; 'There's A Place In Hell For Me And My Friends'; 'That's

Entertainment'; 'Our Frank'; 'Suedehead'; 'Angel, Angel, Down We Go Together'; 'Yes, I Am Blind'; 'Disappointed'. Wembley Arena, 20/7/91.

Nothing To Declare But My Jeans: 'Interesting Drug'; 'Piccadilly Palare'; 'Mute Witness'; 'The Last Of The Famous International Playboys'; 'King Leer'; 'Sing Your Life'; 'Pregnant For The Last Time'; 'November Spawned A Monster'; 'Alsatian Cousin'; 'Will Never Marry'; 'Everyday Is Like Sunday'; 'Asian Rut'; 'The Loop'; 'Angel, Angel, Down We Go Together'; 'I've Changed My Plea To Guilty'; 'That's Entertainment'; 'Suedehead'; 'Our Frank'; 'Disappointed'. Osaka Castle Hall, 28/8/91.

Morrissey In Tokyo: 'Angel, Angel, Down We Go Together'; 'Interesting Drug'; 'Piccadilly Palare'; 'Trash'; 'Mute Witness'; 'The Last Of The Famous International Playboys'; 'Sister I'm A Poet'; 'Alsatian Cousin'; 'The Loop'; 'King Leer'; 'November Spawned A Monster'; 'Everyday Is Like Sunday'; 'That's Entertainment'; 'Cosmic Dancer'; 'Suedehead'; 'Our Frank'; 'Sing Your Life'; 'Disappointed'. Budokan, 2/9/91.

Digital Excitation: 'November Spawned A Monster'; 'Pregnant For The Last Time'; Alsatian Cousin'; 'Interesting Drug'; 'Mute Witness'; 'My Love Life'; 'Piccadilly Palare'; 'Driving Your Girlfriend Home'; 'Everyday Is Like Sunday'; 'Sing Your Life'; 'The Loop'; 'Suedehead'; 'I've Changed My Plea To Guilty'; 'Cosmic Dancer'; 'King Leer'; 'Disappointed'; 'Our Frank'; 'Angel, Angel, Down We Go Together'; 'Asian Rut'. Taken from the Japanese broadcast (WOWOW) of the Hammersmith Odeon concert of 4/10/91.

Dreams I'll Never See: 'Suedehead'; 'Sister I'm A Poet'; 'The Loop'; 'You're The One For Me, Fatty'; 'Girl Least Likely To'; 'Alsatian Cousin'; 'Seasick, Yet Still Docked'; 'Such A Little Thing Makes Such A Big Difference'; 'My Insatiable One'; 'Everyday Is Like Sunday'; 'Interesting Drug'; 'The National Front Disco'; 'November Spawned A Monster'; 'Piccadilly Palare'; 'We Hate It When Our Friends Become Successful'; 'Disappointed'. Leysin Festival, 9/7/92.

I'm A Poet: 'Girl Least Likely To'; 'November Spawned A Monster';
'Certain People I Know'; 'Sister I'm A Poet'; 'Such A Little Thing Makes
Such A Big Difference'; 'Tomorrow'; 'We'll Let You Know';
'Suedehead'; 'He Knows I'd Love To See Him'; 'You're The One For
Me, Fatty'; 'Seasick, Yet Still Docked'; 'Alsatian Cousin'; 'We Hate It
When Our Friends Become Successful'; 'Everyday Is Like Sunday'; 'The
National Front Disco'. All recorded in Colorado, 1/10/92. 'Glamorous
Glue'; 'Suedehead'. Taken from the *Saturday Night Live* television
broadcast, October 1992.

Etchings

The following represent the 7-inch and 12-inch vinyl run-out groove etchings (the words scratched into the centre of the records) from The Smiths and Morrissey rarities catalogue. Though taken from the records themselves and from record company lists, they are not thought to be exhaustive.

'Hand In Glove': *Kiss My Shades/Kiss My Shades Too.*

'This Charming Man': *Will Nature Make A Man Of Me Yet?/Slap Me On The Patio.*

'What Difference Does It Make?': *Sound Clinic.*

'Heaven Knows I'm Miserable Now': *Smiths Indeed/Ill Forever, Smiths Presumably/Forever Ill.*

'William, It Was Really Nothing' and *Hatful Of Hollow*: *The Impotence Of Ernest/Romantic And [ ] Is Hip And Aware.* Reissue of single: *We Hate Bad Grammer.*

'Barbarism Begins At Home' (promo): *These Are The Good Times.*

'Meat Is Murder': *Illness As Art/Doing The Wythenshawe Waltz.*

'How Soon Is Now?': *The Tatty Truth.*

'Shakespeare's Sister': *Home Is Where The Art Is.*

The Queen Is Dead: *Fear Of Manchester/Them Was Rotten Days.*

'That Joke Isn't Funny Anymore': *Oursouls, Oursouls, Oursouls.*

'The Boy With The Thorn In His Side': *Is That Clever, Jim?/Arty Bloody Farty.*

'Bigmouth Strikes Again': *Beware The Wrath To Come!/Talent Borrows, Genius Steals.*

'Panic': *I Dreamt About Stew Last Night.*

'Ask': *Are You Loathsome Tonight?/Tomb It May Concern.*

'Shoplifters Of The World Unite': *Alf Ramsey's Revenge.*

'Sheila Take A Bow': *Cook Bernard Matthews.*

'Girlfriend In A Coma': *Everybody Is A Flasher At Heart/And Never More Shall Be So/So Far So Bad.*

Strangeways Here We Come: *Guy Fawkes Was A Genius.*

'I Started Something I Couldn't Finish': *Murder At The Wool Hall (X) Starring Sheridan Whiteside/You Are Believing You Do Not Want To Sleep.*

'Last Night I Dreamt That Somebody Loved Me': *The Return Of The Submissive Society (X) Starring Sheridan Whiteside/The Bizarre Oriental Vibrating Palm Death (X) Starring Sheridan Whiteside.*

'Some Girls Are Bigger Than Others': *Noh Girl Like Jaguar Rose.*

'Suedehead': *Dreams Are Just Dreams.*

Viva Hate: *Education In Reverse.*

Bona Drag: *Aesthetics Versus Athletics.*

Kill Uncle: *Nothing To Declare But My Jeans.*

'Everyday Is Like Sunday': *Nineteen-Eighty-Hate.*

'The Last Of The Famous International Playboys': *Escape From Vallium/Return To Vallium.*

'Interesting Drug': *Escape From Vallium/Escape To Vallium/What Kind Of Man Reads Denim Delinquent?/Hosscah!* SPM 29 (one-sided promotional 12-inch): *Motorcycle Au Pair Boy* (plus Morrissey etching of Oscar Wilde with sunflower).

'Ouija Board, Ouija Board': *Art Any Road.*

'Piccadilly Palare': *George Eliot Knew.*

'Our Frank': *Free Reg, Free Ron/Drunker Quicker.*

'We Hate It When Our Friends Become Successful': *I Don't Know Anyone That's Happy, Do You?*

Beethoven Was Deaf: Would You Risk It For A Biscuit?

'Certain People I Know': *Why Bother To Keep Clean?*

Bibliography

Primary and secondary sources

Words by Morrissey (booklet), Robert Mackie, 1980-81; also at www.torr.org/moz/letters.htm.

'Crisp Songs & Salted Lyrics', Cath Carroll, *NME*, May 1983.

'Morrissey', Catherine Miles, *HIM Monthly*, July 1983.

'Sorrow's Native Son', Antonella Black, *Sounds*, April 1985.

'Feast Of Steven: Morrissey: Fallen Angel Or Demi-God', Danny Kelly, *NME*, June 1985.

'A Dreaded Sunny Day', Mishka Assaya, *Les Inrockuptibles*, September 1986.

'Home Thoughts From Abroad', Frank Owen, *Melody Maker*, September 1986.

'Who Do You Do?' Diesel Balaam/Sukie de la Croix, *Gay News*, November 1986.

'Morrissey: The Dutch Interview', Martin Aston, *Oor*, January 1987.

'The Band With The Thorn In Its Side', Nick Kent, *The Face*, May 1987.

'Morrissey', Chris Whatsisname, *Les Inrockuptibles*, July 1987.

'Wilde Childe', Paul Morley, *Blitz*, March 1988.

'Shoplifters Of The World', Anon, *Rock Sound Français*, March 1988.

'Morrissey's Revenge: Homo Hymns For Misfits', Adam Block, *The Advocate*, May 1988.

'Private Diary Of A Middle-Aged Man', Shaun Phillips, *Sounds*, June 1988.

'The Light That Went Out', Keith Cameron, *Sounds*, December 1988.

'Morrissey: I'm A Total Sex Object', James Brown, *NME*, January 1989.

'Johnny Remember Me', Dave Haslam, *NME*, March 1989.

'Paradis Perdu', Nick Kent, *Les Inrockuptibles*, January 1990.

'The Deep End', Nick Kent, *The Face*, March 1990.

'Morrissey: Saint Or Sinner/The God That Failed', Kris Kirk & Richard Smith, *Gay Times*, August 1990; follow-up September 1990.

'Bona Contention', Len Brown, *Vox*, November 1990.

'Wake Me When It's Over', Mark Kemp, *Select*, February 1991.

'The Good Lieutenants', David Cavanagh, *Select*, March 1991.

'La Solitude Du Coureur Du Fond', J-D Beauvallet, *Les Inrockuptibles*, April 1991.

'Marr's On Life/The Best Is Fret To Come', Danny Kelly, *NME*, April 1991.

'Morrissey Comes Out! (For A Drink)', Stuart Maconie, *NME*, May 1991.

'Morrissey', interview with New York WDRE Radio, November 1991.

Morrissey Shot: Linder Sterling, Secker & Warburg, 1992.

'Petite Morte', Johnny Rogan, *Les Inrockuptibles*, July 1992.

'Morrissey: Flying The Flag Or Flirting With Disaster', Various, *NME*, August 1992.

'Mad About The Boy/The Fruits Of Misery', David Thomas, *Vox*, September 1992.

'L'Age Christique', E & J Vincent, *Best Français*, September 1992.

'The Man You Hate To Love', Lorraine Ali, *Alternative Press*, October 1992.

'Morrissey Flowers Again', Robert Chalmers, *Observer Magazine*, December 1992.

'Homme Alone', David Keeps, *Details*, December 1992.

'Villain Canard', Hugo Cassavetti, *Rock Sound Français*, February 1993.

'Saying It All With Flowers', Caitlin Moran, *The Times*, November 1993.

Peepholism, Jo Slee, Sidgwick & Jackson, 1994.

Morrissey: Landscapes Of The Mind: David Bret, Robson Books, 1994.

'Nothing To Declare But Their Genius', David Cavanagh, *Q*, January 1994.

'The Loneliest Monk', Dave DiMartino, *Ray Gun*, March 1994.

'Morrissey: Hello, Cruel World', Stuart Maconie, *Q*, April 1994.

'He's A Love, Isn't He?' Rosemary Barratt, *Manchester Evening News*, April 1994.

'Homme Alone 2: Lost In Los Angeles', William Shaw, *Details*, April 1994.

'Hand In Glove', Andrew Harrison, *Select*, May 1994.

'Klaus Nomi', Rupert Smith, *Attitude*, July 1994.

'Out On Your Own', Patrick Fitzgerald & Richard Smith, *Gay Times*, November 1994.

'A Walk On The Wilde Side', Michael Bracewell, *Observer*, February 1995.

'This Charming Mandroid', David Sinclair, *The Times*, February 1995.

'Ma Chienne De Vie', C Fevret & E Tellier, *Les Inrockuptibles*, September 1995.

'Morrissey: Do You Fucking Want Some?' Stuart Maconie, *Select*, September 1995.

'The King Of Bedsit Angst Grows Up', Will Self, *Observer Magazine*, December 1995.

Joyce vs Morrissey & Marr: London High Court Hearing, 2–6, 9–11 December 1996.

'After The Affair', Suzie Mackenzie, *Guardian*, August 1997.

'Heaven Knows He's Miserable Now', Dave Simpson, *Guardian*, July 1998.

A Boy Called Mary, Kris Kirk (ed. Richard Smith), Millivres, 1999.

'Heaven Knows I'm Not Miserable Now', Michael Bracewell, *Observer*, November 1999.

'Morrissey,' interview with Janice Long, Radio 2, October 2002.

The Importance Of Being Morrissey, Channel 4 documentary, June 2003.

'Born To Be Wilde: The Smiths 20th Anniversary', Simon Goddard, *Record Collector*, June 2003.

'Morrissey I-D I-Q', Ben Reardon, *i-D*, July 2003.

'Morrissey', interview with *City Life*, July 2003.

'Morrissey', interview with James Murphy, Tim Goldsworthy, *Index*, October 2003.

'The Morrissey Effect', Andrew O'Hagan, *Daily Telegraph*, January 2004.

'You & I, This Land Is Ours', Ashley Heath, *i-D Drama Queen Issue*, April 2004.

'Somebody Has To Be Me', Dorian Lynskey, *Guardian*, April 2004.

'Morrissey: The Guv'nor Returns', Alex Needham, *NME*, April 2004.

'Morrissey: They Thought I Was A Threat', Alex Needham, *NME*, April 2004.

'Morrissey Mord Encore', Jean-Daniel Beauvallet, *Les Inrockuptibles*, April 2004.

'Morrissey', interview with Sebastian Suarez-Golborne, *Sonic*, April 2004.

'Morrissey: Ik Ben Niet De Enige Mens Die Zich Een Zaam Voelt?' Serge Simonart, *Humo*, May 2004.

'Bigmouth Strikes Again', Robert Sandall, *Sunday Times*, May 2004.

'There Is A Spite That Never Goes Out', Mark Beaumont, *NME*, May 2004.

'If I Can Dream', Victoria Seagal, Paul Slater, *Mojo*, May 2004.

'Morrissey: The Smiths Will End In Murder', Keith Cameron, *Mojo*, May 2004.

'Man At His Best: Morrissey's Back', James Medd, Mischa Richter, *Esquire*, June 2004.

'The Band That Dreams That It Never Broke Up', Andrew Harrison, *Word*, June 2004.

'The Inside Story: The Smiths & Morrissey', Various, *Q Special Issue*, June 2004.

Author interviews

Peter Adams, Martin Aston, J-D Beauvallet, Boz Boorer, Johnny Bridgewood, Murray Chalmers, Robert Chalmers, Spencer Cobrin, Gary Day, Andy Davis, Adrian Deevoy, Gianfranco, Andrew Harrison, Kanako Ishikawa, Kris Kirk, Kirsty MacColl, Stuart Maconie, Mark Nevin, Robert Sandall, Pierre Sankiowski, Linder Sterling, Emmanuel Tellier, Nigel Thomas, Alain Whyte.

Index